True Tales from the West Highlands & Islands

True Tales

from the

West Highlands & Islands

as told by Tony Dalton

Published in 2016 with the help of:

Lumphanan Press

9 Anderson Terrace, Tarland,

Aberdeenshire, AB34 4YH

www.lumphananpress.co.uk

Illustrations copyright of Sarah Bowden-Smith, Jane Wilding, Stephen Cox, David Graham, Douglas Guest & Colin M Baxter respectively. See acknowledgements for details.

Printed and bound by:

Imprint Digital, Upton Pyne, Devon, UK.

ISBN: 978-0-9927468-9-6

Contents

List of Illustrations

Acknowledgements

I am most grateful to the many friends and colleagues who gave so willingly of their time and knowledge in research for this book; and to those who illustrated it and granted permission for their work to be reproduced, including:

Sarah Bowden-Smith: watercolours & maps for tales 3, 4, 7, 10, 11, 15 & 16.

Jane Wilding: tale 14.

Jane Wilding & Stephen Cox: maps for tales 4, 7, 17, 18, 19.

David Graham (www.craignishdesign.com): tales 2, 3, 5, 6, 8, 9, 10, 12, 13.

Mary, Lady McGrigor: tale 17.

Douglas Guest: tale 21.

Colin M Baxter (www.colinmbaxter.co.uk): watercolour of the Maggie Love, tale 20 & cover image.

I am also grateful to Hugh Macleod of Macleod, Dunvegan Castle, for permission to reproduce part of Rory McNeil's original letter in tale 16.

To Alistair Campbell of Airds, Brigadier John Macfarlane and Angus Nicol for encouragement in research and for advice on the Gaelic and on piping.

To Ziz, who loved a good tale, and helped me nick a rib from the remains of the Maggie Love to make a sun-dial base!

To Duncan Lockerbie of Lumphanan Press, whose professional approach and enthusiasm made the complexities of publication seem easy.

And – of course – to Georgina, Rebecca, Iona, James & Tom for putting up with me and my tales!

For my step-brother

Ian Smith

whose generosity made this book possible.

And for all those who have

'Gone up the Bealach before us'

The String of Lorn

A battle between two brothers
The death in 1296 of Sir Colin Campbell – Cailean Mor, Carn Cailean

For many centuries travellers heading south from Oban could take the old drove road that wound from the head of Loch Feochan to Scammadale, and thence to Lochavich and the ferry across Loch Awe. In the final years of the thirteenth century – for that is when our tale is set – the route was already an ancient one, as evidenced by the many Norse place-names. From the sea at Loch Feochan the early Viking invaders would have followed the River Euchar to its source, and there discovered the fertile lands along the banks of the loch. Some, no doubt, would return to settle in this beautiful and peaceful glen and over the years Norse and Gaelic place-names would intermingle.

From Scammadale [Norse *skamm,* short; *dal,* valley] the String of Lorn itself begins, the track hewn from the steep, narrow sides of Coire Geodha [Norse *gja,* narrow creek]. It climbs quickly while far below the pathway the tumbling waters of *Allt Braglenmore* rush down on their way to Loch Scammadale, famed for its salmon and sea trout. Above the traveller the ground rises to *Beinn Chapull* [Norse *kapall,* horse] at 1600 feet visible from the far side of Loch Awe.

It is wild and lonely country, the haunt of raven and eagle, sheep and deer, and the only habitation in all those long miles is the now ruined shepherd's bothy in Fineglen [*Fhionn na ghleann, the white glen*]. The cottage was protected from the north winds by a thin screen of pine and beech trees, for it is aptly named 'The White Glen'. Here the frost and snows of winter lie hard and deep, open as the glen is to the harsh winds which sweep down from the chilly heights of Ben Cruachan. But in summer the moor and glen are achingly beautiful in their fastness, as the waters of *Allt Dearg* tumble over a series of waterfalls, and the faint mewing of eagles floats down on the warm air.

~

It was in Fineglen that the two brothers Selbach and Ancellaig fought for dominance of Argyll in 719 AD, but the actual site of the battle is no longer known. At that time two great Scots tribes held Dalriada – the *Cinel Gabhrain* in south Argyll and Kintyre, and the *Cinel Loarn* in North Argyll. The *Cinel Loarn* were led by Selbach, who had succeeded his father – 'Fearchar The Tall of Lorn' – a scant year before being overthrown by his brother Ancellaig and

'sent bound to Ireland'. Selbach staged a comeback, and at Fineglen, close to the clan boundary, the two tribes met for battle, in the course of which Ancellaig was slain. History has preserved a record in *Blar nam Braithrean* [Battlefield of the Brothers], as also in *Cath Fhionaglean* [The Battle of the White Glen] but no trace of either name has been found on any map.

Selbach was vanquished later that year by the *Cinel Gabhrain* in a sea-battle, the first to be recorded in British history. Although defeated at sea, Selbach continued to reign until 723, when he retired temporarily to a monastery.

~

By the end of the thirteenth century the MacDougalls of Lorn held most of the land between Lochs Awe and Etive west to the sea, as well as considerable holdings in the islands. They controlled this large area from their principal castles of Duart and Dunstaffnage, whilst the critical communications route along Loch Awe was guarded from the castles of Fraoch Eilean, Innischonnell and Fincharn on their islands in the loch. The MacDougalls were a power to be reckoned with, but a small cloud, soon to envelope them, was forming on their horizon – the Campbells. No records document that clan's history until the emergence of Gillespic Campbell in the middle of the thirteenth century; later family historians sought to embellish the pedigree with tales of a Norman knight coming across with William the Conqueror, but little is recorded as fact. Here, however, the Campbells were not alone, for many another upwardly mobile family has sought to improve on their lineage!

The Campbells, by the standards of their time, were no more aggressive or acquisitive than other clans – just more successful. They were led by a series of extremely able chiefs with the ability to recognise that times were changing from Highland to Lowland values and laws; when many a clan chief failed to adapt, as often as not his lands were lost to Campbells.

Gillespic's son, Colin Campbell, shrewdly chose to support King Alexander III and was duly knighted by 1280. Although no landless adventurer – for he held the lands of Menstrie and Sauchrie, near Stirling – it is likely that in Argyll Sir Colin was the King's man when appointed Baillie of Lochawe and Ardscotnish [Kilmartin], rather than holding these lands for himself. It was to be his grandson, Sir Colin Oig, who in 1313 would be granted the free Barony of Lochawe and Ardscotnish by a grateful Robert Bruce.

The Campbells of Craignish probably acquired their lands in the late 1100's when Dougall (Campbell) inherited them from his foster-father, MacEachairn, Thane of Nether Craignish. A later addition was the 'Four pennylands of Lochavich' through marriage with Bridgid, daughter of the *Toiseach* of Lochavich. Be that as it may, Lochavich and Scammadale were certainly an interface between the Campbells of Craignish in the south and MacDougalls to the north and on the small island in *Loch na Streinge* was reputed to be a castle – probably more of a roughly built guardhouse. Whether it was a MacDougall or Campbell outpost will never be known, nor the exact boundaries between the two clans. Wherever they were, high on the watershed between the two was fought a skirmish which cost Sir Colin his life. Whether he was called *Cailean Mor* [Colin the Great] from size or deeds is unsure, but he gave his name to all future Chiefs of Clan Campbell – *Mac Cailein Mor.*

~

Sometime in 1296, probably in the autumn, *Cailean Mor* led a party of Campbells to settle a dispute with the MacDougalls over land. Both sides agreed to meet on the watershed of the String of Lorn, at a burn aptly called *Allt a' Chomhlacaidh* [Burn of the Meeting].

The String of Lorn climbs very steeply from the ancient fort of Duninveran perched high above Loch Avich, and by the time they reached level ground with *Loch na Sreinge* in front of them the Campbells were no doubt out of breath. With relief they saw that no MacDougalls had yet appeared, so they sank into the heather to consume their pieces and wait an hour or so in the warm autumn sun. Still there was no sign of any MacDougall, so assuming the latter had decided to concede the boundaries the Campbells advanced into MacDougall land in order to lift a few cattle. After all, there was little point in coming all this way for nothing! They paused briefly to slake their thirst at the Fiddlers Well, a spring whose ice-cold waters never vary whatever the season. Above them was the ridge of *An t-Sreang* itself, in old Norse *strengr,* and which gave its name to the then narrow path that wound its way over the lonely moor like a length of string.

The MacDougalls were led by *Ian Baccach* [Lame John] son and heir of Alexander MacDougall of Lorn; father and son alike were strongly loyal to Edward I of England, but to their ultimate ruin. On this warm autumn day the MacDougalls stopped to rest beside Loch Scammadale, and here a venerable seer withdrew from his sporran the clan's ancient crystal. In his hands, accompanied by certain rites – conveniently known only to him – the crystal would foretell the outcome of any forthcoming dispute. Imagine their dismay, therefore, when the crystal fell from the hands of the seer, struck a rock, and when recovered was found to be cracked. MacDougall of Rarey, seeing this as a bad omen, immediately returned home with his men for their tea and a quiet evening in front of the fire.

The rest of the MacDougalls, however, were made of sterner stuff and resolved to press on to meet the Campbells and settle the dispute. Hurrying up the slopes of

1.1 Allt a' Chomhlacaidh

Coire Geodha they spied the Campbells approaching, and the two sides met where the String of Lorn forded the burn running down from Fineglen. Battle was joined, and although without Rarey and his men the MacDougalls were heavily outnumbered they fought on ferociously to defend their land. Standing atop his hillock the Campbell piper saw with what courage the MacDougalls fought against greater numbers and how many of them were slain or wounded; when the MacDougall piper himself fell the Campbell composed a tune in sympathy, which is expressed as follows:

Mo dhith! mo dhith! gun tri lamhan,
Da laimh's a phiob is lamh's a chlaidheamh.
Mo dhith! mo dhith! gun tri lamhan,
Da laimh's a phiob is lamh's a chlaidheamh.
Mo dhith! mo dhith! n a shineadth thall ud
Macdhugail's a' phiob's bu mhin leam sgal orr'.

My loss! my loss! that I have not three hands,
Two engaged with the pipe and one with the sword.
My loss! my loss! that I have not three hands,
Two engaged with the pipe and one with the sword.
My loss! my loss! low lies yonder
MacDougall with his pipe, whose sound was soft and
  sweet to me.

So incensed were the Campbells when they heard a tune that was not one of their own – and which was clearly in sympathy with the enemy – that one of them rushed at the piper and with one blow of his broadsword cut the man's head clean from his body. It is said that as the piper's head toppled to the ground his fingers continued to play several notes before piper and pipes fell silent for all eternity.

Meanwhile, back at the battle, the Campbells, not surprisingly, had the upper hand. So fierce was the fight that the bodies of the slain filled the burn so that one could cross dry-shod – which was just as well, for it ran red with the blood of so many dead and dying. The MacDougalls were just about to flee when one of their number behind a boulder transfixed Sir Colin with an arrow, mortally wounding him. Carrying their dying chief, the Campbells retired from the scene of battle with the taunts of the MacDougalls ringing in their ears.

The dead from both sides were buried just north of the ford, where their graves may still be seen. And the ford it-self, from the quantity of blood which had flowed down it, was thereafter called *Ath Dearg* [Red Ford], and the burn was named *Allt Dearg* [Red Burn] – names they bear still.

Tradition has it that the fatal arrow was shot from a boulder high on the slopes of *Creag Dubh* opposite, but at some five hundred yards that was well beyond the range of contemporary bows; even the superior English longbows had a maximum killing range of three hundred yards. It matters not from where the fatal arrow was fired; the end result for Sir Colin was the same – he died. A cairn of stones commemorates the death on that lonely moor in 1296 of *Cailean Mor*, who was born away by his grieving clansmen for decent Christian burial at the nearest church of Kilchrenan.

Sir Colin may have lost his life, but for Clan Campbell it was not in vain. Following success at the Battle of the Pass of Brander in 1309, and the subsequent fall of Dunstaffnage Castle that same year, the lands of Alexander and John MacDougall of Lorn were forfeit. In 1313 King Robert the Bruce granted to Dougall, younger son

1-2 Ath Dearg

of *Cailean Mor*, a great sweep of the former MacDougall lands, comprising the seaboard south of Oban from Kilninver to Melfort. They ran inland to include Scammadale and the String of Lorn, the old boundary of the Lordship of Lochawe. His father may have died over a dispute on this boundary, but for Dougall the lands were now his and his heirs.

Cailean Mor lay peacefully in the quiet of Kilchrenan kirkyard for almost six hundred years, whilst his descendants steadily acquired lands and titles until they were amongst the most powerful in the land. When the 8th Duke of Argyll chose in 1866 to visit the grave of his illustrious ancestor he was, quite naturally, shown the most ancient and impressive stone in the graveyard, into which was carved a claymore. The Duke promptly ordered this stone to be set into the east wall of the church, but when the inscription was deciphered it was found to be not that of *Cailean Mor* but of one Dougall MacKellar, and the stone to date from c. 1500-1560. Undeterred, Duke George erected his own splendid memorial of polished red granite, surmounted by a full-size broadsword, and inscribed with the following:

CAILEAN MOR
SLAIN ON THE
STREANG OF LORNE
AD 1294
ERECTED BY
GEORGE DOUGLAS
CAMPBELL
8TH DUKE OF ARGYLL
26TH BARON OF LOCHOW
1866

And the owner of the original headstone, now firmly built into the east wall? As Moray MacKay so aptly wrote:

It is tempting to see here Sir Dougall McKellar who was vicar of the church in 1556, but the figure represented on the stone carries a sword where a priest usually held a chalice. In any event the vertical stone would seem to have nothing to do at all with *Cailean Mor*.

Sir Dougall must have been a warrior at some stage in order to be knighted, and he may well have preferred a sword rather a chalice on his memorial.

~

Thus died and is commemorated *Cailean Mor*, progenitor of Clan Campbell and the first to whom a memorial was erected. Perhaps the last words should go to Seton Gordon:

> Between Loch Awe and the Firth of Lorne is a wide area of moor, bog and loch, the home of the raven, eagle, and hill fox; of hardy sheep and cattle and a few red grouse. There stands an old moss-grown cairn of stones, known to few, which marks the spot where Great Colin, chief of his clan, was slain in a fierce battle with the MacDougalls.

1-3 Carn Cailean

Map references

- OS Landranger 55, 56. OS Explorer 360:

  Carn Cailean NM 927 176

  Ath Dearg NM 926 183

  Burial site NM 925 183

  Fineglen NM 932 186

  Kilchrenan Church NM 036 229

  Streinge Castle NM 926 169

Historical notes

- The date of the skirmish – and hence the death of *Cailean Mor* – is commonly given as 1294 (and in some accounts 1293). But Alastair Campbell of Airds has unearthed that Sir Colin signed the 'Ragman Roll' demanded by Edward I in the summer of 1296. Whether he attended in person at Berwick that August is debatable, but he was certainly alive in that year, even if dead by the end of it.

- *The Dunstaffnage Papers* refer to Sir Colin's son as *Sir Neil MacChallein Mhor na Streing.*

- There are no contemporary accounts of the event, the earliest being *Ane Accompt* in the mid-seventeenth century. The tale is much embroidered by Victorian romance, but mine is as accurate as I can make it.

- Streinge Castle (Site of). From RCAHMS, *Argyll, Lorn, Volume 2:*

There are no visible remains of this castle which is said to have stood upon the principal island in Loch na Sreinge, having evidently disappeared by 1871. [*Name Book 1871*]. In feudal times, a band of freebooters made this their headquarters, and for nearly a century infested not only the surrounding district, but made predatory incursions to the adjoining counties. [*New Statistical Account 1845*]. Nearby are the ruins of a small, sub-rectangular building of indeterminate age and which appears to have been constructed of dry-stone masonry.

- The 'battle' was more likely a skirmish, with probably no more than 100 men involved at the most. Most versions of the story agree that the fight was at *Ath Dearg*, but some accounts place it further south, nearer *Loch na Sreing*, and that the Campbells were pursuing the fleeing MacDougalls when *Cailean Mor* was mortally wounded at the ford by the arrow (in the library!). The Burial Ground would reinforce the argument for the fight occurring at *Ath Dearg*, as does that name. However, in the bed of the burn there frequently occur red coloured rocks, and it is possible this gave rise to *Allt Dearg* and *Ath Dearg* – but this explanation is mundane and not nearly so much fun!

- Some accounts state that the cairn marks the very spot at which Sir Colin fell. But Lord Archibald Campbell in *Records of Argyll* says that '… a cairn [was] made near that place as a memorial…' and it is more likely to be just that – a memorial, sited at the highest point on the String of Lorn with clears views to north and south. In 1960 it was one-third its current size.

- There is no proof that the 'Burial Ground – Site of' shown on the 6" Ordnance Survey map of 1861 is that of the fight, but RCAHMS [entry 218] repeats the traditional story, and it is thus reasonable to assume it is so. The site today consists of several low mounds, resembling old lazy beds.

- The tale of the piper (from *Records of Argyll*) is possibly confused with another battle. Angus Nicol (piping correspondent of *The Times*) tells me the verse quoted is similar in purport to a very old tune by name *Uamh an Oir* (The Cave of Gold). A common tale throughout the West Highlands has a piper seeking a pot of gold at the far end of a cave, usually guarded by a dragon or monster. Observers above ground followed the sounds of his pipes until they ceased, often accompanied by fierce roarings from the dragon. Where the piper was accompanied by his dog the creature often exited from the cave hairless; his master, needless to say, was never seen again.

• Brigadier John Macfarlane explained:

> Someone once said to me that the pipers were so valuable that they generally had safe conducts particularly if they were notable players but tended to be placed where they could see the fight and yet withdraw tactically if required – to play another day?!

• Sadly my researches commenced soon after the death of Jessie Crerar, the last Gaelic-speaking shepherdess of Fineglen; and the exact location of *Tom-a-Phiobhar* (The Piper's Hillock) appears to have been lost. It was always pointed out to me as close to the boulder high on *Creag Dubh* from which the fatal arrow was reputedly fired. But it seems pointless to me to station your piper five hundred yards from the fight, and across a steep defile as well! It is the *volume* of the pipes, as well as the tune, which inspires men in battle, and no clan chief would place his piper so far away. Seton Gordon, usually very reliable as to local sources, says the site was a small hillock close to the battle, of which there are several such eligible.

• 'The boulder' from which the arrow was fired seems to have moved a few yards more distant with each telling of the tale! I have always understood it was the prominent one high on *Creag Dubh,* five hundred yards from *Ath Dearg.* Lord Archibald in *Records of Argyll* states that a MacDougall crept up behind a boulder and transfixed Sir Colin; this makes far more sense, but far less fun!

• The stone in Kilchrenan kirkyard mistaken by Duke

George for that of Sir Colin bears the inscription:

HIC IACET D

(U)GALL(U)S MAKALL

UR (ET) COLIN(US)

[A]NGUSII CO(N)STR(UXIT.

HERE LIES D

UGALL MACKELL

AR, AND COLINUS,

SON OF ANGUS MADE IT.

The date is c. 1500-1560. [RCAHMS – *Argyll* Volume 2 page 149].

- The MacDougall crystal is about the size of a pigeon's egg, and by tradition was brought back from the Crusades, to Dunollie. Sadly, it was stolen in 1969.

Sources

- *Records of Argyll* – Lord Archibald Campbell. 1885.
- *Highways & Byways in the West Highlands* – Seton Gordon.
- *The Times,* 6 November 1965. Seton Gordon.
- *Kilchrenan and Dalavich* – Moray S MacKay, DFC, BSc, FSA Scotland.
- *A History of Clan Campbell*, Volume 1 – Alastair Campbell of Airds.
- *The Royal Commission on the Ancient & Historical Monuments of Scotland* – Argyll, Lorn, Volume 2.
- *The Lords of the Isles* – Ronald Williams.
- *Eyewitness Guides* – *The Knight*. Dorling Kindersley 1993.
- *The Drove Roads of Scotland* – A R B Haldane.
- *The History of Argyll* – Colin M MacDonald, MA, D.Litt.
- OS 6" Survey 1861.

Caisteal na Nighinn Ruaidhe

The Castle of the Red Haired Girl & why she haunts it

igh on a plateau between the coast at Kilmelford and the vast expanse of Loch Awe lies the isolated glen of Lochavich, some eight miles long, scarcely one mile wide, and nowadays with scant few houses scattered along its length. Towards the western end of Loch Avich lies an hour-glass shaped island, *Innis Luina*; it is now covered by trees, with a small shingle beach in the middle, ideal for a boat landing place. At the eastern end of the island lie the ruins of an ancient castle, probably built between about 1316, as I will explain later.

There is an Ossianic poem – *Cathluina* – said to date from circa 300 AD, which describes *Innis Luina* and it's

castle as '… the hall of the chief, where it lifts its gray head, in the midst of trees, in the green isle of Innisluina'.

One James Macpherson claimed he had discovered ancient manuscripts in the Highlands containing two poems of Ossian, of which he published translations in the early 1760s. They were compared to the works of Homer, sold in several editions, and made Macpherson a small fortune. Unfortunately, he was a fraud, having combined old Gaelic tales of Ossian with his own poetry, but his volumes aroused huge interest in Ossian and his poems.

However, The Reverend John Smith, Minister at Kilbrandon, collected genuine poems, handed down orally through the centuries, and in 1780 published his 'Galic Antiquities'. It contained Ossianic poems, one of which describes Lochavich, *Innis Luana* and *Caisteal na Nighinn Ruaidhe*. There is a footnote to the poem *Cathluina*:

> In the district of Lorn in Argyleshire, there is a lake now called Loch-avich, but anciently Loch-luina, or Lochluana. Near it was probably the scene of this poem. Many places in it's neighbour-hood are still denominated from Ossian's heroes.

Ossian's sword was called Luno, made by Luno of Lochlin, which was described as 'the blade of dark-brown Luno' which indicates Damascus steel.

In ancient Celtic legend Fionn, King of the Alba-men (or Caledonians) was the father of Ossian, a legendary Gaelic warrior. Ossian outlived both his father and his son, and is reputed to have died about 300 AD. In blind old age he wandered the land as a poet and bard, and the Ossianic poems, songs and tales were repeated and memorised down the ages.

True or false, the tale runs as follows:

Two warrior friends, Gaul and Garno, came to Loch Avich and to Moran, toiseach of that time.

> They came to the aid of Moran. They went to the hall of the chief, where it lifts its gray head, in the midst of trees, in the green isle of Innisluina. The daughter of Moran seized the harp, and her voice of music praised the strangers. Their souls melted at the song, like a wreath of snow before the eyes of the sun. The heroes burned with equal love for Annir; but it was upon Gaul alone that she rolled her blue eyes.

And so the die was cast – Annir tries to lure away her unwanted lover by a ruse, but it goes badly wrong. Each mistaking the other's identity, Gaul and Garno end up fighting to the death near Fineglen:

> Blood, mixed with sweat, descends in streams to the ground. It wanders through the green grass, and dyes the passing rill.

Annir comes upon their bodies, and horrified that the ruse has caused the death of her lover and his friend she too dies with them from remorse and grief.

All day, the sun as he travelled through his watery cloud, beheld her grief. All night, the ghosts of rocks faintly answered to her sigh. On the second day her eyes were closed. Death came, like the calm cloud of sleep, when the hunter is tired upon the hill, and the silence of mist, without any wind, is around him.

Two days the father of Annir looked towards the heath [Fineglen]; two sleepless nights he listened to all the winds. "Give me," on this morning he said, "my staff. My steps will be towards the desart". A gray dog howls before him; a fair ghost hovers on the heath. The aged lifts his tearful eye; mournful he spies the lovely form. But, Moran, I will leave thee; I cannot stay to behold thy grief.

Here, son of youth, we laid the three. Here we reared their gray stones. Our sorrow was great for their fall; and our bards gave the mournful song.

One can clearly imagine this tale being told and retold down the centuries; in hall or hut, round the fires of winter, the audiences would be gripped by the poetry and the pathos.

But Gaul and Garno must have been pretty dumb friends to fight to the death without recognising each other!

And so we come to *The Castle of the Red-haired Girl & why she haunts it*. One tale has the builder as a certain Mungan MacFiachar, whose female descendant, Dervail, married a Duncan Campbell sometime about 1100. Sadly – for it is a shame when facts get in the way of a good story – this tale is out by two centuries!

Before the castle was built, Lochavich was protected by two small duns, one at either end of the glen, for in medieval times it was an important route between Loch Awe and the sea at Craignish. Campbell of Craignish family tradition has it that towards the end of the 12th century Dougall Campbell of Craignish married Bridgid

MacCuarrie, heiress of the *Toiseach* of Lochavich, thus acquiring both lands and *Caisteal Na Nighinn Ruaidhe*.

> Dugal who married Brihid or Bridget, daughter to Dugal MacCaurre, Tossach of Lochavich by whom he got the lands commonly call'd the pennies of Lochavich being four in number, or Four Merk land, as also the Old Tower and Fortalice in the Island of that Loch called Castle Lochavich, but of old Castle nahine ruai, or the red maids Castle, some say so call'd from an Apparition or familiar Brounie that was said to frequent it in that Shape in those Days of Dark Ignorance, but rather as I imagine from the heiress who might have been a red hair'd or a Ruddie complexion'd lass.

However, I think it was not an 'Old Tower' but the ancient fort at Duninveran [now Lochavich House]. The late 12th century is too early a date for the building of *Caisteal na Nighinn Ruaidhe*, and over the centuries of tale-telling a turf and timber fort was no doubt transposed into a fine stone-built castle!

Castles and Keeps of Scotland aptly describe the keeps of the time:

> The Scottish keep, like the Norman, usually was a three-storied tower. The basement was invariably vaulted and used for stores, or a stable. Very often its only communication with the hall above was through a trap in the vault.

> The first floor was the hall, and the entrance door opened into this, being reached by a ladder or moveable stair. In this hall retainers, guests and domestics fed and slept indiscriminately, no privacy for man or woman being possible. This hall was usually furnished with a wooden floor midway of its height, forming a chamber in the vault, as is everywhere evidenced by the rows of supporting corbels to be seen in the walls.

> The second floor was the private apartment of the

chieftain and his family, who also had a loft in the roof, as a general thing.

The roof was usually formed of stone slabs laid on a pointed arch, to render the whole fireproof, but in the smaller peels was of wood. The defence was undertaken from the parapet at the roof, which ran completely round the tower, expanding into rounded angles or bartizans at the corners.

The walls were of great thickness, usually carrying spiral staircases, small closets for bed places, retiring rooms, etc., in their structure.

The accommodation of these towers was so circumscribed that they were often added to by a small square projection at one corner, giving an additional room on each floor. Besides this, there is little doubt that practically all these keeps had a courtyard attached, surrounded by a high wall. This contained the stables and offices, and was an additional protection against sudden assault.

Ornamentation was entirely absent from these castles. The parapets and bartizans sometimes were carried on corbels of the simplest kind, and these, with a few plain gargoyles to drain off the rain from the parapet walk, were the only things which broke the stern severity of the grim towers'.

Caisteal Na Nighinn Ruaidhe was a rectangular tower-house of three stories, some 50 feet by 33 feet, with walls 7 feet thick. The main hall was at first floor level, with a fireplace in the south-east wall and a latrine emptying into the loch. Below the hall was a basement, and above it two main chambers for the use of the chief and his family, each chamber having its own latrine. There was a parapet walk around the roof, which would probably have been thatch or heather; the risk of fire from a distant bow-shot from the shore was small, and slate was both expensive and hard to obtain.

The castle was protected by a defensive wall, within which were outbuildings providing accommodation for some fifty men, a sizeable fighting force for the times. The loch is barely waist deep at this point, but was lowered by two feet in Victorian times. Even so, men and animals could have waded or swum from the shore, or possibly crossed a simple wooden bridge, or on stepping-stones hidden below the water.

Seton Gordon records:

> On an island of Lochavich is a ruined castle to which a secret subterranean causeway formerly led. The tradition of the place is that the architect who planned this secret means of approach had his head cut off afterwards, in order that no information might be given as to the position of this causeway.

We do not know who built *Caisteal Na Nighinn Ruaidhe*; certainly it was not local work, but the creation of a skilled mason, trained in defence and architecture. We tend to view Argyll at this time as remote and cut off from the mainstream of events by the hills to the east; but we forget the sea, and the sea-lanes forged by the Vikings. Men who had sailed from the North Cape to Algiers, or traded from the Hebrides to the slave-markets of the Middle East across Russia, provided among all their raiding and destruction a great interchange of ideas. Once integrated into the communities the way was open for native seamen to sail with them and absorb their skills; a marine legacy remaining with the West of Scotland, and particularly the Hebrides.

As Marion Campbell so graphically wrote:

> And a new and powerful magnet was drawing men southwards and eastwards – the Crusades. The sheer scale of the operations, the vast international melting-pot, the interplay of ideas, is apt to be forgotten. For every country in Christendom sent at least some troops, for at least some of the campaigns, and those who stayed at home were kept aware of events in an unimaginably distant country through the narratives of pilgrims or returned crusaders as well as by the repeated appeals for funds or prayers. Those who went out and returned brought back news of Saracen and Byzantine warfare, of mine and countermine under

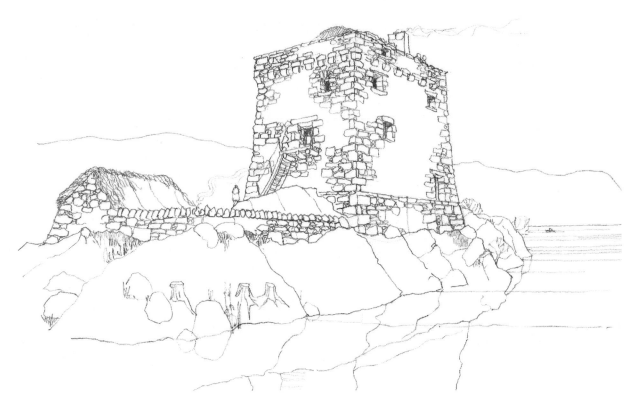

2.1 The Castle of the Red Haired Girl

walls, of garrisons surviving incredible sieges as long as their water-supply held out.

In hall and hut men listened to the tales of battle, and anyone who planned a castle between 1100 and 1300 would have been a fool if he had not inquired into the latest defence-works of Syria; he could be sure that anyone who came against him would know of the latest development in attack. In the kingdoms of England and Scotland no knight could build a castle without his king's leave; if he did so, he might find himself pulling it down again, like any modern builder without planning permission; but on the western seaboard the king's writ scarcely ran.

Here is my version of another story of how *Caisteal Na Nighinn Ruaidhe* was built, originally told by Lord Archibald Campbell about 1895 in *Records of Argyll*:

There once lived in Edinburgh a house-builder who had an only son. Offers were asked for building a castle on a small island in Loch Avich, so the builder sent in an offer, and was successful. When the father and son were setting off to build the castle, his mother said to the latter, "Be sure and have a sweetheart where you are going".

Now, whether he had a weak chest and his mother thought some warm-hearted Argyll girl would care for him, I know not. But the boy followed his mother's advice, and soon after arriving at Lochavich he courted a red-haired servant girl who resided in the house of the man for whom they were building the castle.

After the castle was finished he went to see her, in order to say farewell before his return to Edinburgh. Observing that she looked sad and dejected he asked what the matter was with her. She replied that her master intended to kill him and his father, as he had not the money to pay for the building of the castle.

"But", said she, "do not mention that I told you of it, or they will surely kill me too". The young man revealed to his father the design against their lives, but his father said "I will defeat it".

Next morning he went out and stood gazing intently at the walls of the castle. Presently the laird came to where he was and inquired what he was gazing at.

"I am looking at a stone that has been placed askew", replied the builder, "and which will bring down the whole castle unless it be taken out".

"Then it must be taken out", said the great man in a commanding voice. The builder said that he could not take it out without a special hammer which he had left behind in Edinburgh. The laird said a messenger must be sent for it, but the builder replied that the hammer was so valuable that his wife would not part with it unless the laird's own son and heir went for it.

"I myself will give him a letter to my wife", said the builder, and the wording of the letter ran thus:

"I have sent to you the little hammer, and do not part with it until the big hammer goes home".

"Quite right", said his wife when she read the letter. And forthwith she had the laird's son committed to prison, and did not release him until the builder and his son were paid and reached home in safety.

The laird suspected that it was the red-haired girl who had betrayed the plot, so she was dragged to the top of the castle and flung over the wall to her death on the rocks below. It was from this circumstance the castle got its name of the Castle of the Red-haired Girl. The dwellers in the castle had no rest or peace after this, for on dark and stormy nights torches were seen on the battlements, where no lights should have been. And a long, ghastly scream rang out, followed by a deathly silence'.

When the moon is full, the torches are seen and the scream is heard to this very day.

A great tale, and it *may* even be true. But the more prosaic history of the building of *Caisteal na Nighinn Ruaidhe* is as follows. As the sole documentary evidence for *Caisteal Na Nighinn Ruaidhe* is in one charter of 1414, one reference in a family history written in the 18th century and one tale of its building, then a lot has to be surmised.

The MacDougalls under their Chief, Alexander of Argyll, held great power in the 1200s and many clans suffered, including the Campbells. Indeed, as we have seen in Tale One, the Chief of Clan Campbell, Cailean Mor, lost his life in a skirmish led by John Bacach MacDougall high on the String of Lorn. The King's writ was always weak in the west, but during the Wars of Independence it was almost non-existent. Not until Robert the Bruce triumphed in 1308 at the Pass of Brander and then captured Dunstaffnage Castle was the power of Alexander of Argyll broken. Alexander and his son John Bacach retired to England, where the latter entered the service of Edward II, continuing until his death to strive against Robert the Bruce.

Following Bruce's success in 1308 the MacDougall lands were forfeited, followed by their re-distribution amongst the King's followers, and I think it was about this time the castle was built. On 10th February 1316 King Robert granted to Sir Colin Campbell – grandson of *Cailean Mor* – '… the whole land of Lochow, in one free Barony …' However, less than a decade earlier Edward I had controlled Scotland; the MacDougall Lords of Lorn had been triumphant at Dalrigh, and Bruce's future was uncertain. Although Bruce now looked secure after Bannockburn, a wise man would protect his landholdings as best he could, and I contend that this is exactly what Sir Colin Campbell did at Lochavich. His barony lands extended from Loch Crinan in the south to the head of Loch Awe; various kinsmen in their castles controlled lands in the west as far north as Benderloch, and, on his behalf, the major fortress of Dunstaffnage Castle.

His one weak link was the – then – very important route from Loch Awe through Lochavich and Glen Doin to the sea at Craignish, linking Campbell lands on Loch Awe and at Craignish. His grandfather, *Cailean Mor*, had been killed by the MacDougalls not two miles north of Loch Avich; what if fortunes were reversed and the MacDougalls made a comeback? John of Lorn was actively working for Edward II, so better to fortify his weak flank and prepare for all eventualities. A logical site was the old fort at Duninveran, controlling the strategic route from *Innis Chonnell* over the String of Lorn north to Dunstaffnage; but here there was no water. *Innis Luina*, however, had water in plenty and it also controlled the western approaches to Loch Awe.

So I think that *Caisteal na Nighinn Ruaidhe* was built by Sir Colin Campbell shortly after 1316. Indeed, if Sir Colin did think along these lines he was absolutely correct, for in 1343 John of Lorn's grandson – no doubt helped by his marriage to Joanna Isaac, granddaughter of Robert the Bruce – was restored to the MacDougall former Lorn estates, although not to their former power.

Map references

- OS Landranger 55. OS Explorer 360:

  Caisteal na Nighinn Ruaidhe NM 916 138

  Alt Dearg ('the passing rill') NM 926 183

- OS 6" survey of 1861.

Historical notes

- The Ossianic poem Cathluina: this has a marked similarity with events in Tale One, the battle the two brothers Selbach and Ancellaig fought for dominance of Argyll in 719 AD. If so, this throws doubt on it truly being an Ossianic poem of four centuries earlier – but it's still a good yarn! And in the passage 'Blood, mixed with sweat, descends in streams to the ground. It wanders through the green grass, and dyes the passing rill.' the 'passing rill' is probably Alt Dearg, which features in the account of the death in Fineglen of Sir Colin Campbell, also in tale one.

- The Royal Commission on Ancient and Historical Monuments for Scotland [RCAHMS] entry for *Caisteal na Nighinn Ruaidhe* concludes that:

  The existing structure is so ruinous that its age is difficult to ascertain, but in size and plan-form the building bears a considerable resemblance to the nearby castle of Fincharn, Loch Awe, which may be as old as the 13th century. This was probably built about 1240, when the barony of Fincharn was awarded to Gillescop MacGilchrist.

- Forfeiture of the MacDougall lands following Robert Bruce's success at the Pass of Brander and Dunstaffnage Castle in 1308 was followed by their re-distribution amongst the King's followers. On 10th February 1316 King Robert addressed his:

> beloved and faithful Colin, son of Niel Cambel, Knight, confirming to him 'the whole land of Lochow, in one free Barony, by all its righteous metes and marches, in wood and plain, meadows and pastures, muirs and marshes, petaries, ways, paths and waters, stanks, fish-ponds and mills, and with the patronage of the churches, in huntings and hawkings, and in all its other liberties, privileges and just pertinents, as well named as not named.'

- In 1414 Sir Duncan Campbell, Knight of Lochow, granted to Reginald (Campbell) of Craignish the lands of Craignish and Lochavich previously held by him from the King. The actual Charter cannot at present be traced, but a translation of the Precept of Sasine dated 4th June 1414 reads:

> Duncan Campbell lord of Lochawe sends greetings … Because we have given and granted to our beloved and special cousin Reginald Malcolm of Cragynis, … and to the heirs male of his body lawfully procreated or to be procreated, for homage service and special retinue by him and his heirs male to us and our heirs male for ever to be rendered, of all the lands with pertinents within written, [including] … the four penny land of Lochassy [Lochavich] from the north part of the same, namely, the penny land of Dvaga [Duaig], the penny land of Narachan, the penny land of Killemonna [Kilmun], and the penny land of Duninueran [Duninveran] with pertinents: … together with the office of constable of the castles

of Cragynis and of Lochassy … Given under our seal at Innyschonill, 4th of June 1414. And the three penny nether land of Ardechragynie.

Duke Niall transcribed the actual Charter and for us the critical bit is:

'… and if Reginald or his heirs, or we or our heirs, jointly or separately, should erect or build [up] the castles of Lochaffy and of Cragynse, or either of them, we grant the office of constable of that castle, built, constructed and erected, to him and his heirs'.

Sadly, but in common with charters of that time, there are ambiguities!

Sources

- RCAHMS – *The Royal Commission on the Ancient & Historical Monuments of Scotland* – Argyll 2 (Lorn) item 281.
- *Records of Argyll* by Lord Archibald Campbell, 1895.
- *Castles and Keeps of Scotland* by Frank Roy Fraprie.
- *A History of Clan Campbell*, Volume 1 – Alastair Campbell of Airds.
- *The Kingdom of the Isles* by R Andrew McDonald.
- *Argyll – The Enduring Heartland* by Marion Campbell.
- *Scotland As It Was And Is* – The Duke of Argyll – 1888.
- *Argyll Inventory* Vol. 1 p 310. Inveraray Castle Archives.
- *John of Fordun: History of Clan Campbell*.
- *The Manuscript History of Craignish* – Miscellany of the Scottish History Society Volume IV – 1926.

The White Lady of Craignish

A mother's curse: her seducation of a young lad and dispute over a body

This is a tale of Campbells of Craignish, Mac-Dougall of Lorne, MacNaughton of that ilk, the seduction of young MacIver of Asknish, and a quarrelsome burial party, in which the Campbells – for once – came off worst. So, settle back for a story of an heiress, her marriages, quarrels, imprisonment, escape, pursuit, seduction of a young lad, loss of lands, and, finally, her burial.

~

In 1325 – or thereabouts – there was born to Dougall (Campbell) of Craignish a daughter, called Christina, or Christian in some accounts. *The Manuscript History of Craignish*, written in the eighteenth century, calls her 'the eldest and unhappy daughter', and as such she was heiress to her father's Craignish lands. Being thus very eligible – and very young – Christina was duly married off to John MacDougall of Lorn, by whom she had but a single son in twenty years of marriage.

When MacDougall divorced her for the *much* better catch of Johanna Isaac, cousin of King David II, Christina married again, this time to please herself. Her choice fell on a cousin on her mother's side, *Alexander*

MacNaughton of that Ilk. He held lands at the north of Loch Awe, where the family had probably built their castle on *Fraoch Eilean* shortly after receiving a charter to do so in 1267 from Alexander III. No doubt Christina enjoyed living in a new castle, but her Craignish lands reverted to her uncle Malcolm, although Christina's son contested this. Many were the disputes between the two families over the lifting of rents, MacDougall arguing they were rightly his, great-uncle Malcolm asserting they were his. Being in actual possession, great-uncle Malcolm usually won, especially as he was backed up by his son, *Ranald Mor na h-Ordaig* – 'Big Ranald of the Thumb'. There are lots of tales about *him*, but I must not get diverted.

For some reason, Christina was kept under house arrest by her son in the old fortress at Dunollie – not the present castle, which was only built in the 15th century. Whatever the reasons for her incarceration, Christina decided she had had enough. One night she hitched up her hair, her bosoms and her skirts, made a rope of the proverbial bedclothes, and slid down the castle walls. There a trusty ghillie was waiting with two horses, their hooves muffled with bits of old kilt. Silently they headed south through the darkness, heading for Innischonnel Castle and the succour of Sir Colin Campbell, Knight of Lochawe. At the head of Loch Feochan they followed the old track up and into Scammadale before picking up the ancient drove road known as the String of Lorn. Here they climbed steadily up the steep slopes, the burn rushing far below them. All the while they expected the beat of hoofs in pursuit, or for some sentry to challenge them from behind a rock, but luck was on their side.

As dawn broke they passed the cairn marking the death of *Cailean Mor* in 1296 and Christina shivered as they passed that windswept spot. One last hill and they descended thankfully into Lochavich, then on to the shores of Loch Awe opposite Innischonnel, where the ghillie lit a fire of damp wood to attract attention from the castle. Christina must have breathed more easily, but no sign came from the castle and suddenly they heard the sound of hot pursuit – her son was not far behind. Christina shouted desperately for a boat, and at last one sped out from behind the castle, rescuing the lady and her ghillie in the nick of time. From the safety of the boat the mother hurled abuse at her son fuming on the shore – not the sort of thing a well brought up lady should do, but having only just escaped imprisonment no doubt she had just cause. Infuriated by his mother's taunts, the son swiftly drew his bow and fired an arrow so swift and so true that it pinned Christina's hip to the gunwale. That lady promptly let fly a torrent of curses, which included the following:

> *You with the white bow that frisk upon yonder*
>   *shore, pray God*
> *I may hear the noise of the Fowls of the air feeding or*
>   *picking on your face'.*

Now this is not something a mother should wish on a son, but in due course the curse took effect, for MacDougall was killed by the men of Craignish whilst trying to extract a rent from them. Which only goes to show, never fire arrows at Mum.

~

Quite why we do not know, but in August 1361 Christina made a grant to her 'cousin' the Knight of Lochawe, of

3.1 The White Lady hit

'her part of her late husband Alexander MacNaughton's barony – including the castle of *Fraoch Eilean* – in return for a sum of money and cows already handed over'. At that time Sir Colin had in his service young MacIver of Asknish (now known as Arduaine), for the MacIvers were a sept of Clan Campbell. With this lad Christina fell desperately and passionately in love – for, you see, toy boys are no new fad.

She arranged for MacIver to be her sole attendant on a journey from Loch Awe to Craignish, and the pair duly set out one fine summer day. The track in those days wound along the southern shore of Loch Avich, up the narrow and steep confines of *Bealach Salach nan Airm* (the Pass of the Nasty Place) and into *Glen Domhain* (the Deep Glen). This narrow cleft to the sea at Craignish frames the distant Paps of Jura, and down it runs the burn that eventually swells to become Barbreck River. Not so long ago it was a major route from Loch Awe to the coast, with much additional traffic between the various farms and houses in the glen, now all abandoned.

Just over the march to the Craignish lands, and nearly opposite the ruins of Grianaig is a small birchwood. Being hot and weary from the journey, Christina and young MacIver dismounted and tied the horses to a tree whilst they partook of their pieces in the shade. As he lifted the Lady from her saddle MacIver could not help but observe that in spite of being nearly thirty-five, and thus ancient by the standards of that time, Christina was in excellent trim. Thus it was they partook of more than their pieces, for it was in the wood that Christina seduced the lad – if indeed he needed any seduction. The wood survives to this day, and is known as *Coille na Bhain-tighearna* – The White Lady's Wood.

Christina, however, found herself pregnant, and being determined to marry young MacIver she approached Sir Colin for his consent. There is a suspicion that the Knight of Lochawe had also enjoyed the fair Christina's favours, but Sir Colin drove a hard bargain for the right to re-marriage, and she had to sign away her rights to Craignish, duly registered at Edinburgh in November 1361.

At last Christina died, but knowing her past history one could hardly expect the burial to be a simple matter. Four families attended the funeral – Campbells, MacDougalls, MacNaughtons and MacIvers. The Campbells and

3.2 Glen Domhain with the Paps of Jura in the distance and Coille na Bhain-tighearna on the left

MacIvers set off with the coffin for Kilmory at Craignish; the MacDougalls declared she should rest in their church of Kilbride at Lerags. The MacNaughtons hung back discreetly.

A halt was called for refreshments, set out ready in a convenient barn. No doubt it was pure accident that the MacDougalls were trapped inside by a jammed door, and that by the time they had broken through the wall the other mourners had disappeared. If only they had known where to look for it the coffin was still nearby, hidden under the capstone of a Bronze Age grave. The MacDougalls, however, wasted no time in playing find-the-lady, but rounded up as many Campbell cattle as they could find, and drove them off towards Dunollie. True, they would have to cross MacIver land, but weren't the men of the clan all attending a funeral, and surely they would be some time?

There must have been some amount of refreshments in that barn, for it was only on arriving at Kilmory that the Campbells and MacIvers noticed the funeral procession had no coffin. A smart about-turn, and they set off hotfoot to pursue MacDougalls and lifted cattle alike. Seizing their chance, the patient MacNaughtons now emerged from hiding and bore the coffin away up Glen Domhain, past the roebuck-stone, past *Coille na Bhain-tighearna*, along the shore of Loch Avich and finally home to Loch Awe and burial.

The White Lady – 'this vile woman' as *The Manuscript History of Craignish* called her – was at last at peace.

Map references

- OS Landranger 55. OS Explorer 358, 359 & 360:

  Coille na Bhain-tighearna NM 873 108.

Historical notes

- In fact, in 1361 Christina granted her MacNaughton inheritance to a character called John of Prestwych (whom nobody has identified yet) from whom it seems to have passed to Sir Colin *Iongantach* of Lochawe. He in turn probably granted *Fraoch Eilean* and the supporting lands of Innistrynich, Achlian and Duchollie to his brother Duncan *Sceodnasach* – legend has it that Duncan was fostered in Ardsceodnish, hence his by-name.

- Although Christina had married John *Gallda* (MacDougall) of Lorn, it seems he set her aside when offered the hand of Johanna, grand-daughter of Robert Bruce. John was called *gallda* since he had been brought up at the English court where his family had been exiled after their defeat in the Pass of Brander by Robert Bruce. John *gallda* had been befriended by David II, King of Scots, during David's own exile at the English court; he thus offered John *gallda* his cousin Johanna in marriage.

- The son Christina had with John *gallda* was the first of the family of Dunollie, because by his second marriage John only had daughters.

- Sir Colin Campbell had in fact married Christina's daughter, but later seems to have set her aside for a more advantageous marriage to the heiress of John Campbell of Ardsceodnish.

- Alexander MacNaughton of that ilk appears to have had sons by his earlier marriage before he married Christina. Sir Colin Campbell seems to have granted them land in Glen Shira (?) where they built a castle, but it became infested with the plague so they then built Dunderave Castle. A pile of stones is said to mark the site of their plagued castle. So how Christina managed to end up with Fraoch Eilean castle – instead of the male heirs – is the mystery. But her grant to John of Prestwych is a clear grant.

Sources

- *The Manuscript History of Craignish* – Miscellany of the Scottish History Society Volume IV, 1926.
- *Argyll – The Enduring Heartland*, by Marion Campbell of Kilberry.
- *A History of Clan Campbell, Volume 1*, by Alastair Campbell of Airds.

Three Castles of Skye

Dunscaith: Duntulm: Caisteal Uisdean

The western seaboard of Skye has a series of duns and forts scattered along its coast, all within sight of each other. Probably built by the early Celts to give warning of Viking raids, one was captured and enlarged by a Norse invader, to which he gave his name – Dun Dhaibidh, or David's Fort.

In spite of its area Skye contains few freshwater lochs of any size, and one such – reputed the largest in the island – was located about four miles south-west of Duntulm. In the centre was an island called *Eilean Chaluim Chille*, for on its safety St. Columba founded a monastery, later taken over by the last of the Norsemen, by name Arco Bronmhor.

All attempts to dislodge him failed, and the Lord of the Isles offered a land grant of the Braes – south of Portree – to the man who would rid Skye of the Norseman. A Roag man, one MacSween by name, gained admittance to the island stronghold by posing as a bard, and with songs and tales he lulled to sleep Arco and his men, then promptly struck off the formers head and rapidly made good his escape with it tucked under his arm. Presenting the grisly object to the Lord of the Isles, he was duly rewarded with his land, and this, we are told, was the last Norseman on Skye.

The loch having silted up, attempts were made to drain

4.1 Eilean Chaluim Chille

it in 1716, but were not fully successful until 1825, when it provided the richest land on Skye, requiring no manure for the first twenty years of crops. The New Statistical Account of 1796 says that:

> St. Columba's Lake … was yearly frequented by large flocks of swans … [which] … appeared on 25th October annually, passed the winter on the lake, and remained in all about five months. In autumn, after the lake was drained, they made their appearance at the usual time, but on observing the destruction of their usual favourite haunt, they hovered with a cry of sadness for a brief period over it, then disappeared, and have seldom been seen since near the place.

Nowadays the great ditches, many feet deep, have silted up, but their banks are home to damp-loving plants that blossom in profusion during spring and summer. The many acres of land, won at such labour and once so fertile for crops, are now grazing for cattle and sheep. The marshy conditions are a haven for snipe, curlew and the elusive, crepuscular corncrake – five pairs when we were there.

The beheading of Arco Bronmhor saw, in theory, the last of the Norsemen, but of course one man does not represent the sole legacy of several hundred years. The Norsemen arrived in the 9th century, at first to plunder, then to trade and settle, for Norway was overcrowded and the inhabitants were fine and adventurous seamen. In time Norway controlled – and claimed – the Orkneys, Shetlands, Outer Isles, Inner Isles and much of the western Scottish mainland. But the hold of the Norwegian king was tenuous, and the local princes and chiefs remarkably adept at ignoring his commands, for the king in Norway was far away. And as Scottish kings increasingly strengthened their own hold on the emergent kingdom, so did the grip from Norway weaken. In 1266, Norway finally ceded to Scotland all the lands she claimed there.

For the common people a change of king made no difference at all – life was equally hard and unforgiving, and the local chief just as rapacious. But for those at the top this change of allegiance brought new opportunities as well as dangers. The king in Edinburgh was distant and

Duntulm

Loch
Callum
Chille

Uisdean

Dunvegan

Portree

Ramsay

SKYE

Scalpay

Cuillins

Dunscaith

Soay

Camus

4.2 Three castles on Skye

his own hold on the western margins of his kingdom just as tenuous as had been Norway's. Leod, son of a Norse prince, was granted Dunvegan and much of Skye and from him descended the MacLeods of Dunvegan. Much of the later history of the island is of the struggle between MacLeods and Macdonalds for Skye – on the one hand to hold the lands, on the other to acquire them.

For with the emergence of Somerled in about 1130 the Macdonald Lords of the Isles – based at Finlaggan on Islay – increasingly gained control by marriage and conquest of most of the western seaboard and islands. In their latter days they gained the vast and rich lands of the Earldom of Ross, although this eventually contributed to their downfall. Indeed, from 1353 – the date accepted as the start of the medieval Lordship of the Isles – theirs was, in effect, a principality within the Kingdom of Scotland, although at times they treated directly with the English kings as if independent rulers. However, as the Kings of Scotland became progressively stronger they were anxious to bring under control this Celtic mini-kingdom fringing their western margins

In 1493, James IV forfeited the Lordship of the Isles, although intermittent risings followed Donald Dubh – grandson of John, Earl of Ross, last Lord of the Isles – until Donald's death in 1545 without an heir. With the abolition of the Lordship their central control was dispersed and a power vacuum formed, which the clans contentedly filled with almost constant warfare for the next two generations. For as the bards recounted, 'It is no joy without Clan Donald. It is no strength to be without them'.

Early reports said that Trotternish, the north-eastern peninsula of Skye *'is a most pleasant, profitabl and most fertill Countrey both of corne and abundances of milk'*. So it is no surprise that with their increasing strength the Macdonald Lords of the Isles soon attempted to evict the MacLeods from Skye.

Dunscaith

Although the Lordship itself had been forfeit, strong branches of Clan Donald survived, and one such was Macdonald of Sleat, originally based at *Caisteal Camus*, now known as Knock Castle. This was the first stronghold on Skye to be wrested from the MacLeods by the Lords of the Isles, and the Macdonalds took great care to hold it tight. Indeed, as late as 1617 *Donald Gorm* Macdonald held his Skye lands from the Crown on condition that *Caisteal Camus* should at all times be ready to receive the King or his representative.

When, in time, the rest of the Sleat Peninsula fell into their hands, the Macdonalds moved from *Camus* to *Dunscaith*, previously occupied – according to legend – by an Amazon queen by name *Sgáthach*. Folklore has the castle as having:

> seven great doors and seven great windows be-
> tween every two doors of them, and thrice fifty
> couches between every two windows of them, and

4.3 *Dunscaith*

thrice fifty marriageable girls in scarlet cloaks and in beautiful and blue attire attending and waiting upon Sgáthach.

Queen Sgáthach was a warrior without equal, and she trained many in the art of battle. Over the sea in Ireland dwelt one Cuchulainn, Knight of the Red Branch of Ulster, renowned 'for the melody of his language, for the beauty of his face, and for the loveliness of his look'. Cuchulainn determined to visit Queen Sgáthach and receive instruction from her, and after many adventures he did so. For this he was awarded the title 'Chief of the Isle of Mist', for the poetical name for Skye is *Eilean a' Cheó* – Isle of Mist. It is tempting to link the name of Cuchulainn with the mighty Cuillin range, but in fact their name more aptly comes from *cuilinn* or holly. Seen from Dunscaith Castle the peaks of the Black Cuillins are etched jaggedly sharp against the northern skyline, clearly resembling the shape and spines of a holly leaf.

One tale has Dunscaith occupied for a short time by the crew from a Roman galley, and certainly a Roman fleet did circumnavigate Britain. What is almost certain is that it started life as a Celtic *dun*, built as protection against the Norsemen. When Norway ceded to Scotland all her Scottish lands the original vitrified fort was probably enlarged with a keep by MacLeod of Dunvegan about that time. MacLeods in turn were ousted by Macdonalds, who later enlarged and fortified the keep into a castle. It is an excellent site, washed on three sides by the sea, and on the fourth separated from the land by a deep gully. Across this was built an arched causeway with space for a wooden drawbridge, and as long as the freshwater held out Dunscaith was all but unassailable.

A charter of 1449 confirms Hugh Macdonald in his Sleat lands in south Skye, so it was probably at some prior date that the tale I am about to unfold occurred. For Macdonald of Sleat – weary at the incessant warfare with MacLeod of Dunvegan – determined to marry his daughter to MacLeod's son and heir. The daughter, however, was violently opposed to the match, but in the way of the times her views were totally disregarded – after all, what was the point of daughters if not to keep house and make advantageous marriages? The handfasting duly went ahead, and in spite of the daughter's deep hatred of both husband and father, in time two sons were born, flaxen-haired, sturdy lads, as befits a MacLeod heir. And in time Macdonald invited them all back to Dunscaith for a great deer drive, for he doted on the two lads, his only grandchildren.

It was a foul day for the deer drive, with lashing rain driven by a westerly gale, and the Cuillins constantly hidden behind low cloud. On their sodden return they were thus delighted to be met by Mistress MacLeod, bidding them hurry to the supper table, for she had made with her own hands a great fawn pasty in honour of the day. Ravenous with hunger they fell upon the pie and pronounced it delicious; only when they had mopped up the last bit of succulent juice with hunks of bread did Mistress MacLeod reveal the truth. In the depth of her hatred for the father who had given, and the husband who had taken her in marriage, she had cooked, and they had eaten, her own sons.

"No heirs for Macdonald. No heirs for MacLeod," she screamed, and the poor, demented woman flung herself from the window to welcome death on the rocks below. Far above, husband and father stared down through the shattered window in horror and disbelief, whilst on the rocks below gale-driven spray washed the blood from her lifeless corpse. The fitful moon shone but intermittently through the racing clouds, and as its last beams disappeared for that night, a ferocious gust of wind blew out every last guttering candle in the great hall of Dunscaith Castle.

And they do say, that on dark and stormy nights there can be seen wandering amongst the ruins of Dunscaith the ghostly forms of a bloodied woman holding the hands of her two flaxen-haired sons, searching, always searching. But what they have lost, no one can say.

~

Several generations later, in about the 1520s, the Macdonald of the day was *Donald Gruamach* (Moody Donald, 4th of Sleat), married to a Clanranald. One day she was entertaining twelve of her kinsman who just happened to have dropped in for tea when a cousin of her husband's also dropped in, one Ranald Macdonald from North Uist. He too stayed the night, but arose early next morning and prepared to depart. *Donald Gruamach* urged him to stay longer, but Ranald was adamant that he must depart.

"At least stay and say goodbye to my wife," remonstrated Donald.

"If I stay, she will not thank me," retorted Ranald enigmatically as he hurried down to his waiting birlinn.

And thank him she did not, for on drawing back the curtains of the solar Lady Macdonald beheld her twelve kinsmen strung up in full view, each and every throat slit by Ranald Macdonald's dirk. Ranald, it appears, nurtured a feud with her family of Clanranald, and had taken this heaven-sent opportunity to even the score by a round dozen.

Lady Macdonald, not surprisingly, was somewhat miffed at this display of bad manners from a guest, and immediately despatched her steward to assassinate Ranald, which the faithful man duly accomplished. Good staff are *such* an asset!

~

In ruins for many centuries, Dunscaith Castle is well worth a visit, for it is steeped in history, and an easy walk out. The road from Ostaig is firstly over moorland, then through old woods of hazel, birch and oak past Tarskavaig. Here, Seton Gordon recorded, 'there is a small church, built at the water's edge, and during the Sabbath service the roar of the surf mingles with the mournful cadences of the Gaelic psalms'.

On a clear day the views westward from Dunscaith Castle to the Small Isles and northward to the Cuillins are amongst the most dramatic on Skye.

Dunscaith commanded the approaches between Skye and the mainland, but it was many miles from the vital sea-route between Skye and the Outer Isles. Besides, Macdonald of Sleat coveted the rich lands of Trotternish – *'fertill Countrey both of corne and abundances of milk'*. So it came as no surprise that in 1539 *Donald Gruamach* seized both Duntulm and Trotternish, for in a spot of early ethnic cleansing he drove out at spear point every single MacLeod inhabitant of Trotternish.

Some accounts credit Donald as building Duntulm keep into a castle. But whether enlarged by Angus, Master of the Isles in 1485 or by Donald Gruamach in 1539, the latter was the first Macdonald of Sleat to leave Dunscaith and make Duntulm his official residence, the better to hold his newly acquired lands. He had not long to enjoy his new castle, for Donald Gruamach died that same year, mortally wounded by an arrow whilst unsuccessfully besieging Eilean Donan Castle (see Tale Sixteen – Eilean Donan). He was succeeded by his son, Donald Gorm (blue eyes).

Duntulm

We have seen how the Viking fort of *Dun Dhaibidh* (David's Fort) became in Gaelic *Duntulm* (The fort of the knoll or eminence). One report has Angus, Master of the Isles, capturing and enlarging the fort of Duntulm into a castle in 1485, but the Macdonalds in due course were themselves turned out by MacLeod of Dunvegan. In 1498 'Alexandro Makloid de Dunbegane' was required to have ready for the Crown one galley of twenty-six oars and two galleys of sixteen oars, but, interestingly, the charter of lands specifically reserved to the King all falcon's nests.

In 1539 Donald Gruamach was the first Macdonald of Sleat to leave Dunscaith and make Duntulm his official residence. Perched on a rocky headland rising sheer from the restless waters of the sea, from a distance the castle might be the cliff itself, so firmly embedded are the weathered stones. From it is one of the finest views in the islands, for the hills of Harris rise clear across the Minch, while to the south the cone of Eaval in North Uist lies on the western horizon. But as we will see in Tale Fifteen,

Donald Gruamach did not enjoy Duntulm for long, for he died that same year.

In the summer of 1540 James V determined on a show of strength to this unruly part of his realm, and embarked in the *Salamander*, 'which the French king gave him', along with a fleet of fifteen other ships. From Lewis James made his Skye landfall at Dunvegan Loch, where *Alasdair Crotach* (Hunchbacked) MacLeod wisely submitted to this show of force. Together with several other chiefs he embarked in the *Salamander* with the king, and the whole fleet sailed for Score Bay and Duntulm.

Perched high on its clifftop, Duntulm commanded the bay into which James V and his fleet sailed that summer day over four-and-a-half centuries ago. James much admired Duntulm's great strength, size and beauty, and no doubt took note of its potential as a fortress, whether for him or against him. From Duntulm the fleet sailed north about Skye to *Loch Columcille* and the hamlet of *Kiltarraghan*; in honour of the king's visit the hamlet was renamed *Port an Righ* (Port of the King), and in what is now Portree Square the king held his court. There he summoned all the island chiefs to do homage and vow fealty, but in spite of this, when he sailed away he carried with him both MacLeod's heir and Clanranald himself as hostages to good conduct.

Donald Gorm had died by 1546 and was succeeded by his son, *Donald Gormson* (son of Donald blue-eyes). In the bay below Duntulm Castle lies Tulm Island (sometimes called Holm Island), of which Martin Martin wrote in 1549, 'Ellan Tuilm, haff mile lairge or thereby, good for corn and store, pertaining to Donald Gormsone'.

It provides scant shelter from the prevailing south-westerly's, so the birlinns from Duntulm used to be drawn up on the smooth rocks below the castle, where in time their iron-shod keels wore two parallel grooves, still to be seen. A harbour was cut from the solid rock to provide further shelter for the galleys, today used by local fishermen.

Donald Gormson did much to further the interests of Clan Donald, and it was probably he who built the garden at Duntulm with soil imported from seven kingdoms – England, Ireland, Spain, France, Germany, Norway and Denmark. When Seton Gordon lived there in the 1930's, two hundred years after the castle was abandoned, the garden was a hayfield, from which good crops were cut from the soil of the seven kingdoms. As for Tulm Island – 'good for corn' – none was grown there after the Macdonalds moved to Monkstadt in about 1730.

Donald Gormson died about 1573, and was succeeded by his son, *Donald Gorm Mor* (Macdonald, 6th of Sleat), a child, but who in manhood history does not remember kindly. For although *Donald Gorm Mor* had three wives, none produced for him the coveted son and heir, perhaps because he was such an unpleasant character. One of his wives was sister to Rory Mor MacLeod of Dunvegan, one Margaret, who had had the misfortune to lose an eye. Such was his dislike of this poor woman that at the end of the year's handfasting Donald returned the unfortunate Margaret to her brother – without, one assumes, her dowry. He mounted her on a one-eyed horse, escorted by a one-eyed man followed by a one-eyed dog. This calculated insult naturally led to an uprising of clan fighting, which became known as *Cogadh na Cailleach Caime* or the War of the One-eyed Woman. So hurt and so bitter was the despised Margaret that her ghost returned to haunt the Castle of Duntulm, and on moonlit nights her weeping is heard still.

Donald Gorm Mor died in Edinburgh, but his wraith appeared at Duntulm the following night and informed his family and followers:

> *I was in Edinburgh yestreen,*
> *I am in mine own hall tonight,*
> *And as much as the mote in the sun,*
> *There is not of harm in my corpse.*

Having failed to produce an heir, the chieftancy passed to his nephew, *Donald Gorm Og*; with it young Donald inherited all the vast lands and holdings of the Macdonalds of Sleat, but he had one vital problem – no title deeds. His uncle had hidden them for safety, but totally neglected to tell anyone of their place of concealment, least of all his nephew. In times past this would have been no problem, as lands were chiefly held by the sword; but in 1597 James VI in far-away Lowland Edinburgh had decreed that all Highland Chiefs must produce titles to their lands as proof of ownership – no deeds, no land.

This left Donald in somewhat of a quandary, but worse was to follow, for his uncle continued to haunt Duntulm

Castle. Not only that, but he brought with him a couple of ghost-friends, and so drunken were their revels and so loud their singing that the more earthly inhabitants of the castle seldom got a wink of sleep. Things became progressively worse until at last *Donald Gorm Og* sought the advice of a priest, who blessed seven flaming torches of pine-wood. With six of his most stalwart men Donald confronted the three ghosts in the middle of his uncle's favourite and noisiest song.

The ghost of uncle was so impressed by the sanctity of the torches and the courage of his nephew that he not only agreed to moderate the noise level, but he also revealed where the deeds were hidden. Parchments in hand, *Donald Gorm Og* of Sleat high-tailed it for the fleshpots of Edinburgh and the Court of James. There he duly registered his lands together with:

> the woods, fishings, sheallings, grassings, mosses, muirs, meadows, annexis, connexis, pairts, pendicles, and pertinents of the said heal lands.

And that is why, to this very day, his descendant is known as 'Chief of the Name and Arms of Macdonald of Macdonald and High Chief of Clan Donald'.

Quite why Duntulm Castle was abandoned is unclear, but as the ghosts of *Donald Gorm Mor* and Margaret Macleod were a century later joined by a third (and some say a fourth), perhaps all these hauntings made life in the old castle unbearable. For in the early years of the eighteenth century a great ball was given to celebrate the birth of an heir to Macdonald, at which the oldest tenant was to propose the toast. The old man was brought in, the music ceased, and all gathered to raise their glasses as the nurse brought in the baby. The first words only of a Gaelic toast passed the lips of the old retainer before he collapsed to the floor.

"Merely a faint," said the doctor.

"Too much excitement," said some.

"Too many drams," said his relations.

Others were not so sanguine. "What did he see?" they asked. "What omen does it portend?"

Within months the baby was dead, accidentally dropped by his nurse from an upstairs window onto the rocks far below. Macdonald in his grief ordered the nurse

4.4 *Duntulum*

to be bound tightly and cast adrift upon the Minch in a leaking boat. Her shrieks as she was dragged off still haunt the castle, although one account says she was merely taken by her kinsmen to the dungeons whilst a dummy was set adrift in the boat, and the nurse later conveyed to her father's croft at Treaslane under cover of darkness.

Some say this was the last great happening in the castle, others that it was a ball given by Sir Donald Macdonald – *Domhnall a' Chogaidh* or Donald of the War – when the clan came out for the '15. Following defeat at Sherriffmuir the estates were forfeit the following year; about fifteen years later Macdonald of Sleat abandoned draughty old Duntulm and moved to the less impressive but infinitely more comfortable house of Monkstadt.

Certain it was that the old tenant had seen something, but whether the death of the child, the failure of the '15, the abandonment and ruin of Duntulm or the exile of Macdonald we shall never know. And although these events seem to us far in the distant past, Seton Gordon, writing at Duntulm Lodge in the 1920's, knew of an old woman in the neighbouring village of Conista whose father, as a young boy, recalled seeing lights blazing from the windows of Duntulm Castle.

No doubt the MacArthurs played at that final great ball, for they were hereditary pipers to the Macdonalds, and:

> from time immemorial occupied the lands of Hunglader in virtue of their office. In 1773 these lands were valued at eighty-four merks of silver duty.

The MacArthurs (sometimes spelled MacKarter) vied with the MacCrimons, hereditary pipers to Macleod of Dunvegan Castle, and although less famous were renowned throughout the piping world. During his tour of Skye in 1772 Pennant wrote:

> took a repast at Sir Alexander MacDonald's piper, who, according to ancient custom, by virtue of his office, holds his lands free. His dwelling consists of several apartments – the first for his cattle during winter; the second is his hall; the third for the reception of strangers; and the fourth for the lodging of his family.

The MacArthurs played the pipes at the funeral of Flora Macdonald in 1790, but that is the last we hear of them. Their burial place was Kilmuir Churchyard, close to their lands of Hunglader, and in there is a flat gravestone, heavily weathered and moss-grown, of which the inscription reads:

HERE LY

THE REMAINS OF

CHARLES MAC

KARTER WHOSE

FAME AS AN HON

EST MAN AND

REMARKABLE PIP

ER WILL SURVIVE

THIS GENERATION

FOR HIS MANNERS

WERE EASY & REG

ULAR AS HIS

MUSIC & THE

MELODY OF

HIS FINGERS WILL

And there the inscription stops, for Charles' son Donald was drowned whilst ferrying cattle across the Minch from North Uist. Donald was paying for the inscription at – so it is said – sixpence a word, and no one saw fit to complete this memorial to his father.

Caisteal Uisdean

Unpleasant though *Donald Gorm Mor* Macdonald may have been, his nephew was even worse. This was *Uisdean mac Gillespic Chleirich* (Hugh, Son of Archibald the Clerk), a giant of a man whom history remembers as dark, dishonest and devious. His grandfather had been *Donald Gruamach*, 4th of Sleat, and Hugh fostered a deep belief that he himself should be the chief, not his uncle.

South of Uig Bay, twelve miles from Duntulm, he started to build himself a keep, perched on the very edge of the sea cliff, with its landward side protected by boggy ground through which none could pass easily or swiftly. Standing four-square to the sea and all the gales driven in from the Sea of the Hebrides, the only entrance was nine feet high, from which door a ladder was lowered for anyone requiring entry. Naturally enough the keep became known as *Caisteal Uisdean* (Hugh's Castle) although it was never actually completed, as my tale will reveal.

Now, castles are expensive to build, and Hugh's elder brother was likely to inherit the rich Macdonald lands held by *Donald Gorm Mor*. Thus Hugh took to piracy, raiding vessels in the Minch and mooring his galley *An Ealadh* (The Swan) in a sheltered inlet half a mile north of the castle, known to this day as *Pol na h-Ealaidh*. Whenever he acquired sufficient booty he built up the castle walls a bit more, but things came to a halt in 1585 when he was outlawed by *Donald Gorm Mor*, for his depredations on the Minch shipping threatened the trade of all.

Later that year *Donald Gorm Mor* sailed to visit his kinsman and ally, Angus Macdonald of Islay, but storms forced him to seek shelter on Jura, which then belonged to Maclean of Duart. By sheer bad chance Hugh and another outlaw were also on Jura, and seizing their chance they made off with some of Maclean's cattle, certain that *Donald Gorm* would be blamed – as he was. In the dead of night the Macleans fell upon the Macdonalds, and many men of Sleat were killed, *Donald Gorm* himself only escaping because he had chosen to sleep onboard his galley. From this event followed years of intermittent warfare between Macleans and Macdonalds, and 'for a while they did continually vex one another with slaughter and outrages to the destruction almost of the countries and people'.

Finally Hugh was sufficiently reconciled with *Donald Gorm* to be allowed his return to Skye and the further building of *Caisteal Uisdean*. However, Donald continued to regard his nephew with deep suspicion, and justifiably so; Hugh was, in fact, plotting to murder both Donald and his own elder brother in order to gain the chieftancy. In 1602, as the castle was nearing completion, Hugh wrote a friendly invitation for *Donald Gorm* to attend a house-warming feast and to let bygones be bygones. At the same time he wrote explicit instructions to one William Martin of East Trotternish to murder Donald once ensconced within the castle. Now, his father may have been a Clerk, but Hugh himself was pretty hopeless at filing, for he confused the two letters, and sent the murder instructions to his intended victim, *Donald Gorm Mor*.

Not surprisingly, Donald took a dim view of this murderous plot, and he instantly despatched to arrest Hugh the best swordsman in Skye, a chap called *Domhnall MacIain ic Sheumais* (Donald, son of Ian, son of James). His descendants became the Macdonalds of Kingsburgh who were to gain immortality by sheltering Bonnie Prince Charlie and Flora Macdonald. (The room wherein the Prince slept was kept intact until Johnson and Boswell came to stay, when the good Doctor unwittingly lit and burnt the carefully preserved half candle from the Prince's bedside!)

Now Donald, son of Ian, son of James was not only the best swordsman on Skye but he also thought ahead a bit. Thus he equipped the raiding party with ladders, and in time they managed to fight their way into *Caisteal Uisdean*. Hugh sought to conceal himself in woman's clothing, sitting in the kitchen grinding corn at a quern, but his great stature gave him away and he was roughly seized. Shrugging off the cloak he fought his way to the door, leapt down the ladder and raced across the moor to his galley moored in *Pol na h-Ealaidh*. Safely onboard *An Ealadh* he sped cross the Minch to Newton, in North Uist, where he hid out in the ruins of the appropriately named *Dun Sticer* (Fort of the Skulker).

This proved to be Hugh's undoing, for some years earlier he had rooted out from their farms on that island the MacVicar family, in the process killing Donald MacVicar, along with his sons Angus, Donald, Hector and John. Early one morning the Widow MacVicar was turning out her one remaining cow to graze on the moor when she observed Hugh swimming ashore from his hiding place. Not surprisingly the good widow made all haste to lead Macdonald's men to the islet on which stood *Dun Sticer*, and there they duly captured Hugh and bound him securely.

Dragged back to face the wrath of *Donald Gorm Mor*, the latter instantly threw Hugh into a dungeon below Duntulm Castle. There he was starved for many days before being lowered a large chunk of salt beef on a pewter plate; ravenous with hunger he wolfed down the lot, but being denied any water he died a horrible death from thirst, chewing the pewter plate to pieces in his anguish. For his many crimes and murders Hugh was denied Christian burial, and the corpse was left above ground in Kilmuir kirkyard for the ravens to pick at. As late as 1827 his skull and great thighbones lay on a windowsill of that church before finally being buried.

There is a marvellous waulking song ascribed to a sister of the slain MacVicars, of which the first and last verses are

4.5
Caisteal Uisdean

a pretty good curse, and one which all too rapidly came true:

Thou tall man from the Coolin hills,
Strong art thou, mighty thy blow;
My seven curses on thy foster-mother
That she did not press on thee with knee or elbow
Before thou didst slay all the brothers!

Tall Hugh, son of Archibald the Clerk,
Where thou liest down, arise not whole!
May the news of thy death reach the women of Sleat,
May thy entrails be in the tail of thy shirt,
And may I have my share in it!

Thus it was that *Caisteal Uisdean* was never completed, but the ruins remain, perched high above the waters where Great Northern Divers feed on their journey north to Iceland. Almost as big as a goose and seldom seen in flight, the fishermen of old considered they were unable to fly, but swam the whole eight hundred miles to their nesting sites. Indeed, it was said by some on Skye that the birds were the souls of men murdered by Hugh, son of Archibald the Clerk, returning to haunt the waters below the very castle where he lived. Who am I to gainsay this?

Map references

- OS Landranger 23 & 32.
- OS Explorers:

  408 – *Duntulm* Castle, *Eilean Chaluim Chille, Caisteal Uisdean*.

  412 – *Caisteal Camus, Dunscaith* Castle.

- OS Grid references:

  Duntulm Castle NG 409 742

  Eilean Chaluim Chille NG 376 68

  Caisteal Uisdean NG 381 583

  Pol na h-Ealaidh NG 378 603

  Dunscaith Castle NG 595 121

  Caisteal Camus NG 671 086

Historical notes

- DUNSCAITH: The legend of Queen Sgáthach is, of course, myth. As far as I know the tales of Mistress Macleod cooking her own sons and Clanranald murdering then stringing up twelve Macdonalds are both based on fact.

- DUNTULM: *Alasdair Crotach* Macleod: during a skirmish with the Macdonalds, in which there were heavy losses of life as well as ten Macdonald galleys, Alasdair was wounded in the back by one Evan MacKail, who wielded a battle axe. But as the wounded Alasdair fell he grabbed hold of Evan MacKail and brought him to the ground, killed him with his dirk and cut off the dead man's head as a trophy. But the wound crippled him the rest of his life, hence crotach, meaning 'humpbacked'. In 1830 there were still heaps of skulls and bones where the battle took place!

- Years before his death, *Alasdair Crotach* gave up the

leadership of the clan to his son, William, then retired to the monastery of Rodel, on Harris. He endowed the monastery with lands and restored the church, where his tomb is one of the most magnificently carved tombs of its era in Scotland. *Alasdair Crotach* was the first MacLeod chief not to be buried on the island of Iona.

• JAMES V'S 1540 PROGRESS TO THE ISLES: There were 3-4000 men embarked for this visit to 'the north and south isles for the ordouring of thame in justice and gude policy'. Almost all the nobility were ordered to attend upon the King, including the Earls of Argyll, Huntly, Atholl, Arran, Errol, Moray, Cassilis and the Earl Marischal; and Lord Maxwell, Admiral of Scotland. There were merchant ships for the lords and gentlemen, three ships for victuals, a hulk for baggage, and a bark to be the 'scurior' before the fleet. The record of expenses includes twelve shillings for grey cloth to line a coloured coat for the King 'quhen he zeid [went] to the Ilis', for someone must have warned him that the wind might be cold when he rounded Cape Wrath.

• The fleet sailed in early June, James having delayed for the safe birth of his son James by Mary of Lorraine on the 22nd of May. This was a royal progress, intended to impress the further reaches of the Kingdom, and the King dined on gold plate to the sound of music. For on a progress, whether by sea or on land, he expected to be entertained with as much splendour as if in his own palace. The voyage ended in mid-August at Dumbarton, and was adjudged a great success in strengthening the King's hold on his outlying regions.

• CAISTEAL UISDEAN: All true! The castle is on a working farm but of easy, if somewhat damp, access.

Sources

- *Skye – The Island and Its Legends* – Otta F Swire.
- *The Charm of Skye, The Wingéd Isle* – Seton Gordon.
- *Highland Days* – Seton Gordon.
- *Highland Summer* – Seton Gordon.
- *The Heather and the Gale* – Ronald Williams.
- *The Lords of the Isles* – Ronald Williams.
- *A rutter of the Scottish Seas* circa 1540 – Alexander Lindsay. National Maritime Museum monograph No. 44-1980.
- *Carmina Gadelica* (485) – Alexander Carmichael.
- Ibid. Volume II – 1928.
- *West Over Sea* – D C Pochin Mould.
- *Exploring Scotland's Heritage* – Argyll and The Western Isles – Graham Ritchie and Mary Harman.
- *The Royal Commission on Ancient & Historical Monuments of Scotland* (RCAHMS). The Outer Hebrides, Skye and the Small Isles – 1928.
- *Clan Donald* – Donald J Macdonald of Castleton.
- *Burke's Peerage, Baronetage & Knightage and Scottish Clan Chiefs* – 107th Edition.

How the Macleans came to Mull

And of murder, kidnapping & coercion – and a happy ending, at least for our two heroes

The Macleans first came to Mull from the Isle of Seil, near Oban, where *Iain Dubh* (Black John), third chief of Clan Maclean, held lands from John of Lorn, head of Clan MacDougall. *Iain Dubh* was obviously a man of trust with MacDougall, for the latter's son was fostered with Maclean.

Iain Dubh had two sons, *Eachann Reaganach* (Hector the Ferocious) and *Lachlan Lubanach* (Lachlan the Wily). In about 1360 he sent them to Ardtornish Castle, on the eastern shore of the Sound of Mull, where they were to attend upon John of Islay, Lord of the Isles, who had planned a great *tircal*, or deer hunt.

For some reason the Macleans fell out with the Master of the Household, one Niall MacGillebride Mackinnon, Chief of Clan Mackinnon, and holder of great lands on Mull and the adjoining mainland. So deep was Mackinnon's hatred that he resolved to do away with the young men, and accordingly instructed two of his best archers to shoot the brothers during the thick of the deer drive, thus making it seem an accident.

Word leaked out, however, and one who was obliged to Lachlan drew him aside and confided, "Should you and Hector be taking part in the deer drive, it is whispered in this castle that Niall Mackinnon has told his bow-men to cull two young stags that have recently become troublesome in the herd. Even the best of archers can sometimes miss their aim." And so saying, the man withdrew as silently as he had come, leaving the brothers to decide their next move.

At the deer drive, Lachlan and Hector Maclean were so assiduous in their attendance upon John of Islay that not for one moment did they leave his side; even the most skilled archer dare not risk a shot for fear of hitting his Lord.

Their chance for revenge came next day, when John of Islay determined to visit his castle of Aros, and embarked in his *birlinn* to cross the Sound of Mull. He took only a few men, for Mackinnon was to follow in his own galley with the main bodyguard. But no sooner had the Lord of the Isles sailed than the Maclean brothers promptly slew the unfortunate Mackinnon, along with any of his followers who got in the way. Taking (the late) Mackinnon's place in the galley, they rapidly overhauled John of Islay's *birlinn* and drew alongside.

"My Lord" said Lachlan as he and Hector boarded, "we have discovered Mackinnon was a traitor all along, so we have come to offer our protection". And as he looked around, John of Islay noted the galley filled with Macleans, a hefty Maclean standing over each of his own oarsmen, and, what's more, a Maclean had already replaced his own helmsman by the simple manoeuvre of nudging him over the side.

"Will Mackinnon be joining us?" he asked.

"I think not" replied Lachlan truthfully. And as John was mulling this over he noted the *birlinn* had altered course under the command of the new, Maclean, helmsman.

"I say," interposed John of Islay. "Aren't we going the wrong way for Aros Castle? It's that way," he said, pointing behind him.

"I think not," answered Lachlan, "for Mackinnon may well have had a surprise in store for you there. I suggest we go to your castle of Dunconnel until we are certain it is safe for you to return."

"Purely for your own safety, you understand my Lord", explained Hector the Ferocious, absentmindedly fingering the razor-sharp edge of his great battleaxe.

"And of course, of only a temporary nature, my Lord", added Lachlan the Wily, smiling oilily.

By all accounts John of Islay was a pragmatic man, and he thus accepted the situation for what it was, a *fait accompli*. Without his own men in command there was little he could do anyway, he reflected, so he leant back on the cushions and gnawed at a chicken leg as his *birlinn* sped south on the last of the ebb tide.

Now, Dunconnel (*Dun Chonnuill*) is dramatically sited on the northern end of the Isles of the Sea, perched on a small island with sheer cliffs plunging to the sea. The galley with Hector the Ferocious went ahead to warn the small garrison on the island of the change of plan – principally by dirking anyone who challenged him! There is a small creek between the two islands, and into this the helmsman guided the *birlinn* carefully, for by now both wind and sea were rising appreciably. John of Islay drew his cloak about him as he made his way up the steep path to the lower postern gate, noting as he passed that his own guards had been replaced by Macleans.

"Ah well" he thought, as he strode across the wind-blown summit of the island to the welcome shelter of his hall-house, "nothing to be done just now."

That night the wind rose to a gale and it was well that Hector had sent the boats to the shelter of Ardlarach, on the nearby island of Luing. But that meant they were stranded on Dunconnel, and as the gale grew in ferocity and the torrential rain seemed endless even Lachlan wondered if their supplies would hold out. The peat fire smoke drifted upwards to escape through a hole in the roof, and the rain made a constant hissing as it dripped on the embers.

After supper Lachlan approached John of Islay. "My Lord," he began, "as we seem to be stuck here for some days, perhaps we could discuss who will become your new Chamberlain, now that Mackinnon has so sadly vacated the post?"

"And what about his lands?" interrupted Hector, much to the annoyance of Lachlan, but who took care not to show it.

"Of course," continued Lachlan, "you'll need someone strong – and loyal of course – to hold those lands for you, just in case Clan Mackinnon tries to seize them. And you'll need someone you trust to run your Household and *Court*," he emphasised. "Finding the right staff is *such* a bore for a busy man like you, my Lord. And all those *endless* negotiations with other clan chiefs – you'll

5.1 The birlinn approaching Dunconnel

need someone diplomatic to negotiate for you."

John of Islay was flattered by the use of the word 'Court' – as was intended – for it had a regal sound to it. "Let's all sleep on it," he suggested. "After all, none of us is going anywhere!"

The gale blew all that week, but just as the cheese ran out and the last hen on the island had been killed for that night's supper they reached agreement.

"Lachlan, you will be Chamberlain of my Household," announced John of Islay.

"And?"

"Constable of Duart, Dunconnel and Carnaburg castles?"

"And?"

"Lands on Mull, Coll, Tiree and the mainland to support them?"

"And?"

"My daughter Mary in marriage?"

"*Thank you,* my Lord," bowing so low he nearly put his back out.

"But what about *me*?" interjected Hector "I *am* the older."

"My dear chap," replied John of the Isles, noting out of the corner of his eye that Hector's great axe was well within his reach. "I've got something *far* more up your street – how about Commander of my forces?"

"And?" queried Hector.

"How about 80,000 acres of Mull?"

"And?"

"How about Christina Macleod, from Harris? I hear she's quite a looker, and I can have a word with her father. Not a bad sort is old Murdoch."

"*Thank you,* my Lord," replied Hector, echoing his brother, but completely forgetting to bow.

Having reached a *very* satisfactory agreement, and the wind and sea having dropped, the Maclean brothers took John of Islay to the sacred Isle of Iona. There, with due solemnity, the unfortunate Lord of Isles was made to swear on a certain black stone to forgive and forget the murders committed by the brothers, and to confirm their demands for lands and offices.

Once restored to power one does wonder why John of Islay did not repudiate this agreement, which, after all, he had not made of his own free will. But times were difficult then, for bubonic plague had swept through Scotland in previous years, taking nobles and common men alike without favour. Good men were scarce, and John of Islay had need of strong and clever men to govern the vast new lands he had acquired on marriage to Amy MacRauri, in addition to those lands forfeited by John of Lorn, Chief of Clan MacDougall. Along with MacDougall, many of his relations had backed the wrong side during the Wars of Independence, and been forced to flee to Ireland. John of Islay's own children were either too young, or already engaged in administering his lands.

The Maclean brothers were certainly strong, as they had all too effectively proved; and, moreover, they were his cousins, albeit distant.

"Better to keep it in the family", mused the Lord of the Isles to himself. "Lachlan is not called 'The Wily' for nothing – I can do with his brains. And Hector, for all his coarseness, is a dab hand with the battleaxe. Nothing will bring back Mackinnon, so best to make do with what I have".

~

Thus Lachlan, as befits the more crafty brother, was given, in 1367, the hand of Mary Macdonald, daughter of John of Islay. He was also awarded MacKinnon's large holdings on the mainland and on Mull, and there he enlarged the castle at Duart to guard the vital seaways. So, all in all, our Lachlan did not do too badly.

As for his brother, Hector was indeed granted 80 merklands (about 80,000 acres) of land at Lochbuie, on Mull, but unfortunately it was already occupied by the chief of the MacFadyen. As these were fine and fertile lands MacFadyen was hardly likely to give them up, so Hector devised a plan.

"Look old chap," he said to MacFadyen one fine spring day, "there is my brother building himself a castle at Duart. What if he was to attack you sometime? Why don't you let me build a castle here in Lochbuie, then I could protect you too." As he spoke, he fingered the edge of his battleaxe, looking pointedly at MacFadyen's neck.

Now, MacFadyen was not too bright, but he knew that Hector the Ferocious was not called that for nothing. Besides, he had a dozen clansmen at his back, all fingering the edges of their weapons too.

"If I only offer him a *wee* bit of land," MacFadyen thought to himself, "he can only build a *wee* castle on it, which I can easily enough take if I need to".

"Youcanhavethelandwithinacowhide" he blurted out in one anxious rush. Then, in a more seemly tone for a Chief, he added "There's a splendid rock down by the shore, with a perfect slip for your galley. Why don't you build there?"

Hector looked at the rock, which would indeed be covered by a cow hide but that would barely give him room to lie down. However, he and MacFadyen shook hands on the deal and MacFadyen went off to his own house, chuckling inwardly.

"I certainly fooled that big sap" he thought to himself, "but no one beats a MacFadyen for brains".

Hector lost no time in slaughtering the largest cow he could find – one of MacFadyen's, naturally – flayed the hide, chopped up the meat and started a good fire for supper. Whilst it was stewing in a big pot Hector got his men to cut the hide into thin strips – about the width of a bootlace – so that when MacFadyen came back in the morning the cow's hide enclosed not only the rock but a fine piece of land called *Magh* (field, hence Moy).

MacFadyen could hardly admit he had been outwitted, for Hector had kept his side of the bargain.

So Hector the Ferocious built his own keep, known as Moy Castle, but with MacFadyen as an all too close neighbour. So one fine morning Hector climbed the winding stone stair to the parapet walk, whence he spied MacFadyen below, happily gnawing at a cold haunch of venison for breakfast. Aiming carefully, he sent an arrow straight through the bone, and MacFadyen took the hint.

"Time I was off", said he. So MacFadyen, his wife and his children packed their bags and gathered their cattle – less one of course – and with barely a farewell wave to Hector, they left. I know not to where, but as that's the last we hear of them in our tale, it doesn't matter much anyway.

As well as the fair lands of Lochbuie, Hector also acquired a wife, Christina Macleod, whose brother Torquil was the first Macleod chief of Lewis. And that's the last we hear of big Hector the Ferocious as well, now snug in his Castle of Moy – at least in this tale – but from Hector and Christina are descended the Maclaines of Lochbuie.

Map references

- OS Landranger 49. OS Explorer 383:

  Aros Castle NM 564 449.

  Ardtornish Castle NM 692 426.

- OS Landranger 49. OS Explorer 375:

  Moy Castle NM 616 248.

  Duart Castle NM 749 354.

- OS Landranger 55. OS Explorer 359:

  Dunconnel NM 681 127.

Historical notes

- *Burke's Peerage* has John Dubh as holding lands at Duart, Isle of Mull but this is unlikely; it was almost certainly his son *Lachlan Lubanach* who was granted Duart by John of the Isles, probably in 1267 when *Lachlan* married Mary, John's daughter.

- The Lords of the Isles controlled much of the western seaboard of Scotland from the time of Somerled in the mid-12th century until the abolition of the Lordship by James IV in 1493. [Although the title is still held by the Prince of Wales] In the first half of the 1400's they controlled all the islands and the western mainland from Kintyre to Cape Wrath. Although the final rebellion against the Crown was in 1544, the island clans still hoped for a resurgence of their power until the final defeat at Culloden in 1746.

- DUNCONNEL CASTLE: At the northern end of the Garvellachs – or Isles of the Sea – is a small cliff-bound island heavily fortified with the remains of perimeter walls where the cliffs were not vertical. Nothing much is left of the actual castle, which was probably more a collection of buildings on the summit of the island, within the protection of the cliffs and walls. In those days it was of major strategic importance, commanding the seaways from the south to Mull and Lochaber.

- Originally held by the MacDougalls of Lorn from King Hakon of Norway, in 1343 David II granted to John, Lord of the Isles the royal castles of Carnaburg and Dunconnel. In 1390 John's son, Donald, granted to Lachlan [*Lubanach*] Maclean of Duart the half constabulary of Dunconnel, along with lands in the area to support and supply it.

- *Lachlan Lubanach* was not known as 'The Wily' for nothing, and as Chamberlain to John of the Isles his skills as a negotiator between fractious clansmen was legendary.

- In 1367 Lachlan was granted a Papal Dispensation to marry Mary, daughter of John, Lord of the Isles; by all accounts it was a love match, rare in those days, and they had not waited to produce children, as the Dispensation makes clear!

- The office of Chamberlain of the Household to the Lords of the Isles was held by successive Macleans of Duart for 100 years, until the abolition of Lordship of the Isles in 1493.

- Nearly 600 years later, in 1943, the direct descendant of *Lachlan Lubanach* and Mary Macdonald, Fitzroy Maclean, was appointed as Brigadier commanding the British Mission to the Yugoslav Partisans, a post requiring negotiating skills equal to Lachlan's! Fitzroy Maclean was the 15th Hereditary Keeper and Captain of Dunconnel in the Isles of the Sea. He was Chamberlain to Queen Elizabeth II, and in 1957 was created the 1st Baronet Maclean of Dunconnel.

- DUART CASTLE: following the marriage of Lachlan Maclean to Mary, daughter of John of Islay, the original

Macdougall wall of enceinte was probably strengthed about 1367 with the great tower house.

- MOY CASTLE: Hector was granted a charter of Lochbuie in 1360 by John of Islay and may well have built a small defensive keep at Moy. But the RCAHMS say the present Moy Castle was probably started in 1400-1450, and first appears on record in 1494. It was abandoned as a residence in 1752, when a new house was built nearby, itself abandoned in 1793 when it was adapted as stables for the new mansion house built by Murdoch Maclaine, 19th of Lochbuie.

- In *Recollections of an Argyllshire Drover,* Eric Cree recorded many tales in the mid-20th century for the School of Scottish Studies from Donald Morrison. Donald was born in 1885 and came from a long line of Mull crofters and he relates the tale of cutting the cowhide into thin strips.

Sources

- *West Coast Cruising* – John Maclintock.
- *The Isles of the Sea* – Sir Fitzroy Maclean.
- *Hebridean Journey* – Halliday Sutherland.
- *Warriors and Priests* – Nicholas Maclean-Bristol.
- *Summer Days among the Hebrides* – Alasdair Alpin McGregor.
- *The Royal Commission on Ancient and Historical Monuments in Scotland* – Argyll 5. [RCAHMS]
- *Recollections of an Argyllshire Drover and other West Highland Chronicles* by Eric R Cregeen, edited by Margaret Bennett.
- *Burke's Peerage, Baronetage & Knightage and Scottish Clan Chiefs* – 107th Edition.

How landless Lachlan Maclean gained Coll and a rich wife

And how his son – John Garbh – regained the island and seized Barra and Boisdale from his wicked stepfather

As we have seen in the fifth tale, *Lachlan Lubanach* (Lachlan the Wily) and his brother *Eachann Reaganach* (Hector the Ferocious), had established themselves firmly on Mull after abducting John of Islay, Lord of the Isles. John of Islay, however, was a pragmatist and so appointed these useful brothers to positions of power as well as granting them considerable lands. John of Islay died in 1387 and was succeeded by his son, Donald, who re-appointed *Lachlan Lubanach* as his Chamberlain and Constable of several castles.

At Duart Castle, *Lachlan Lubanach* was much involved in the affairs of the Lords of the Isles, and there is many a fine tale to be told of him. Our story, however, is of his third son, also Lachlan, just to confuse you; he turned out to be a strapping lad, but being only a third son, landless. One fine summer's day in the early 1400's he was sent by his father to the Island of Tiree, for *Lachlan Lubanach* was Baillie of both Coll and Tiree for Donald, Lord of the Isles.

Young Lachlan forgot to pack himself a piece for lunch, and finding himself hungry he stopped off at Coll for a meat tea. Knocking at a cottage door and asking for succour, you can imagine his surprise when he was soundly turned on by the old woman within.

"Call yourself a Maclean?" she berated him. "When there are Norsemen living on Coll. What are you? A man or a mouse?" And so saying, she slammed the plank door in his face, leaving him meatless and as hungry as ever. More so, in fact, for he had caught a whiff of the stew bubbling on the old woman's hearth, and oh boy, it smelt good, especially after a sea voyage.

Angered by what she said – for it had a strong element of truth – Young Lachlan sat himself down to think, then instructed his companions in a plan. The Norsemen on Coll went by the name of Macaulay (*Mac Amhlaidh)*, and their main stronghold was on a crannog in Loch Amhlaidh, an almost impregnable place to attack. So Lachlan disguised himself as a harper, for he was no mean player, and just happened to have one with him. Striding up to the loch he asked for food and shelter in exchange for playing, and was duly guided across the hidden causeway and onto the island on which the crannog was built. Now, a travelling harper was an occasion for a feast, for they brought not just music but stories of daring deeds from far lands, as well as the odd juicy bit of gossip as to whose wife was sleeping with whom. Lachlan, however,

took care to pour most of his ale onto the floor, and some very happy deerhounds were soon snoring at his feet.

When all the company had drunk themselves into a stupor, Lachlan quietly gathered all the weapons he could find, and dropped them silently into the loch. Stealing back across the causeway, he alerted his companions, regained the crannog, and slaughtered all the inhabitants – men, women and children alike. With their chief and his warriors dead, the rest of the Macaulays put up scant resistance to Lachlan and his men, and those few who survived fled to North Uist.

And that's how Young Lachlan, landless third son of *Lachlan Lubanach*, became the first Maclean of Coll.

~

Having acquired himself an island, Lachlan also set about acquiring a wife – preferably a rich one – and his choice fell on an heiress, one Anna Macleod. True, she was divorced from her first husband, and widowed by the death of her second, but divorce was common and easy among the upper classes of that time. Suitable marriage

6.1 *The Viking crannog in Loch Amlaidh*

partners were not prolific, for wars, plague and clan battles took a steady toll. A child-bearing, eligible woman not too closely related was an asset silly to waste on just one husband, for marriages tended to bind the clans more closely. That said, the number of siblings and cousins – of both sexes – who happily murdered each other is endless!

Lachlan and Anna obtained papal consent to marry in 1403, and with her dowry they set about building on Coll that essential commodity, a castle. In keeping with his importance as a new laird, Breacachadh Castle was a four-storey rectangular keep, with a curtain wall connecting it to a three-storey circular tower. Positioned at the head of a sea loch it guarded both his galleys and his cattle, and was designed to impress as well as to defend the lands of Maclean of Coll.

Lachlan probably completed Breacachadh Castle, but died within a few short years; but Anna soon married again, and the lucky chap this time was Roderick MacNeil of Barra. Anna took to Barra her young son by Lachlan, who later was called *Ian Garbh* [pronounced Garve – meaning Rough John] on account of his great size and strength. But Roderick had a son by a previous marriage,

and he determined that this *Gilleonan* should inherit both Coll and Barra. MacNeil was so wicked to his stepson that *Ian Garbh* began to fear for his life, and he determined to flee for the safety of Coll and his own people.

Ian gathered to himself the five Coll men he could trust, and on a still summer's night they slipped quietly away from Barra in a six-oared boat. All night they rowed, for the sea was glassy calm, but with that oily swell that presages a gale soon to arrive. They stopped only to partake of some oatcakes and water, then on into the night they went, heading for Coll on the far horizon. Eventually the moon rose, flooding the Sea of the Hebrides with light almost as bright as day, and in the very distance they spied MacNeill's galley in pursuit.

For when MacNeil discovered that Ian had escaped his fury was immense and Kisimul Castle echoed to his roared orders.

"Make ready my galley", he bellowed. "Man it with the fittest rowers I have, and *fetch me that brat alive*. For by God, I want him to suffer. Slowly. And painfully".

"Roddy dearest", interposed his wife sweetly, "don't you think you're being the teeniest bit unreasonable?" All the reply she received was a back-hander from his fist which sent her staggering into an arras, for Roderick MacNeil was not in the mood to be reasonable.

Ian and his companions were now rowing for their very lives, but the safety of Coll was still some miles away, and the galley with its eight oarsmen was gaining fast. Desperately, Ian searched for deliverance, but not a boat could be seen anywhere, save only MacNeil's galley in hot pursuit, and soon to be within bowshot. By now the sun was rising and Ian had a sudden inspiration; he headed for a narrow gap between two small islands.

"Do *exactly* what I say", he commanded, "and do it fast, for our lives hang on this one chance".

On the two boats sped, fear lending the pursued super-human strength, and brute force combined with sheer numbers enabling their pursuers to gain rapidly. Ian headed straight for his chosen gap, and at the very last moment he shouted "Toss oars". Each oarsman bore down heavily on the loom of his oar, and all six were tossed vertically up into the boat, just as she shot though the gap.

MacNeil's helmsman though, not knowing these waters, and with the newly risen sun full into his eyes, totally misjudged the width of the gap, and with a mighty splintering of oars the galley came to an abrupt halt. And ever since that day, the place has been known as *Caolas Bhristeadh Ramh* – The Sound of the Breaking Oars.

As for Ian, he and his men eventually escaped to Ireland, that refuge of many a clansman. MacNeil's galley, with barely a serviceable oar on board, was driven far to the north in the great gale that sprung up, and many were their travails before they limped home to Barra and the wrath of MacNeil.

Ian Garbh remained in Ireland some three years, earning his living as a *gallowglas* or hired mercenary. All the while he perfected his skill at fighting, especially with the great battleaxe, and it was now that he really lived up to his name of Rough John. Finally he was ready to return home and claim his patrimony of Coll, so he and a few faithful men made their way to Duart Castle, on Mull. There he asked his elder brother for help, but Duart refused, and Ian was forced to proceed with only his men and the inevitable few extras always ready for a scrap.

They landed secretly on Coll at *Acarsaid Fhalaich*, and

6.2 Tossing Oars

6.3 Caolas Bhristeadh Ramh (The Sound of the Breaking Oars)

found that MacNeil was away at Grishipol on the north coast. There he was building a house more suitable than Breacachadh for journeying to and from Barra, with a bay more sheltered from the south-west for beaching his galley. *Ian Garbh* challenged his stepfather to single combat, and so sure was MacNeil of winning that he instantly accepted and battle was joined. Long and fierce was the fight, but it gradually became clear that MacNeil was gaining the upper hand. A lad from Dervaig on Mull was watching the fight with some trepidation – he had joined Ian at Duart, and was known as *Gille riamhach* (Brindled Lad). The combatants getting dangerously close to where he stood, this lad suddenly jumped the Grishipol burn backwards, and so surprised MacNeil that he was momentarily distracted. With one swing of his battleaxe Ian lopped off MacNeil's head, thus claiming the fight, Coll, Barra and Boisdale.

The Brindled Lad was rewarded for his intervention by Ian granting him a croft at Dervaig rent-free for life, and many was the time in old age that the lad recounted how he had jumped the Grishipol burn backwards.

Some tales say that Anna MacNeil, now husbandless yet again, came out from Grishipol House bearing in her arms MacNeil's infant son to show his half-brother. And that Ian Garbh, not wishing to share Barra, promptly skewered the babe on his dirk. Some tales, however, also say that Anna had murdered MacNeil's sons by a previous marriage, in order that her own son might inherit – so who are we to believe? But I've told that tale in the Postscript below, for she is remembered on Barra as 'Marion of the Heads'.

MacNeil being dead, *Iain Garbh* occupied Barra and Boisdale, holding them for seven years, and building the small castle of Calvay on the southern shore of Loch Boisdale. His mother he kept under close watch – as well he might – but so fussy was her taste that she demanded a fresh calf's tongue each day, with disastrous results to the herds on the island. She is reputed to have been buried standing up so that she might forever see her beloved Coll. If so, she must have been buried halfway up *Ben Sheabhal* to be able to see low-lying Coll 40 miles distant, but facts seldom get in the way of a good Hebridean tale!

The boring old truth is that Anna married yet again in

1426, when papal permission was granted for her to marry John Maclaine of Lochbuie as her fifth husband. And, thankfully, that is the last we hear of Anna.

The following year Alexander of Islay, Lord of the Isles, restored to MacNeil's son, *Gilleonan*, his rightful lands of Barra and Boisdale, and *Iain Garbh* reluctantly withdrew to Coll. There he lived quietly enough, and the last we hear of him – appropriately enough – is on his death-bed. Adjured by the priest to "Worship God and Fear the Devil", *Iain Garbh* raised himself up and seized his vast pantaloons from the chair.

"Do you think", he roared, "that the man who can fill these is afraid of the Devil?"

Postscript – Marion of the Heads

Anna MacNeil got the nickname not just for her demand for a fresh calf's tongue each day – hence, I presume, a fresh head each day – but also from the following grisly tale. Anna had a son by Roderick MacNeil and she was determined that her son *Ruari* would become chief rather than his step-brothers.

One fine warm day the two step-sons went duck shooting in *Bagh Chorneig* in Vatersay, just across from Kisimul Castle. Marion ordered one of her Maclean retainers to go to Vatersay and bring back the boys' heads to her. The two boys, tiring of duck shooting, went to sleep in the warm sun and the retainer carried out his order, throwing the heads into a sack and the bodies into the bay.

Marion was delighted when her servant untied the sack and out tumbled the heads onto the flagstones of her solar, for her son *Ruari* would now become Chief of Clan Neil. But being very religious she determined to give the heads a Christian burial, so she took them back to Vatersay, to the well near the burial ground of *Cille Bhrianain*. There the ancient rite of washing the heads was carried out and there they were interred, with Marion as chief mourner. From thence forth she was known as 'Marion of the Heads,' the well is known as the 'Well of the Heads', and the chapel is known as *Caibeal Moire nan Ceann* – Chapel of Mary of the Heads.

There is another tale of her burial, in that she instructed her burial to be at *Cille Bhrianain*, within sight of her beloved Coll – and with maybe a belated twinge of guilty conscience? So the burial party carted Marion over by boat from Kisimul Castle, then way along the shore to splash across the sands to the burial ground on the islet of *Uinessan*. There they belatedly saw that the island of *Muldoanich* blocked any view of Coll – but being tired they buried her there anyway!

Map references

- OS Landranger 49. OS Explorer 383:

  Ardtornish Castle NM 692 426;

  Duart Castle NM 749 354.

  Moy Castle NM 616 248.

- OS Landranger 55. OS Explorer 359:

  Dunchonnel NM 683 128

- OS Landranger 46. OS Explorer 372:

  Loch Amhlaidh NM 189 558

  Breacacadh Castle NM 160 539

  Grishipol NM 195 595

  Caolas Bhristeadh Ramh NM 277 650

- OS Landranger 31. OS Explorer 452:

  Kisimul Castle NL 665 970.

  Cille Bhrianain is on Uinessan, a small tidal islet at the extreme east of Vatersay. NL 644 957

Historical notes

- We don't have exact dates for when all these events occurred, but I checked the various versions of this tale for facts against Warriors and Priests, the definitive volume on early Macleans by Nicholas Maclean Bristol. He had previously argued convincingly that 'Landless Lachlan' was the 3rd son of Lachlan Lubanach, 1st of Duart, and I agree.

- However, many versions of this story and the 107th edition of *Burke's Peerage, Baronetage & Knightage and Scottish Clan Chiefs* state that John Garbh (*Ian Garbh*), 1st of Coll, was in fact the 3rd son of *Lachlan Bronnach* [Big bellied Lachlan, who died circa 1472], 3rd of Duart, by his second wife, Finovolva, a daughter of Macleod of Harris. If so John Garbh's eldest brother would thus have been *Lachlan Og*, 4th of Duart. And if so, John would only have been about 5 when he supposedly fought and killed MacNeil in about 1420! For Lachlan Bronnach's father, Hector Ruadh, only had Papal Dispensation to marry in 1393, so we can assume Lachlan Bronnach was already born or born about then. Even if he fathered John Garbh aged 14, John would barely be seven in 1420 and fourteen in 1427, when Barra was restored to Gilleonan MacNeil.

- *The Royal Commission on Ancient & Historical Monuments of Scotland* Argyll Volume 3 states that 'Sometime during the second quarter of the 15th century, however, Alexander, Lord of the Isles, granted the island [Coll] to John Garbh, son of Lachlan Maclean of Duart and founder of the family of Maclean of Coll, and the tower-house and courtyard were probably built at this period'.

- The firm dates we do have are as follow. In 1390 *Lachlan Lubanach,* 1st of Duart, was appointed Baillie of Coll and Tiree and constable of Carnaburg Castle, with meal and cheese for the garrison to be provided from Tiree. In 1403 'a' Lachlan Maclean had Papal Dispensation to marry Anna Macleod. In 1409 Donald, Lord of the Isles, granted to *Lachlan Lubanach's* son – Red Hector

Maclean, 2nd of Duart – 6 merklands in the south of Coll instead of the meal and cheese. And in 1427 Alexander, Lord of the Isles, restored to MacNeil's son, *Gilleonan*, the lands of Barra and Boisdale which *Ian Garbh* had seized.

• Another reputable source says:

> Early in the fifteenth century Alexander Earl of Ross appears to have granted the lands and barony of Coll to John Maclean, styled Garve, the son of Lauchlan Maclean of Dowart, and founder of the family of Coll. The same John is said to have slain Gilleonan MacNeil of Barra, who disputed his possession of Coll.

• *Ian Garbh's* son, *Iain Abraich* (Lochaber John) was killed in an affray with Cameron of Lochiel at Corpach and his pregnant wife given shelter by a family MacElonich. Hence Coll had the lintel stone at Breacacadh Castle carved, 'promising succour to any of the MacElonich family in need and this pledge was honoured right down to the eighteenth century. This stone has disappeared but there is a vacant space above the eastern doorway from which it may have been removed.' As we will see, similar such 'lintel tales' are told of Moy and Eilean Donan castles.

• So there we have it – Lachlan, 1st of Coll, was *probably* the landless 3rd son of *Lachlan Lubanach*, 1st of Duart; *sometime* in the early fifteenth century he gained Coll and a rich wife, then built himself Breacachadh Castle. *Iain Garbh* [pronounced Garve and often written as John Garbh] was *probably* his son; was *probably* born about 1403; *probably* recovered Coll from MacNeil of Barra about 1420; *definitely* seized Barra and Boisdale, but lost them in 1427. And *probably* died a cantankerous old man!

Sources

- *Burke's Peerage, Baronetage & Knightage and Scottish Clan Chiefs* – 107th Edition.
- *Coll* – a booklet by Betty Macdougall.
- *Six Inner Hebrides* by Noel Banks.
- *West Coast Cruising* – John Maclintock.
- *The Isles of the Sea* – Fitzroy Maclean.
- *Hebridean Journey* – Halliday Sutherland.
- *Warriors and Priests* – Nicholas Maclean-Bristol.
- *Summer Days among the Hebrides* – Alasdair Alpin McGregor.
- *The Royal Commission on Ancient & Historical Monuments of Scotland:*
  Argyll Volume 3 – Mull, Coll and Tiree.
  The Outer Hebrides, Skye and the Small Isles – 1928.
- *Origines Parochiales Scotiae.*
- *West Highland Notes & Queries* – The Society for West Highland and Island Historical Research.
- *The Lords of the Isles* – Ronald Williams.

The Lady's Rock

And how another Lachlan MacLean of Duart tried to drown his wife
An Lethsgeir / Sgeir na Baintighearna

f you take the ferry from Oban to Mull you will pass between the tall lighthouse on *Eilean Musdile,* at the south-western end of Lismore, and a smaller whitewashed tower perched on a lonely rock. The views are spectacular in any direction, but three tidal streams converge at this point, and their waters swirl ominously round and over the rock, which dries at low water. Nor are the tides all that is ominous about the rock, for it was the scene of a dastardly attempt at murder, which I shall recount in all its grisly detail. There are, as always in Hebridean tales, several different versions, but the basics are that a Maclean of Duart, wishing to dispose of is wife, marooned her on this tidal rock, leaving her there to drown.

Luckily – for her, if not for him – the lady was rescued, by whom is unclear after all these centuries. One tale has it that some Maclean clansmen were unable to withstand the piteous cries of the lady, rescued her and landed her safe on the Point of Knap. Fearful of their Chief's vengeance they fled ever further south, rounded Kintyre, and landed at Southend. On being asked their name they inserted an r into Maclean, disguising it to Maclaran, and thus hoping to throw Duart off their trail. A nifty twist to the tale, but, sadly, a modern invention, for it is highly unlikely they were literate; and in any event, Macleran is the anglicised version of *Mac Gille Eadharain,* which would not transpose so readily from Maclean.

Be that as it may, the following version (in spite of my embellishments) is probably the most accurate.

~

On a sunny day in 1514, *Lachlan Cattanach* Maclean of Duart, 10th Chief of Clan Maclean, married Lady Catherine Campbell, the daughter of Archibald, second Earl of Argyll, who had died at Flodden the previous year. Lady Janet's brother, Colin Campbell, thus succeeded as the 3rd Earl, and by this marriage he hoped to gain control of the Maclean lands. The Campbells had long coveted these extensive holdings on their western seaboard, but did not actually gain them until much later. The union was no love match, as events were to prove, but merely a political alliance normal between powerful clans at that time. Not for Lady Catherine was this to be a Barbara Cartland romance, swooning in the arms of the debonair and handsome *Lachlan Cattanach* as he clasped her to his manly chest. Rather, it was the exchange of one draughty castle for another, with the added disadvantage of having to share Lachlan's bed.

The years passed, but this did not soften the Clan Maclean hatred of all things Campbell – including their chief's wife – and matters were not helped by rumours that the lady had in her retinue a young lover, thinly disguised as a monk. The final straw was that Lady Catherine failed to produce an heir, despite Lachlan's best efforts. Things became so bad between the couple that Lachlan took to sleeping with a sword in his bed lest the lady should attempt to murder him. Now a sword in the bed is almost as uncomfortable as having a dog lying on it, and thus one can hardly blame the lady for attempting to poison her husband, not once but twice – Sir Fitzroy MacLean says she used the then little-known drug cavale.

Now, Macleans are known as pretty tolerant sorts of chaps, but this was all too much for the Chief. The story goes that Lachlan had two foster-brothers, by name *Eachan Mor na Suil* (Big Hector of the blue eyes) and *Charles Cuom lionach* (Charles crooked flax) 'two stout big men always attending himself, *coaltan* (foster-brothers) of

Morvern

Lismore

Leith
Sgeir

Duart
Castle

Mull

○ LADY'S ROCK
Sgeir na Baintighearna

Dunstaffnage
Castle

● Oban

Kerrera

7.1 *The Lady's Rock*

his own'. One evening, after a hard day hunting the deer with his brothers, Lachlan called for drink, which his lady prepared with her own hands and gave to Hector to carry into the hall. Hector, however, was suspicious, and

> made an old woman that was in the house to take a mouthful of it. After taking it she immediately expired. Before then Maclean's lady made up a plan to drown him in a river. Eachan and Charles proposed to the laird of Dowart to get quit of his lady… to which the Laird of Dowart agreed'.

So one night of the full moon in about 1520, Big Hector of the blue eyes bundled the Lady Catherine over his shoulder and scrambled down the steep path from Duart Castle to the small jetty at the foot of the cliff. The Campbell girls are not renowned for their slight build, and this one objected strongly to the indignity of being carted like a sack of peats. So she beat with her hands upon Hector's back and anything else within reach, including those blue eyes, but all to no avail. For, besides being a 'stout big man', Hector was well used to carrying off protesting

females, be they human or sheep – for rape and pillage then was as popular as soccer now – and often had the same results. Lady Janet also kicked out lustily with her legs, managing one well-aimed blow at his crutch, but all he said was "Oof". Hardy sons of Albion those Macleans.

Arriving at the jetty Hector threw the lady into a boat, and with Charles at the oars they rowed out towards the south end of Lismore. About a mile from Duart there is a rock, then known as *An Lethsgeir* (The half-rock), for it only covers at spring tides – that is, the extra high and low tides occasioned by full and new moons. It being low water Big Hector heaved the Lady Catherine onto the skerry without so much as a "Goodbye my lady", then rowed back for home, his supper and his bed.

"Bother", said the lady, for the rock was hard, damp, and covered with smelly, slippery seaweed – not at all the sort of place on which she was accustomed to spend the night. Although battered and bruised, Lady Catherine forbore to cry out, for she was, after all, an earl's daughter. But as the rising tide lapped round her ankles she decided that Hector and Charles were safely ashore in Duart, that her pride would no longer be compromised, and that a good yell for help would not go amiss. So she shouted, but the only answer was the mournful cries of gulls, sounding so very like the lost souls of the ship-wrecked mariners they are reputed to be. As the waters reached her waist she yelled even louder, for there is nothing like cold water as an incentive to the lungs. When the swirling, inky-black water finally reached her breasts she began to think the end was nigh – but still she cried for help. Truth to tell, there is little else to do with your feet scrabbling for a foothold on a slippery, rapidly submerging rock.

The water reached her chin just at the breaking of dawn, and she resigned herself to death by imagining what she would like to do to her husband, now safely tucked up in bed with his Teddy Bear. But just when she had finally given up all hope, out of the early morning mists loomed a wee fishing boat from Tayvallich, after the cuddies, and manned at the oars by a chap called Macleran along with his two sons.

"Hulloo", said they, "it's a braw nicht for swimmin". Now the Lady Catherine, being a well brought up sort of gel, knew that swearing was unladylike, but she *had* had rather a trying evening, and what's more, she had missed her supper. So her reply, I am ashamed to say, is unprintable; but the result was that within minutes she had been hauled into the boat, rubbed down with the least fishy bit of sacking, and bundled into an old horse blanket that was handily lying in the bilges.

Being now the beginning of the ebb, the Maclerans abandoned the fishing and high-tailed it for home, fearful that Lachlan should observe them from Duart Castle, perched high on its cliff and commanding a view of all these waters. In any case, an earl's daughter was fair swop for a basket of cuddies any day. By mid-morning they were at Carsaig, and a pony found for the lady, who was sheltered by the Campbell laird at Oibmore until she recovered sufficiently for the journey to Inverary and her father's castle.

Meanwhile, back at Duart, Lachlan Cattanach drew aside his bedroom curtains, observed the rock was bare of his pestilential wife, and descended the spiral stairs to bacon and eggs for breakfast. "And mushrooms. And tomato ketchup", he thought to himself, humming his favourite tune and kicking with good humour at the deer hounds. Later that day he sent a message to the earl that,

"Hulloo, It's a braw nicht for swimming"

7.2 *The Lady being rescued*

with immense sadness, he had to report that his sister had met with a boating accident.

"Never pays to lie", thought Lachlan. "At least, not too much".

In due course there came a reply from Argyll, commiserating with his misfortune, and inviting him to Inveraray so that husband and brother could mourn their mutual loss. So *Lachlan Cattanach* set out, accompanied by a retinue suitable for one chief visiting another, and in a day or two they all arrived at Inveraray Castle – the old castle of course, not the one we know today, which was only begun in the 1740's. There the two grieving men sat down to drown their sorrows in many refreshments and a huge banquet; no sooner were all seated than in came the Lady Catherine herself, magnificently gowned and very much alive.

"Whoops", thought Lachlan, "something's gone wrong here". And without saying goodbye-and-thank-you-for-supper he and his men beat a hasty retreat out of the nearest windows. Now, one version of this tale has him being caught, imprisoned in a bottle-dungeon, and fed on salt beef with no water until he went mad and died a lingering death. Sad to say, the facts belie the case, for he did escape, and, what's more, married again – but that is another complete story.

Lachlan Cattanach eventually died in November of 1523, in his Edinburgh bedroom, although certainly not peacefully in bed. Sir John Campbell of Cawdor, also brother to the Lady Catherine, burst in the bedroom door with the help of fourteen of his men; Cawdor then 'thrust the sword, sheath and all, through his body. These things gave rise to a song composed in these days (take up MacLean and prick him in a blanket).' Another version has him still being stabbed by Campbell of Cawdor, but this time in an inn brawl; whichever version is true, the end result was the same for *Lachlan Cattanach* – he died.

~

That doughty and most accurate recorder of folk-lore, MEM Donaldson, was told the tale in the 1920's, just before oral tradition disappeared under the onslaught of wireless and vastly improved communications in the West Highlands. In her splendid 1927 volume, *Further*

Wanderings, Mainly in Argyll, she states that Tayvallich tradition had it the men were MacLerans from that village, and were rewarded by Argyll with the Mill of Taynish, whose 'very desolate ruin' she visited. AA Currie, writing a century earlier, has Argyll giving the MacLerans the Mill of Oib, and although there was a Donald Roy McLeran as 'Miller in Oib' in 1720, that was two centuries after the date of our tale.

Whichever mill Argyll rewarded the MacLerans with – and I am inclined to Oib – there is little doubt that they were able to give up the fishing and live happily ever after, for a mill was a valuable sinecure.

And as for the rock, ever since our tale it has been known as *Sgeir na Baintighearna,* The Lady's Rock. And it was from this story that the poet, Thomas Campbell, formed his poem, Glenara.

> I dreamt of my lady, I dreamt of her grief,
> I dreamt that her lord was a barbarous chief;
> On a rock of the ocean fair Ellen did seem;
> Glenara! Glenara! now read me my dream!

Map references

- The Lady's Rock: OS Landranger 49. OS Explorer 376.
- OS Explorer 375. Admiralty chart 2814a:

  Duart Castle NM 772 344
- OS Landranger 55. OS Explorer 358:

  Mill of Taynish   NR 737 849
- OS Landranger 55. OS Explorer 358:

  Mill of Oib NR 778 897

Historical notes

- THE LADY'S ROCK: Ever since it has been known as *Sgeir na Baintighearna,* The Lady's Rock. In Gaelic *Baintighearna,* (Ben-tyurn-a) is a lady, especially a Chief's lady.

- By Mull tradition, before this event the rock was known as *An Lethsgeir* (The half-rock). About a mile north of Eilean Musdile is *Liath Sgeir* [Grey Rock] and there is a question over whether the latter is in fact the Lady's Rock.

- In 1520 the rocks were two feet and six inches deeper, but even at Equinoctial Spring High tides *An Lethsgeir* (The half-rock) would barely be 4 feet underwater. *Liath Sgeir* [Grey Rock] would be covered by 8' 6" of water, ample to drown an unwanted wife!

- Did the original 19th century Ordnance Survey confuse *Liath Sgeir* with *Lethsgeir* and the locals quietly smile at the error of the clever English surveyors who could not even speak Gaelic? It would not be the only occasion!

• Maclean / *Mac Gille Eadharain*: The Marquess of Lorne in *Adventure in Legend* (about 1890) gives the name as *Mac an Learen*.

• MILL OF TAYNISH: sited on the shores of Loch Sween and fed by Lochan Taynish above. The mill was abandoned in 1886, reflecting the influence of cheap grain from America, but much of the ruins remain.

• MILL OF OIB: known as one of the 'treasures of Knapdale' due to its unfailing water supply fed by rock-cut lade from Loch *Coille-Bharr*. The RCAHM says that 'the south-west gable remains with a cart archway, but most of the building has been demolished'. In fact a considerable amount remains, giving a good idea of how important a mill it was to the surrounding area. Oib Mill was described as 'newly built' by the 5th Earl of Argyll in a charter of 1549.

• Mills as a sinecure: as a form of taxation Alexander II in 1284 had enacted that:

> na man sall presume to grind Quheit or Rye with a Hand Mylne (quern) except he be compellit be storm, or be in lack of mylnes quilk suld grind the samen.

This taxation on a crofters grain was extracted by the miller on behalf of the laird as multure – a proportion of the meal ground, varying from about one-tenth to one-twentieth part. The tenant was also subject to thirlage, whereby he was bound to use the laird's mill and no other.

> When mills were erected, the authorities destroyed the querns in order to compel the people to go to the mills and pay multure. This wholesome and inconsiderate destruction of querns everywhere entailed untold hardships of thousands of people living in roadless districts and in distant isles without mills, especially during storms.

So it was not surprising that querns were used in many isolated parts of the Highlands and Islands for many centuries after the Act. Alexander Carmichael, writing in about 1900, but of events occurring many years earlier, recorded:

Among other expedients to which the more remote people resorted was the searching of ancient ruins for the *pollagan* (mortar mills) of former generations. The mortar is a still more primitive instrument for preparing corn than the quern. It is a block of stone about twenty-four inches by eighteen by eight. The centre and one end of this block are hollowed out to a breadth of about six to eight inches, and a depth of four or five, leaving three gradually sloping sides. The grain is placed in this scoop-like hollow and crushed with a stone. When sufficiently crushed, the meal is thrown out at the open end of the scoop, and fresh grain is put in to follow a similar process. When using the mortar the woman is on her knees, unless the mortar is on a table.

I first saw the quern at work in October 1860 in the house of a cottar at *Fearann-an-leatha*, Skye. The cottar-woman procured some oats in the sheaf. Roughly evening the heads, and holding the corn in one hand and a rod in the other, she set fire to the ears. Then, holding the corn over an old partially dressed sheepskin, she switched off the grain. This is called *gradanadh* (quickness), from the expert handling required in the operation. The whole straw of the sheaf was not burnt, only that part of the straw to which the grain was attached, the flame being prevented from going further. The straw was tied up and used for other purposes.

Having fanned the grain and swept the floor, the woman spread out the sheepskin again and placed the quern thereon. She then sat down to grind, filling and relieving the quern with one hand and turning it with the other, singing the while to the accompaniment of the *whirr! whirr! birr! birr!* of the revolving stone.

In a remarkably short space of time the grain from the field was converted into meal, and the meal into bannocks, which the unknown stranger was pressed to share. The bread was good and palatable, though with a slight taste of peat, which would probably become pleasant in time.

The meal obtained from this process is called *pronn, pronnt, prontach, min phronntaidh* (bruised meal), to distinguish it from *gradan, gradanach, min ghradain* (quick meal), *min brath, min brathain* (quern meal), and *min mhuille* (mill meal).

The quern and mortar are still used in outlying districts of Scotland and Ireland, although isolatedly and sparingly.

• *Lachlan Cattanach* Maclean of Duart, 10th Chief of Clan Maclean met his death in Edinburgh, in November 1523, at the hands of Sir John Campbell, 1st of Cawdor, another of Lady Catherine's brothers. Cawdor, with a party of fourteen men, surprised Lachlan in bed and,

thrust the sword, sheath and all, through his body. These things gave rise to a song composed in these days (take up MacLean and prick him in a blanket).

Sources

- Lady Catherine Maclean married as her 2nd husband Archibald Campbell of Auchinbreck.
- *Hebridean Journey* – Halliday Sutherland.
- *Notes & Queries* – The Society for West Highland and Island Historical Research.
- *Further Wanderings, Mainly in Argyll* – MEM Donaldson.
- *West Coast Cruising* – John Maclintock.
- *The Isles of the Sea* – Sir Fitzroy Maclean.
- *A History of Clan Campbell* – Alastair Campbell of Airds.
- *Warriors and Priests* – Nicholas Maclean-Bristol.
- *Carmina Gadelica* – Alexander Carmichael.
- *The Scottish Country Miller 1700-1900* – Enid Gauldie.
- *Royal Commission on Ancient and Historical Monuments, Volume 7 – Knapdale*.
- *Popular Tales of The West Highlands* – J F Campbell.
- *Warriors and Priests* – Nicholas Maclean-Bristol.
- *Burke's Peerage, Baronetage & Knightage and Scottish Clan Chiefs* – 107th Edition.

Of Macleans and Maclaines

Ian the Toothless & his incarceration, Allan of the Straws, The Headless Horseman, and how Dumpy Murdoch finally gained his rightful inheritance and lived to a grumpy old age

There is a tale of how the Maclaines acquired Lochbuie, and although bits are not true (as I'll tell you at the end) it's a cracking yarn anyway! As we have seen in Tale Five, *Eachann Reaganach* (Hector the Ferocious) and his brother *Lachlan Lubanach* (Lachlan the Wily) kidnapped John Macdonald, Lord of The Isles, and held him captive in one of his own castles. Recognising a *fait accompli* Macdonald not only forgave them but granted them high offices, large lands and advantageous marriages. Lachlan got the lands of Duart, and Hector those of Lochbuie, but they were already occupied by one MacFadyen. One fine June day Hector wandered up to MacFadyen, who was leaning on a gate happily watching his men cutting peats.

"Look old chap" said Hector "I've nowhere to keep my sheep. Do you mind if I build a fold for them down on the shore? Promise we won't get in each other's way".

"Wheeel – just for the noo", replied MacFadyen, stroking his beard. "Jest til ye find yer feet, d'ye ken?"

Now, MacFadyen must have been pretty stupid, for instead of a sheepfold Hector built himself a snug castle in a field *(Magh,* hence Moy Castle*)* running down to the sea and easy access to his galley.

Somewhat belatedly, MacFadyen noticed the keep.

"Hey. Yon's a castle, no a sheepfold like we agreed".

"Sheepfold?" queried Hector. "So sorry, I thought you said castle. It's my tinitus you see – makes me very hard of hearing. And very bad-tempered" he added, fingering the edge of his axe.

"Time I was off" thought MacFadyen, and promptly left for pastures new. So, as Hector had promised, they didn't get in each other's way!

Having ejected the incumbent chief Hector then acquired a fair wife, Christina Macleod of Lewis, and from Hector and Christina are descended the Maclaines of Lochbuie, who spell their name differently just to confuse us!

~

And now we get to our tale. Nearly two centuries later – about the 1530's – *Hector* Mor Maclean, 7th Chief of Duart, and John Maclaine, 5th Chief of Lochbuie, were constantly in arms against each other. In particular, Maclean of Duart coveted the good lands of Lochbuie, for so fertile was the ground it was known as 'The Garden of Mull.'

Maclaine was known as 'Ian the Toothless', and had four sons, of whom two feature in our tale, John and Ewen; they were at constant odds with their father, egged on – of course – by Duart. John was killed by *Lachlan Cattanach's* younger son, *Ailein nan Sop*. Allan of the Straws got his nickname from his mother giving birth early when travelling by horse, and by Allan grasping a handful of straw which had been hastily laid as her bed. Or it may have been from his habit of using straw when burning down houses – in March 1533 Allan was remitt for 'treasonable raising of fyre and birnyng of houses in the Ile of Mull'. According to one Maclean account 'this desperate character was by nature of the most ferocious and desperate disposition and even more tales are told of him that his equally worthless father'.

As a youth Allan of the Straw tried to rape Barra's daughter when staying on his mother's home of Carnburgh, but a man seeing this pushed him over a cliff. Luckily for Allan – but unluckily for John Maclaine and numerous others – he landed on a ledge, henceforth known as *Uirigh Ailein nan Sop* [Allan of the Straw's couch]. Seemingly he was a handsome man and is said to have seduced MacIan of Ardnamurchan's wife; then – on promise of marriage – Allan persuaded her to murder both her husband and infant son. Once done Allan dismissed her – "Go home woman. You who would murder your husband and babe may well murder me".

His mother – Marion, daughter of Maclean of Treshnish – married as her 2nd husband Neil Maclean of Lehir, dismissed by one scribe as 'a weak effeminate man, and had no issue tho married at the time of his death'. Following a violent disagreement he was killed by Allan, who then fled to a life of piracy at sea. Luckily for all concerned this violent man was dead by January 1552, but too late for John Maclaine, whom Allan had murdered some twenty years earlier.

Ian the Toothless' next son, Ewen [or Hugh] continued the quarrels with his father until matters came to a head in 1538. Ewen had married a daughter of Macdougall of Lorn, a carping and penurious woman by all accounts; as a home Ewen's father gave the couple a crannog in Loch Squabain, in Glen More. She, however, was not happy with this and repeatedly urged Ewen to demand a larger portion of the estate; his father repeatedly refused and a bitter quarrel ensued, one which could only be settled by battle.

On battle's eve Ewen was studying the ground on which they would fight when he heard sweet singing coming from a girl washing clothes in the burn. Only as she turned did he realise that this was no girl but old *Ludeag*, the fairy washerwoman, pummelling bloody shirts on the smooth boulders.

"Who will win the battle tomorrow?" he asked politely, for that is how you must speak to old *Ludeag*, lest she cast a spell on you. Ewen summoned up all his courage as she approached him and fixed her great staring eyes on his before she replied.

"If at breakfast butter is on the table without you yourself asking for it, then the day will be yours". And with that utterance she vanished; the burn, which moments before was red from the bloody shirts, now ran crystal clear.

Next morning his penurious wife provided no butter on the table, so it was with a heavy heart that Ewen assembled his men and set off down Glen More to Craig. There he found that Hector Mor of Duart – ever ready to stir up trouble – had sided with his father against him.

Although outnumbered a fierce battle ensued, and during it someone managed to lop off Ewen's head with one stroke of his broadsword. Ewen's headless corpse slumped over the horse's neck, the feet jammed in the stirrups – the terrified beast galloped nearly four miles for home and only stopped when exhausted, just above the Falls of Lussa. There the headless horseman finally dropped to the ground, and there Eoghan a chinn bhig was buried for a few days before being moved to Iona, where his graveslab can still be seen. Where the body fell is marked by a small mossy cairn, about 150 yards along the path towards the Falls from the ruins of Torness Farmhouse.

According to legend – and to those who have seen him – *Eoghan a chinn bhig* is still riding about in this world and is present when any of the Lochbuie family is in distress or about to die. He frequently attends the funerals of that family, wearing his old cloak about him summer and winter, and always carrying his trusty sword. He is still without his head and rides a dun horse, the same horse on which he rode to battle and from which he eventually fell. This horse has no equal in Arabia, or anywhere else, and travels over sea and land with equal

8-1 The Headless Horseman

ease. Ewen does not confine his wanderings to Scotland but has been frequently in Ireland, Spain, and other countries. He complains that his restlessness is because "he fell fasting, his cross and worthless wife having given him no breakfast on the morning on which he left home for Glen Cainnir."

With the only two of Ian the Toothless' legitimate sons now dead, Maclean of Duart decided to ensure Ian had no more sons. Rather than kill Lochbuie outright, which might upset the King, even if he was in far-away Edinburgh, Duart imprisoned Ian in his castle on one of the remote Treshnish Islands, *Cairn na Burgh Mhor*. And with Ian the Toothless safely out of the way, his younger brother, Murdoch Maclean of Scallasdale seized the Lochbuie lands and installed himself in Moy Castle.

Carnaburg Mor is at the northern end of the Treshnish Isles, more of a rock pinnacle than an island, and beset by skerries and strong tides. It is thus ideal for confining a neighbour whose lands you wish, or whose wife you covet, or who just has the television on too loud. At the very top the pinnacle had been fortified into a small keep, and here it was that Duart conveyed his captive one dark and stormy night. Lochbuie being not only toothless but at 68 elderly (for those times) and also now heirless, Duart ordered that only the ugliest old woman on Mull be sent to share his captivity and to wait upon him. But within a twelvemonth she was with child, much to the surprise of Lochbuie and to the great annoyance of Duart, who promptly ordered her removal to Torloisk, on Mull, and instructed the midwife as follows.

"See here," he commanded, "as you value your life, if it is a male child, smother it at birth. I want no heir to Lochbuie." In due course the old woman gave birth to a daughter, who was, of course, no interest to Duart, and he promptly retired to his castle and the pleasures of lifting cattle from as far afield as Gigha. But an hour or two after he left the old woman produced another child, this time a boy, who was swiftly conveyed to safety to a remote cave, guarded by a faithful clansman of Lochbuie, his wife and their seven sons.

But you can't keep a secret on Mull, and before many years were out Duart heard of the birth of an heir to his enemy, Lochbuie. He ordered the island to be searched and the young boy slain; by the banks of the River Lussa they came upon Lochbuie's faithful clansmen and his seven sons. Stalwartly refusing to reveal the whereabouts of the child the man and his sons were cut down one by one in a great battle, enabling the child to be hastily removed to safety and a MacGillivray foster-mother in Glencannel.

The boy was known as *Murchadh Gearr* (Stunted or Dumpy Murdoch) for although strong he was a short, stout lad. And when he approached mans age – his father in the meantime having died – his foster-mother told him of his lineage, that he was the true heir to Lochbuie, and advised him for safety to quit Mull. So off he went to Antrim and remained there a time, gathering round him twelve trusty friends, to whom he related his circumstances, and his determination to win back his lands.

With this small band of followers he landed on the shores of Lochbuie – on yet another dark and stormy night! But the Castle of Moy was too strongly garrisoned for his small force to attack; furthermore, the only entrance door was protected by a massive iron yett, making an assault on this only entry impossible. Reconnoitring in the dark he came across a woman returning from tending the cattle, who he recognised as his MacGillivray foster-mother from Glencannel. Great was their rejoicing and Murdoch drew her aside to explain his plans.

"You know the castle" he whispered. "How can I take it?"

She thought for a moment then replied.

"The calves and their mothers are kept separate, the calves on one side of the castle, their mothers on the other. When the last light is out and the garrison asleep, station some men by the door, whilst others loose the calves and the cows. The noise whilst the cows bellow for their own calf will alert those within, who will think the cattle are being lifted. Those by the castle door can kill those within as they emerge".

"But what about your husband? How will I recognise him?" asked *Murchadh Gearr*, not wishing to cause distress to his foster-mother by killing her husband.

"Ach! Leig an t-urball leis a'Chraicionn" (Ach! Let the tail go with the hide) she replied with a shrug.

When the last light was out Murdoch did as she suggested and soon the castle was his, but Murdoch of Scallasdale escaped and soon prepared to do battle for the

8-2 Regaining Moy Castle

Lochbuie lands; in this he was aided by his wife's clansmen, the Stewarts of Appin. Old friends and clansmen of Lochbuie rallied round Dumpy Murdoch, who by chance heard of where his wicked uncle was. At dead of night he and his trusty lieutenant, an Irishman called MacCormick, crept into the cave where Scallasdale slept, sheltering from the Mull rain no doubt. There he was sleeping, fully clad in his armour ready for the morrow's battle, clasping his broadsword. Very gently, inch by cautious inch, Murdoch eased the sword out of his hand and exchanged it for his own. When he awoke Scallasdale realised he had been spared and vowed he too would spare the clan from what was bound to be a very bloody battle. He disbanded his men and sought friendship with *Murdoch Gearr*, which lasted all their lives – or so some say!

The faithful MacCormick was not forgotten, for Murdoch ordered that anyone of that name was to be given hospitality at Moy Castle. Lest anyone forget he had cut into the door lintel these words:

Biath agus Deoh do MhacCormig
Food and Drink to MacCormick

Thus, with the aid of friends from Antrim, did Dumpy Murdoch get back his lands and his Castle of Moy. He married the sister of the 1st Earl of Antrim, and lived to become a belligerent old man. In 1576 he was described as *'a agit decrepit man of four scoir yeris'* when the father complained that his son, John, *'hes usit himself verie uncourteous'*. I don't really blame John, for he sued his father for casting him in chains in Moy Castle. In 1578 John, Bishop of the Isles lodged a complaint against him, and that's the last we hear of Dumpy Murdoch.

~

Although the Lochbuie lands are no longer in Maclaine hands, twenty chiefs later the line goes on, in South Africa – Lorne Gillean Iain Maclaine of Lochbuie, 26th of Lochbuie, Chief of Maclaine of Lochbuie (the *Siol Eachainn* – The Race of Hector) and Representer of the baronial house of Maclaine of Moy.

Map references

- OS Landranger 49. OS Explorer 375:

  Moy Castle NM 618 247
- OS Landranger 48. OS Explorer 374:

  Cairn na Burgh Mhor NM 448 306
- OS Landranger 49. OS Explorer 375:

  Falls of Lussa NM 648 325

  Airidh na Sliseig [Arinasliseig] NM 655317

  Loch Sguabain crannog NM 631 307.

Historical notes

- Timescales: According to *Clan Gillean*, published in 1899: Ian the Toothless was born c. 1470 and died c. 1539 – some accounts say he died in 1538 fighting against his son Ewen. Ian's son John was killed by Allan of the Straws in 1526; and Ewen of the Little Head died in battle against his father in 1538. With both his legitimate sons dead Ian set about legitimising his two sons by a handfasting marriage [Murdoch and Charles] and both were legitimised in 1538.

- Hugh Maclean of Scallasdale seized the Lochbuie lands in 1538, presumably with Duart's consent. Dumpy Murdoch was born about 1498; regained his lands in 1540; and died about 1578, *'a agit decrepit man of four scoir yeris'*.

- *Ludeag* – the fairy washerwoman: The *bean nighe* (washer woman), is a Scottish fairy, seen as an omen of death and a messenger from the Otherworld. She is a type of *bean sith* (in Irish bean *sídhe*, anglicized as "banshee").

- By legend, as the 'Washer at the Ford' she wanders near deserted streams where she washes the blood from the grave-clothes of those who are about to die. A *bean nighe* is described in some tales as having one nostril, one big protruding tooth, webbed feet and long-hanging breasts, and to be dressed in green. If a mortal passing by asks politely, she will tell the names of the chosen that are going to die. While generally appearing as a hag, she can also manifest as a beautiful young woman when it suits her, much as does her Irish counterpart the *bean sídhe*. [Wikipedia].

- Some accounts say Dumpy Murdoch's mother was a Macphee, and that mother and child were swiftly conveyed to a cottage in remote Glencannel, way up at the head of Loch Ba, where they were cared for by a family called MacGillivray.

- The ruins of the croft where the 'Battle of the Seven Sons' took place are still standing, and are known as *Airidh na Sliseig*, which Alasdair Alpin MacGregor says means Shieling of the Slashing – and who am I to argue with him! The site is on the west bank of the River Lussa, and marked as *Arinasliseig*. However, the name more probably means 'Shieling of the Shavings', as a family of boat builders once lived there, carrying or floating their boats to Loch Spelve.

- Some accounts have *Hector Mor* Maclean of Duart seize the Maclaine lands, but it was Hugh Maclean of Scallastle, in 1538, not when Dumpy Murdoch was born c. 1500.

- So although Ian the Toothless may well have been imprisoned at some stage on Carnaburg Mor by Maclean of Duart it's unlikely he had a child there by 'the ugliest old woman on Mull' – but it's still a cracking good story!

- MOY CASTLE: Hector was granted a charter of Lochbuie in 1360 by John of Islay [Burke's] and may well have built a small defensive keep at Moy. But the RCAHMS say the present Moy Castle was probably started in 1400-1450, and first appears on record in 1494. It was abandoned as a residence in 1752, when a new house was built nearby, itself abandoned in 1793 when it was adapted as stables for the new mansion house built by Murdoch Maclaine, 19th of Lochbuie. [RCAHMS]

• In *Recollections of an Argyllshire Drover* pp. 164-171 Eric Creer details the many tales he recorded for the School of Scottish Studies from Donald Morrison in the mid-twentieth century. Donald was born in 1885 and came from a long line of Mull crofters, one of whose ancestors had come over from Antrim with *Murchadh Gearr* and his trusty band – indeed he was the steersman of the boat.

'The chiefs of Lochbuie kept up a close connection with the descendants of the original warrior-band, and, until his grandfather's time, would regularly invite the Morrisons to a great week-long New Year feast at Lochbuie.'

Donald also confirmed that a MacCormick was indeed one of those who came over from Antrim. He relates the tale of

cutting the cow-hide into thin strips, the imprisonment on Carnaburg Mor of Ian the Toothless, and the re-taking of Moy castle with the use of the cattle. However, all three tales are often recounted in different versions in national and international folklore.

• Carved lintels: a similar tale is told of Breacachadh Castle on Coll. *Iain Abraich* (Lochaber John) was son to *Iain Garbh*, 2nd Maclean of Coll; *Iain Abraich* was killed in an affray with Cameron of Lochiel at Corpach and his pregnant wife given shelter by a family Mac-Elonich. Hence Coll had the stone carved:

promising succour to any of the MacElonich family in need and this pledge was honoured right down to the eighteenth century. This stone has disappeared but there is a vacant space above the eastern doorway from which it may have been removed.

• From Eilean Donan Castle, where a panel above the entrance door reads: *As long as a MacRae is in, a Fraser will not be out.* This refers to the time before the MacRaes moved to Kintail but were on Lovat land south of the Beauly Firth. Seemingly carved above the entry to the Fraser stronghold was:

Fhad 'sa bhiteas Frisealach a stigh,
na bitheadh MacRuath a muigh

As long as Fraser lives within,
let not a MacRae remain without

Sources

- *Encyclopaedia of Scotland* – John Keay and Julia Keay.
- *Somewhere in Scotland* – Alasdair Alpin MacGregor.
- *The Place Names of Mull* – Duncan Macquarrie.
- *Scottish Islands* – Hamish Haswell-Smith.
- *Warriors and Priests* – Nicholas Maclean-Bristol.
- *West Highland Notes & Queries*, Series 2 No 4.
- *Recollections of an Argyllshire Drover and other West Highland Chronicles* – Eric R Cregeen edited by Margaret Bennett.
- *Tall Tales from an Island* – Peter MacNab.
- *Highways & Byways in Mull & Iona* – Peter MacNab.
- *Royal Commission on Ancient & Historical Monuments for Scotland* – Argyll Volume 3.
- *Burke's Peerage, Baronetage & Knightage and Scottish Clan Chiefs* – 107th Edition.

The loss of Lewis by the Macleods

And of how various Macleod brothers murdered each other or were duly hanged for piracy & rebellion, and of the failure of the Fife Adventurers

he Clan Torkil [Macleod] in Lewis were the *stoutest and prettiest men, but a wicked bloody crew, whom neither law nor reason could guide or modell, destroying one another, till in the end, they were all expelled that country, and the Mackenzies now possess it.'*

So goes an old saying, and if you sitting comfortably for a complex true medieval saga of piracy, family feuding, theft and murder, then pin back your lugs for a story that makes Eastenders look like a fairy-tale! There is a chart below of who did what to whom.

Viking control of the Hebrides, either directly from Norway or from the Kings of Man, extended from about 880 AD until The Treaty of Perth in 1266, when Norway ceded the Hebrides to Scotland. The Macleods of Lewis – and their kinsmen of Harris and Dunvegan – were descended from Leod, a son of Olaf the Black, King of Man.

Our tale starts in 1532, when Ruari (Roderick) Macleod – known as Old Rory – succeeded as the eleventh, last, and worst chief of the Macleods of Lewis. He quarrelled incessantly, fighting not only with his own family, but with the Brieves (Hereditary Judges) of Lewis, a clan called Morison; with the Mackenzies of Kintail, who rather fancied adding Lewis to their already extensive mainland holdings; and with the King, which was not always a smart thing to do. Indeed, so enraged was James V at the unruly outreaches of his kingdom that in 1540 he embarked on a show of strength to the Northern and Western Isles, '*for the ordouring of thame in justice and gude policy*'. At Stornoway, Old Rory was forced to accompany the King on his progress, but was later released and a new charter granted for his lands. The ink had barely dried for a few years when Old Rory was treasonably engaged with the King of England, seeking to transfer his allegiance to him; no doubt he thought a King in London was even further away than a King in Edinburgh.

Old Rory had three wives and eight sons, of whom only three [(B), (C) and (D) in the chart] were legitimate, and this caused endless problems, as our tale will unfold. Quite how many daughters he produced is not recorded, for girls at that time counted for little – unless of course she was an heiress who could be profitably married off to an impecunious son.

He wed when young a flighty widow, one Janet Mackay, whose morals seem to have been about equal to his own. She bore a son, Torquil (known as *Torquil Conanach*), but Old Rory refused to acknowledge the child as his heir, claiming that the real father was the Brieve, Hugh Morrison – probably true. This Torquil was a definite baddie, and held Old Rory '*in maist miserable captivitie in mountains and cavernis of craigis far distant from the societie of men, [where he] almaist pereised wt [with] cauld and famine.*'

Finally, after two years captivity, Old Rory accepted *Torquil Conanach* as his heir, but on his release he promptly revoked the agreement.

Meanwhile, back at the castle, Janet had run off with John Macleod of Raasay, so Old Rory divorced her, married again, produced a son, and bewilderingly also called him Torquil. To avoid confusion he was known as *Torquil Oighre*, or Torquil the Heir; this Torquil was seemingly a TNC [thoroughly nice chap], but as often happens to the goodies, he was drowned at sea in 1566. So we can forget about him.

Old Rory was without an heir, so he married yet a third time and produced two sons, yet another Torquil (known as *Torquil Dubh*) and Norman. Of the five illegitimate sons, three were killed in family squabbles, leaving only Neil (*Niall Odhar*) and Murdo to interest us for our tale.

~

Against all odds, and at the ripe old age of ninety-five (in about 1595), Old Rory finally popped his clogs, peacefully in his own bed. Long before his death the sons had followed their father's example, and were happily murdering each other, the Morisons, and anyone else who got in their way. At the death of Old Rory the Macleod succession was still unsettled, and the 'Clanleyid of Lewis' joined the MacGregors and a few others on the list of broken clans.

One legitimate son, *Torquil Oighre*, had been drowned at sea; another, *Torquil Dubh*, was murdered by his illegitimate half-brother Murdo. In this foul deed he was aided by John Morison, the Brieve, acting at the instigation of Mackenzie of Kintail – not that this nefarious pair seemed to need much encouragement. Having got rid of *Torquil Dubh*, Mackenzie of Kintail promptly kidnapped Norman, the only legitimate Macleod heir, in his way to gaining Lewis. The lad was thus dragged from his school in Perth to close confinement in Kintail, and there he languished for many a long year.

Which left the illegitimate Neil Macleod (*Niall Odhar*, or Sallow Neil) in charge of affairs in Lewis, and happy to pursue his vendetta against the Morisons, whom he proceeded to kill one by one. And from his base at Stornoway Castle he sallied forth to raid shipping in the Minch, the Mackenzie lands on Skye and the mainland – and indeed anywhere that took his fancy.

However, a small cloud appeared on the horizon, in the shape of King James VI in far-away Edinburgh. Not only was James fed up with the constant warfare of the Macleods, and his lack of revenue from them, but there landed on his desk at Holyrood a most timely e-mail. It described the island of Lewis as *'inrychit with ane incredibill fertilitie of cornis and store of fischeingis and utheris necessaris, surpassing far the plenty of any pairt of the inland.'*

Now if there was one thing King Jamie liked more than pretty young men it was money, and the Treasury being empty – as always – he swiftly accepted the report without checking the truth. The image of all these riches in Lewis just waiting to be tapped and taxed became like a Holy Grail, and the King set in motion a devious plan for garnering them in without any cost to him.

First, he passed an act that all landowners in the Highlands and Islands should present themselves and their title deeds to the Lords of the Exchequer by 15 May 1598, together with security for their future behaviour. No deeds – no land. This caused somewhat of a problem for our Neil, as his elder half-brother, *Torquil Conanach*, had nicked the deeds for Lewis from Old Rory and had given them to his mother's family, none other than Mackenzie of Kintail. So Neil was hit by a treble whammy – illegitimate, proscribed, and disinherited; not that he cared overmuch, for his main pursuits of piracy, reiving and murder were not affected much by a King so far away.

The King thus having gained vacant possession of Lewis he proceeded to the next stage by offering this El Dorado rent-free for seven years; he also threw in as part of the bargain the remote Isle of North Rona, and Trotternish on Skye. The takers were a group of merchants from Fife who hoped to make a tidy profit from this land flowing with 'cornis [and] fischeingis.' True, the Lewis men had 'given themselves over to all kynd of barbaritie and inhumanitie,' (which was correct) but part of the deal was to bring Lowland civilisation to Lewis. If the islanders did not like it, they could leave for the mainland and be replaced by more worthy – and taxpaying – Lowlanders.

The group were called The Fife Adventurers, for it was surely a Great Adventure, Lewis being then as remote to the merchants of Fife as the Darien Peninsula – and equally unprofitable. They landed in Stornoway in late October 1598, and were met by the recalcitrant islanders, led by Neil and Murdo Macleod, winter gales, rain and bitter cold. Six hundred mercenaries beat back the Macleods, the artisans built a base camp, and the Minister – one Robert Drurie of Anstruther – presumably administered to his flock. The settlers, however, were rapidly awoken to the true realities of the land, the threatening islanders. They also had a distinct lack of provisions, for they had expected from the glowing reports that Lewis would provide a cornucopia of food. Silly men!

Neil Macleod enjoyed a profitable year of raiding the settlers with his brother, but he had never forgiven Murdo for a couple of family murders. Early in 1600 he captured his half-brother, in the process slaying Murdo's twelve Morison followers, whose heads he lopped off and popped into a handy sack. Then he did a deal with the Adventurers;

in exchange for Murdo, they promised Neil a share of the land, and to intercede with the King for a pardon.

"Done," said Neil, and off he went to Edinburgh with his new settler chums, his sack of heads, and brother Murdo under close arrest. Neil duly got his pardon, but Murdo lost his head. Not only that, but he was hanged, quartered and drawn, and his head fixed above the Nether Bow at Edinburgh, as an example to others 'to abstain from the like treasonable, barbarous and heinous attempts in the future.'

The Adventurers expected a quieter life now that Murdo was dead, and Neil on their side, but he soon fell out with them and resumed his old habits of piracy and raiding the settlers. And from the wings Mackenzie of Kintail continued stirring the pot to his own advantage, pretending to be friend of King, Adventurers and Macleod alike.

As we heard, Mackenzie had held in captivity for some years the last remaining legitimate son of Old Rory, Norman Macleod. Knowing full well that the islanders would rally to one of their own and attack the Adventurers, he released Norman, who promptly surprised the settlers 'prettie towne', killing many of them and setting fire to the encampment. For eight months they held the remaining settlers captive, finally releasing them on condition that they never returned, handed over title for Lewis to Norman Macleod, and obtained the King's pardon for all the Macleod past misdeeds.

King Jamie, however, had no intention of agreeing to this blackmail, and in July 1602 he raised the Northern Counties with powers of fire and sword to subdue 'sic ane tyrannous byke of rebellious lymmaris'.

But about that time King James was rather preoccupied with the little matter of inheriting England, so it was to be three years before they landed in Lewis. In the face of such a strong force Norman capitulated, much against his Uncle Neil's advice, who, as ever, fancied a good scrap. Under safe conduct Norman was conveyed to London, where he made a favourable impression on the King; instead of lopping off Norman's head James merely imprisoned him in Edinburgh for ten years. In 1615 Norman was allowed to move to Holland, where he later died; exit Old Norman's last legitimate son.

Meanwhile, Mackenzie of Kintail was not content to let matters rest, for the few surviving Adventurers were so pissed off at the climate, constant feuding and poor soil that they decided to withdraw. Mackenzie chose this moment to produce the deeds of Lewis, given him by his nephew, *Torquil Conanach*. Kintail just happened to have as a chum the Lord Chancellor, and persuaded that worthy to use the Great Seal to convey Lewis to Kintail. Then, as now, it was ever handy to have a politician in one's pocket! However – King James was not too pleased at these shenanigans, forced Mackenzie to resign the title to the Crown, and promptly conveyed it to the remaining three Adventurers, Lord Balmerino, Sir James Spence, and Sir George Hay.

Murdo Macleod's hanging had left just Neil from Old Rory's nine sons, and if you think he was ready to retire to a bungalow in Stornoway, think again! He continued to create such mayhem that the Northern Counties were called out again in 1609 to help the colonists and to capture Neil. However, Mackenzie was up to his old tricks, and whilst on one hand he sent the beleaguered colonists a shipload of much-needed provisions, on the other hand he informed Neil, who – being a good pirate – promptly captured it.

With supplies running out, Hay and Spence dismissed the men from the Northern Counties, left a small guard at the fort, and themselves sailed for Fife to procure more men and provisions. This was just the opening Neil had been looking for, so with his nephew Malcolm – an up and coming young pirate and murderer in true Macleod fashion – and backed by a strong band of islanders, Neil captured the fort and sent the survivors packing back to Fife.

This was the last straw for the Fife Adventurers, and they sold the title of Lewis to Mackenzie of Kintail for 10,000 merks in 1610. Lord Kintail promptly crossed to take possession of Lewis, and most of the islanders accepted the change – except for Neil Macleod, his three nephews, a chap called Torquil Blair, and about thirty-four followers.

The Lords of the Privy Council were pretty cheesed off at this further rebellion; and I suspect Neil was equally cheesed off at losing Lewis to his old rival, Mackenzie of Kintail. The latter was issued,

with fire and sword and all kind of hostility, to search, seik, hunt, follow and persew, the said

Neil [Macleod] his complices, assistaris and per-takers by sea and land, quhairever they may be apprehendit.

Thus pursued, Neil and his followers eventually found sanctuary on the tiny island of Bearasay [Berisay, *Bearrasaigh*], situated at the western end of Loch Roag.

From Ordnance Survey maps Bearasay looks an inhospitable base, more of a rock outcrop than island, rising steeply to 150 feet, surrounded by outlying skerries, bleak, and exposed to the full force of the Atlantic. There Neil held out for three years, for he had previously stockpiled provisions and weapons against just such an eventuality. But Bearasay was so small that the wives, camp followers and children had to be left on neighbouring Berneray, and it was this fact that led to Neil's eventual downfall.

In 1611, however, he had cause to rejoice when his old adversary, Lord Kintail, died. As Kintail's son was a minor the boy's uncle, The Tutor of Kintail, had the commission of fire and sword renewed on his behalf. This Tutor was a more ruthless man than his late brother, and on Lewis they said that the three worst evils that could affect a tenant were May frost, July mist, and the Tutor of Kintail.

Meanwhile, back on Bearasay, Neil had met up with the English pirate Peter Love (or Lowe), who had arrived in Lewis with a 'shippe furnished and fraughted with great wealth'.

The men soon became firm friends, having been outlawed for similar reasons, and they plotted how best to become masters of Lewis by land and sea.

All too soon, as thieves are wont to do, they fell out; Peter Love and his ship Priam were captured and his erstwhile friend Neil had Love and his crew sent to the Privy Council, who promptly hanged them at Leith as a job lot. Neil hoped by this action to gain a pardon for himself and the release of his half-brother Norman from Edinburgh Castle. Neil was eventually pardoned and invited to Edinburgh, but knowing what had happened to Norman and others of his clan he wisely refused, even though he thereby relinquished the pardon.

In one last attempt to dislodge Neil and his supporters, the Tutor of Kintail rounded up the wives and children of those holding out on Bearasay. Within sight of the

9-1 '… they tied to a rock the boat containing the hostages …'

island they tied to a rock the boat containing the hostages, and left them to drown when the tide rose. The cries and screams of these women and children created such a *'pit-iefull spectakll [that] did so move Niell and his company to compassion'*.

They gave in and evacuated Bearasay, seeking refuge in the wilds of Harris.

Now, Rory Macleod of Harris was a distant kinsman (some accounts say an uncle), but he was also *under payne of treasone to delyver Niell McLeod to the privie Counsell'*, and to him Neil finally surrendered. Maybe he expected his kinsman to harbour him; maybe he expected his pardon to be renewed; maybe he was just getting too old for life on the run. Anyway, Rory Macleod promised to take Neil to the King in London and plead his cause; but when they arrived in Glasgow they were directed to Edinburgh and trial on counts of fire raising, murder, burning, theft and piracy.

Neil pleaded guilty, and was sentenced to be hanged at the Market Cross in April 1613 *'and thaireftir, his heid to be strukin frome his body, and affixt and set upone ane priket'* at Nether Bow Port. His half-brother Murdo's head had been stuck there twelve years before, so the brothers were starting somewhat of a family tradition.

By pleading guilty to the long list of crimes Neil had expected a reprieve, and he was hoping for this to the last moment. Wishing to get matters over with, one of the officials said to Neil

"Hurry up old bodach" (old man). To which Neil replied "If I was on the slanting deck of my galley you would not call me bodach" and promptly struck the man down. This apart, Neil was reported to have died *'verie Christianlie'*.

~

Thus died Neil Macleod, by his own admission a pirate, murderer, arsonist and thief, but one can't help having a sneaking admiration for the thug he undoubtedly was, for it was an age of fellow thugs. Mackenzie, Lord of Kintail was equally guilty of just such crimes, but was high enough and crafty enough to get away with them; he and his heirs ended up owning Lewis for two hundred years. Created Earls of Seaforth in 1628, they were staunch Jacobites, and Lewis suffered dearly for it. One reputable account states that 'during the whole Seaforth regime, proprietor and tacksman alike exploited the people with little or no consideration for their welfare.'

Whilst Neil lost his head, his kinsman Rory Macleod of Harris gained a knighthood for delivering him to the Privy Council. But we must not be too hard on Sir Rory, as the choice was either deliver Neil or be attainted for treason and risk losing his own head.

Neil's sons Donald and *Ruairidh Dubh* had been imprisoned with him, but were released on condition they banished themselves from Scotland. Some chance! Instead of doing this they returned to Lewis, where *Ruairidh* was promptly killed, and Donald fled to Holland.

Neil's nephew Malcolm, who had been in Bearasay with him, continued the family tradition of piracy, harrying fishermen and merchant ships in the Minch. He also enjoyed plaguing the Tutor of Kintail for many a year – just possibly because the latter had executed Malcolm's two brothers? In 1616 Malcolm led a rebellion in Lewis with the support of some of his late Uncle Neil's old cronies, but this the Tutor savagely repressed, and Malcolm eventually

went to Spain. In 1621 he was back at his old trade of piracy in the Minch – what else is a poor boy meant to do? – and is presumed to have died in Holland.

~

Although Old Rory died in his bed at ninety-five, his quarrelsome sons and grandsons fared less well, and a chart of the family tree is scattered with murders, counter-murders, hangings and executions. Of the sons, *Torquil Conanach* was disowned as legitimate and caused mayhem ever after. *Torquil Oighre* – the most promising – was drowned at sea. *Torquil Dubh* was murdered by a half-brother, Murdo; and Norman, the final legitimate son, was imprisoned for years, released to encourage and lead a rebellion, pardoned by the King, and finally died in Holland.

Of the five illegitimate sons, *Tormod Uigeach* was murdered by his half-brother Donald, who was later executed at Dingwall. Murdo, who murdered his legitimate half-brother *Torquil Dubh*, was hung, drawn and quartered at Edinburgh. Neil was merely hung for his many misdeeds, although the end result is the same. And *Ruairidh Og* was made captive by *Torquil Dubh*, given to MacLean of Duart for safe-keeping, escaped, and died in a snowstorm.

The grandsons fared no better. John (son of *Torquil Conanach*) was murdered by *Ruairidh Og*, his uncle; *Ruairidh Dubh* (son of Neil) was killed in battle, and his brother Donald fled to Holland; William and *Ruairidh* (sons of *Ruairidh Og*) were executed by The Tutor of Kintail; and we have already heard how their brother Malcolm fled to Holland after a life of piracy and rebellion.

~

An old Gaelic saying succinctly summed up the Macleods in two lines:

> *It is my opinion of Clan Leod that they are like pikes*
>   *in water.*
> *The oldest of them, if the larger, eats the younger.*

Map references

- OS Landranger sheets 13 & 14. OS Explorer 456, 457,

  458, 459:

  Bearasay NB 122 425

Historical notes

- It's all true!
- James V's Expedition to the Isles: In 1540 James V embarked on a show of strength to the Northern and Western Isles, '*for the ordouring of thame in justice and gude policy.*' Most of the nobility were commanded to attend, accompanied by 3-4,000 men in a fleet of sixteen ships led by the Royal Yacht of that time, 'the Salamandry which the French king gave him.' Merchant ships accommodated the lords and gentlemen, three ships were for victuals, a 'howk' [hulk] for baggage, and a well-trimmed bark to be the 'scurior' before the fleet. The record of expenses includes twelve shillings for grey cloth to line a coloured coat for the King 'quhen he zeid [went] to the Ilis.' Someone must have warned James that the wind might be cold when he rounded Cape Wrath!

Sources

Old Rory Macleod's sons

- *Behold The Hebrides* – Alasdair Alpin Macgregor.
- *Lewis – A History of The Island* – Donald Macdonald.
- *Harris and Lewis* – Frances Thompson.
- *A Rutter of the Scottish Seas* – Alexander Lindsay. [c.1540].
- *Collins Encyclopaedia of Scotland* – edited by John Keay and Julia Keay.

Legitimate sons

- Old Rory = [1] Janet Mackenzie of Kintail, widow of Mackay of Reay. Their son – *Torquil Conanach* (A) – was disowned, as his natural father was Hugh Morrison, the Brieve.
- Old Rory = [2] Barbara Stewart, daughter of Lord Avondale. Their son – *Torquil Oighre* (B) – was drowned at sea in 1566.
- Old Rory = [3] Jeannette MacLean of Duart and had by her two sons.
- *Torquil Dubh* (C) = captured by the Brieve and Murdo Macleod (2). Executed by Mackenzie of Kintail July 1597.
- Norman (D) = died in Holland after 1615.

Illegitimate sons

- *Torquil Conanach* was disowned, as his natural father was Hugh Morrison, the Brieve. Imprisoned his father in a bid to get recognised as heir and continued to cause havoc.

- (1) *Tormod Uigeach* – murdered by Donald (3).
- (2) Murdo – murdered legitimate *Torquil Dubh* (C); hung, drawn and quartered at Edinburgh 1601.
- (3) Donald – murdered *Tormod Uigeach* (1); executed at Dingwall.
- (4) Neil (*Niall Odhar*) – actually murdered none of his brothers; but killed rather too many Fife Adventurers for the King's liking and was duly hung at Edinburgh, 1613.

Of Niall Odhar's sons
- Donald – escaped to Holland.
- *Ruairidh Dubh* – killed on Lewis c. 1614.
- (5) *Ruairidh Og* – made captive by *Torquil Dubh* (C), handed to MacLean of Duart, died in a snowstorm when escaping.

Of Ruairidh Og's sons:
- Malcolm – a pirate, escaped to Holland.
- William – executed by the Tutor of Kintail.
- *Ruairidh* – executed by the Tutor of Kintail.

The Fletchers of Achallader

How the Fletchers lost a castle through Campbell duplicity – but kept the door
The treaty of Achallader / the massacre of Glencoe

At the very head of Glenorchy, a mile to the north-east of Loch Tulla, stand the ruins of Achallader Castle [*Caisteal Achaladair,* field of hard water] once the home of the Fletchers of Achallader. Fletcher comes from the French word *flechier,* meaning arrow maker, in Gaelic *fleisdear* [*leisdear* or *leisdeir,* pronounced leshjer] which by the 18th century was anglicised into Fletcher.

Sometime after the eleventh century a band of *Mac-an-leisdears* [sons of the arrow maker] settled in Glen Orchy, where they became arrow makers to Clan MacGregor. Indeed, the birch woods of Glenorchy provided those early Fletchers with ample material to fashion arrows, not only for their own use but for others. An old Gaelic verse details the needs of a bowman:

Bogha a dh'iubhar Easragain,
Sioda na Gaillbhin
Saighead a bheithe an Doire-dhuinn,
Ite fìrein Locha Treige
Bow of the yew of Easragan,
Silk of Gallvinn
Arrow of the birch of Doire-donn,
Feather of the eagle of Loch Treig,

10-1 Glen Orchy, with Beinn Achaladoir in the distance

Easragan is by Ardchattan Priory, on the north shore of Loch Etive, and it was here that Robert Bruce held his first Parliament after success at the Battle of the Pass of Brander in 1308. Gallvinn is possibly Dunkeld, famous for its wax and silk. *Doire-donn* (brown grove) is in Glen Orchy, renowned for its birch woods. Loch Treig is deep in the wildness of Rannoch Moor, and any eagle living here would need strong feathers.

MacGregor country it may have been, but there is an ancient saying which runs thus: *Se clann-an-Leisdar a thog a chiad smuid a thug goil air uisage on Urcha'* (the Fletchers were the first to raise smoke to boil water in Glenorchy).

Boiling water was an early form of staking a claim to land, and the main holdings of the Fletcher chiefs were at Achallader and Barravurich, the highest and most mountainous parts of Glenorchy. It was hard country, with the heights of *Beinn Achaladoir* to the east, the great peaks of Black Mount to the west, and the vast wilderness of Rannoch Moor to the north. Only to the south-west, down Glen Orchy, was the land kinder, for on the straths there was good grazing, and the river provided many salmon and trout for salting down in preparation for the long, harsh winters.

The first recorded chief was *Angus Mac-an-Leister*, born in about 1450, and in due course he built the Castle of Achallader – quite when is unknown, but the Fletchers had lost the superiority of their lands to the Campbells sometime between 1497 and 1523. For in the latter year,

> … the fortalice of Glenurquhay was confirmed along with the lands, by Colin, Earl of Argyle, to Duncan, son and heir of Sir Colin Campbell (third laird of Breadalbane). [Origines Parochiales].

So it is possible that *Angus Mac-an-Leister* himself chose the site for the castle, beneath the lowering slopes of *Beinn Achaladoir* and *Beinn an Dothairdh*, close by the burn that tumbled between them. There he and his settled down to the normal clan life of farming, raiding, hunting deer and lifting their neighbour's cattle.

However, Sir Duncan Campbell of Glenorchy coveted not just his neighbour's wife, but also his castle and lands, so he devised a cunning plan. Sir Duncan was responsible to King James VI for the ordering of the law in that area, and also for the peacefulness of the clans. So, on the surface, he made friends with the Fletchers, then one day he set off for Achallader, taking with him three 'strangers', men unknown to the Fletchers. Arriving at the castle, he remained concealed, but said to his men, "Do you turn the horses into yon field of oats close by the castle, and take no orders from any but me".

Naturally Angus Fletcher was enraged at the spoiling of his crop, and rushed from the castle wherein he was breakfasting.

"Remove those animals instantly, or it will be the worst for you", he cried in a loud voice to the 'strangers'. But when they ignored his commands, as ordered by their own chief, Angus became so furious that he seized an iron tethering-peg and hurled it at the nearest man. Such was his strength and so sure his aim that the man fell instantly dead upon the spot.

Sir Duncan, emerging from his place of concealment, came up to Fletcher in the pretence of his 'just happening to be passing'.

"How now", said he, "this is indeed a sorry day, for as the King's man I must see justice done for this murder". Then he appeared to think awhile, and continued, "Although you are my friend and neighbour, and that man but a knave, the King will surely hear of the matter, and so this is what I counsel. Go you into Rannoch Moor until this blows over, and I will away to the King and plead your cause".

The Fletcher chief was much pleased with this friendly concern, and they repaired to the castle to seal the arrangement with a dram – as any two gentlemen would surely do. But whilst they were there, Sir Duncan appeared deep in thought, and finally said, "It would appear better to the King as if you had repented of the deed, and signed over your lands to my care. I, of course, will return them to you as soon as this matter is over and you return to Achallader".

Trusting and unsuspecting, Fletcher called for pen and ink and paper, and signed away his lands to Sir Duncan.

"Now, make haste," said the knight, "and be off into the wildness of Rannoch till I send word".

Angus Fletcher hid many months on the Moor of Rannoch, but Sir Duncan at once repaired to Edinburgh. There he promptly registered the lands in his own name, and a reward of two hundred marks was offered by the

Privy Council at Stirling for the head of the Fletcher chief. When Angus was finally able to return to Achallader Sir Duncan absolutely refused to transfer back castle or lands but allowed the Fletchers to rent them back. In 1587 Angus Fletcher [probably the 3rd chief] is described as *'Angus Mcinleister in Auchalladour'*; in the Black Book of Taymouth the Muster Roll for 1658 includes 'John Fletcher in Auchalladour'. [The term 'in' was used for a tenant, whereas had they still owned the land or been tacksmen the term would be 'of' Achallader].

Deprived of their lands by trusting a Campbell, the Fletchers later moved a mile east to another farm they once owned, Barravurich, and there successive chiefs lived until moving to Dunans in the early 18th century.

~

On account of his black hair, his nefarious deeds, and his habit of building or acquiring castles Sir Duncan became known as 'Black Duncan of the Seven Castles,' but died peacefully in his bed in 1631, at the ripe old age of seventy-eight.

About 1587 he rebuilt the tower of Achallader, which now rose to three storeys and a garret, well defended by shot-holes.

'He biggit [built] the toure of Auchalladoure for the warkmanfchip [workmanship] of the quhilk [which] he gaif ane thousand markis'. [The Black Book of Taymouth].

Barely was the paint dry than the castle was raided by retainers of Grant of Ballindalloch, Simon Fraser Lord Lovat, and others in 1595, resulting in 'the slaughter and injury of several person in the lands of Auchallander and spoilation thereof'. Among the names of the claimants for damages against the raiders are 'Angus McAngus V'eane (Fletcher) and John McIlliespikis (Fletcher) son'. [Reg of Acts and Decreets V.156 fol 254 and V.151 fol 32]

It was then burnt by Clan MacGregor, out to avenge the hanging of their chief, Alasdair MacGregor of Glenstrae. Following the proscribing of the *Gregarach*, Black Duncan and his sons had been assiduous in hunting them down, although it was Argyll himself who committed the

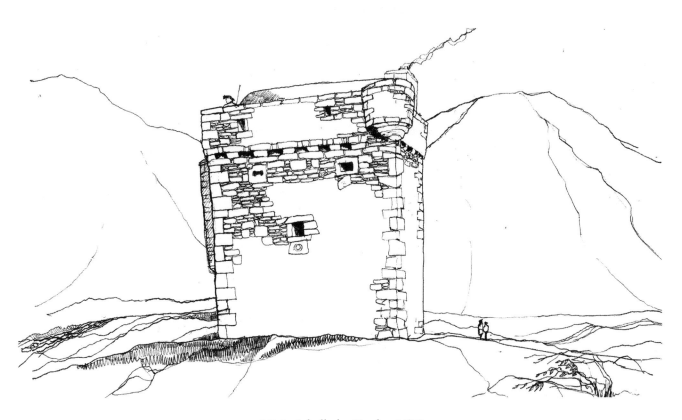

10-2 Achallader Castle c.1600

final treachery that led to Alasdair's death in October 1603.

It was damaged by fire again in 1646 by Montrose's forces [some accounts say by the MacGregors again] but the Earl of Breadalbane had it rebuilt. In the summer of 1683 a Commission for the settlement of the Highlands stayed at the castle, led by Sir William Drummond of Cromlix. He welcomed, among other chiefs, Alistair MacIain of Glencoe, whose clan was a sept of the Macdonalds. The MacIain lands were poor and the men were notorious cattle lifters, particularly from the herds of Campbell neighbors.

The end for the castle came in 1689, following the Glorious Revolution of the previous year, for with William and Mary now reigning, but not yet secure, there was a Jacobite Rising. The MacIains, returning from victory at Killiecrankie but repulse at Dunkeld, took great delight in pulling down what they could of a Campbell castle. It was never restored and much of the stone was used to build the present farmhouse. But the castle ruins were still serviceable enough to host a remarkable meeting in the year before the Massacre of Glencoe.

A treaty and a massacre

Even after defeat at Dunkeld the Highland clans remained in arms. King William – ever one to demand a quick solution to a complex problem – was unwilling to commit the resources and time to winning a peace in the Highlands. The obvious solution was to buy peace from the impecunious and debt-ridden chiefs, but this proposal would have to come from one who understood both their language and their mentality. The man chosen for this delicate task was none other than the son of our old friend – but not to the Fletchers – Black Duncan of the Castles. John Campbell of Glenorchy was by now the first Earl of Breadalbane, 'fated to be one of the most maligned and misunderstood men in Scottish history'.

John Campbell was an ambitious man, and as a member of the Scottish Privy Council he could see that backing William and the new regime was the sensible option. However, he hedged his bets, because the chances of James reclaiming the crown were not impossible either. His nickname of 'slippery John' was appropriate, for one could never be certain which side he was on.

His aim was to persuade the chiefs to sign an oath of allegiance to William and Mary; and in June 1691 Breadalbane met at Achallader with various chiefs, amongst them the elderly Alastair MacIain of Glencoe. Much secret plotting went on in the makeshift accommodation that had been contrived amongst the ruins, for in essence the chiefs would relinquish their ancient rights and privileges in favour of the Crown in exchange for payments of gold. Cameron of Lochiel asked for £20,000 on behalf of the chiefs but Breadalbane beat him down to £12,000, the sum authorised by King William. [Many, many millions today]. In discussing the individual amounts, Breadalbane abruptly told MacIain that his share would be set against some cows he had stolen the previous December – in fact, he would get nothing. The two men quarrelled and MacIain departed, later telling his sons that 'he feared mischief from no man as much as Breadalbane'.

Other than how much gold they would get, each chief had another concern; what would happen if King James returned? Eventually, on the last day of June, a truce was agreed until the end of October, and messengers were sent to the exiled James in France to gain his permission for the clans to take the oath. It was waiting for this consent that delayed MacIain from taking the oath until past the due date of 1 January 1692, and which subsequently led to the Massacre of Glencoe on the 6th of February that year.

As for the gold, the chiefs saw little of it, for Breadalbane was thought to have kept most for himself! When later he was asked to account to Parliament for the vast sums of money he had been given to pacify the chiefs Breadalbane replied 'The money is spent, the Highlands are at peace and there is no accounting between friends'.

The Treaty of Achallader was little more than a breathing space, allowing more time to reach a final settlement, but Breadalbane was pleased with his success and left for William's camp in Flanders. Soon after he left an unholy alliance formed among his enemies, for too many people had too much to lose by the Treaty. It was spread about that a second, secret, treaty had been signed at Achallader, whereby if James did return all oaths of allegiance to William and Mary were invalid – furthermore, Breadalbane himself would bring out 1,000 men for James.

Clearly the allegations were a forgery; the original 'secret treaty' was never produced and William believed Breadalbane. But the damage was done; William, ever impatient for results, decided not to wait until October for the truce to end. On 27 August 1691 he offered all Highland clans a pardon for their part in the Jacobite uprising, as long as they took an oath of allegiance before 1 January 1692 in front of a magistrate. Those who did not would be 'answerable at their highest peril.'

James delayed answering the chiefs, convinced that he was close to returning to Britain to reclaim his throne. Finally, on 12 December, James replied but his letter was intercepted and read in London before being resealed and sent on – slowly – to Edinburgh. It reached Edinburgh on 21 December, ten days before the deadline, but it still had to travel into the highlands, in the middle of winter. When it finally arrived with Lochiel there were scarcely 24 hours left to get it to MacIain at Glencoe. With the deadline upon him there was no way he would make it to the signing at Inveraray, so he made haste to Fort William and Colonel Hill. The latter advised MacIain that as he was not a magistrate he could not accept his oath; MacIain must appear at Inveraray before Sir Colin Campbell. On went the elderly chief, detained by bad weather and by Campbell of Barcaldine, in spite of Colonel Hill's safe conduct.

By the time he reached Inveraray it was the 2nd January, but Sir Colin had left town for Hogmanay and was not due back for 3 days. When Sir Colin returned he accepted MacIain's explanation with the letter from Colonel Hill, and allowed MacIain to add his signature to the oath. Sir Colin wrote recommending that MacIain's oath be accepted, agreeing with Colonel Hill that the spirit of his oath and his effort to make it had been genuine. With relief MacIain and his men returned to Glencoe, satisfied their safety was assured. The package with the oath signatures, the letters, and other business was sent to the Privy Council in Edinburgh; Colonel Hill wrote to MacIain that his clan was now under the protection of the garrison at Fort William.

However, technically MacIain was in default, and all was not over for him. Time to introduce another character into our tale, Sir John Dalrymple, the Master of Stair and Secretary of State for Scotland.

Dalrymple was one of those amoral figures of whom the modern world is only too well aware. Cynical, self-assured and ambitious, and a man of no great conviction himself, he was impatient of it in others. He had a cold, rational mind, intolerant of all political and religious enthusiasm, serving James and then William with equal ease, and without any trouble of conscience. Above all, he served himself.

Dalrymple was determined to make an example of someone and in December 1691 had revealed the murderous direction to his thoughts:

> It may be shortly wee may have use of your garrison, for the winter time is the only season in which wee are sure the Highlanders cannot escape us, nor carry their wives, bairnes, and cattle to the mountaines. The Clan Donald is generally popish…' He further expressed the hope that the soldiers 'would not trouble the government with prisoners.

By early January, Dalrymple was aware that some rebels had submitted, and expressed his sorrow that Keppoch and Glencoe, whom he seems to have singled out as his particular targets, were now safe. However, on the evening of 11 January 1692, the Earl of Argyll gave news that caused him to exult:

> Just now, my Lord Argyle tells me that Glenco hath not taken the oathes, at which I rejoice. It's a great work of charity to be exact in rooting out that damnable sept, the worst in all the Highlands.

Other clans had not taken the oath either, but Dalrymple had his prey – the Macdonalds of Glencoe. Not because they were the most culpable, but because they were the most vulnerable. Not only were they were a small clan, but the narrow valley of their homes was a trap rather than a fortress.

The story of the Massacre of Glencoe is so well recounted elsewhere as to not warrant repetition here. But the orders were explicit:

You are hereby ordered to fall upon the rebels the Macdonalds of Glenco, and put all to the sword under 70. You are to have special care, that the old fox and his sons do upon no account escape your hands; you are to secure all the avenues, that no man escape.

MacIain was one of the first to die – in all, thirty-eight people were murdered, men mostly, but also some women and children. Most fled across the snowbound passes, including John and Alasdair, the 'fox's cubs'.

As a piece of political terrorism it enjoyed quick success. Before long, Clanranald, Sleat and other chiefs were hastening to submit. The only senior figure to express any real sense of outrage was Breadalbane, who described the crime as 'barbarous, illegal, imprudent'. He did not keep these views to himself, but wrote that the Massacre had undermined all his attempts to secure peace in the Highlands. Yet after the king was forced to agree that Commissions of Inquiry be set up, Breadalbane was to find himself singled out as one of the chief targets.

The 1693 and 1695 Commissions were never a serious attempt to discover the truth, but to exonerate the king. In the search for scapegoats, Dalrymple was the obvious choice, for he stood condemned by his plentiful and public correspondence. He lost office, but suffered no other penalty. Breadalbane, too, was singled out, although there was absolutely no evidence against him. He was, however, arrested and imprisoned for a time because of the uncertainty surrounding the Achallader negotiations in 1691. Parliament determined that the Massacre had been 'slaughter under trust' and asked William to send home the responsible officers for trial – no trials were ever held.

~

And what of the Fletchers, with whom our tale opened?

In 1715 the Fletchers were out on the Jacobite side, headed by Archibald, eldest son of the 8th chief. He not only survived but seemingly prospered, for he married in 1717 and soon after bought the property of Dunans, in Glendaruel. Archibald was born at his father's home, Barravurich, in 1675, and was known among his contemporaries locally as *Gillesp-na-Crannaich* [Archibald of Crannach, a reference to Crannach Wood, which lies quite close to Barravurich].

Before they left Achallader for Dunans the Fletchers carried away the great door of Achallader Castle, made of oak from the forests of Crannach, hard by the Waters of Tulla. Carrying it off was an indication that they would one day return to Achallader, but when it came on the market in the 1920's no offer was made. Ian Fletcher of Dunans merely commented that he was 'quite comfortable' at Dunans.

In 1745 the Fletchers followed the banner of Prince Charles, under the leadership of Archibald's younger brother, John of Inveroran.

~

So there you have it – no doubt there are myriad other tales these roofless old ruins of Achallader could tell us. The south end and east side are entirely dilapidated, but one of Black Duncan's angle-turrets, several loop-holes and the remains of a turnpike stair can still be seen.

And the great oak door of Achallader Castle? I'm happy to say it's still in the possession of Angus Fletcher of Dunans.

Map references

- OS Explorer 377. OS Landranger 50:

  Achallader Castle NN 322 442

Historical notes

- Note: my mother was a Fletcher, so I have a vested interest in this tale!
- Sir Duncan Campbell of Glenorchy, ordinarily called *Donacha Dhu nan Curich* (Black Duncan of the Cowl) or Black Duncan of the Castles. He was Laird of Glenorchy for forty-eight years prior to his death in 1631 at an advanced age, a man of considerable force of character, and, for his time, large means. The household books of this great Celtic chief exhibit his style of life, with his rents principally paid in kind; the corn, cattle, and poultry supplied by the tenants went directly to the support of the laird, his family and household. The family enjoyed food such as chickens, brawn, venison, mutton, smoked ham, wildfowl, rabbits, salmon, herring, and butter, with spices such as saffron, mace, ginger, sugar, and pepper. They drank claret, white wine, ale, and aqua vitae. They slept on feather beds, with bolsters, blankets, linen, and bed hangings. All of this was luxurious living by the standards of the day.

He was a very advanced landlord and estate improver who bred excellent horses, established fallow deer, maintained a small flock of sheep and planted numerous trees, including oak, fir, and birch. The regulations for tenants were decidedly enlightened but there is a feudal note about them which was alien to the old Highland way of life, foreshadowing the changes in relationship between chieftain and clansmen which were to take place in the eighteenth century. [http://www.wikitree.com/wiki/Campbell-6404]

• Archaeology Note from Canmore:

Achallader Castle, a small tower house, was built by Sir Duncan Campbell shortly before 1600. The castle was attacked and burnt by members of the Jacobite army in 1689, and is now fragmentary. While the north and east walls stand almost to their original heights, only a small portion of the west survives and the south wall has disappeared completely.

The tower is oblong on plan, measuring 8.7m from east to west by 6.7m transversely over walls which vary in thickness from 0.91m to 1.07m. The accommodation comprised three storeys and a garret, the side-walls rising to a height of 9.3m. The masonry is of random rubble laid in lime mortar, with dressings of schist. [RCAHMS 1975, visited 1970]

• In *The Peat Fire Flame* Alasdair Alpin Macgregor writes:

'As proof of this story of how the Fletchers came to lose Achallader, the old shepherds there used to point to the green hillock close to the farmhouse, wherein the 'stranger' slain by Fletcher was interred, and known in Gaelic as 'The Grave of the Stranger'.

• In 1658 John Fletcher is described as 'in Auchalladour'; his son Archibald was born at Barravurich, in 1675; so presumably the Fletcher chiefs moved from Achallader sometime between those dates. I imagine that the then Mrs Fletcher preferred a cosy farmhouse to a draughty castle!

- Crannach Wood is now an SSSI:

  Lying approximately 15 km north of Tyndrum [Crannach Wood] is comprised of ancient Scots pine woodland. The native pinewood is a small relic of an extensive forest which formerly covered large tracts of land, including substantial sections of Rannoch Moor. The woodlands support a rich diversity of invertebrates and the rare Northern emerald dragonfly is also present at this site.

- Sir John Dalrymple: Although forced to resign over ther Massacre, by 1700 his reputation had been rehabilitated and he was appointed a member of the Privy Council of Scotland; in 1703 he was made the first Earl of Stair by Queen Anne. Dalrymple went on to exert his considerable influence in favour of the Act of Union with England which, despite widespread opposition across Scotland, was passed in 1707.

- John Campbell, 1st Earl of Breadalbane: Although made a scapegoat for the Massacre – along with Dalrymple – he was one of the few men to recognize the political damage the episode caused in the Highlands.

- Breadalbane did not vote for the Union in 1707, but was chosen a representative peer in the parliament of Great Britain of 1713–1715.

- When summoned to appear at Edinburgh in the 1715 Jacobite rising he excused himself on grounds of age and infirmity but then next day visited Jacobite camps. His real business, according to the Master of Sinclair, was 'to trick others, not to be trickt, and to obtain a share of the French subsidies'. He took money to provide 1200 men to the uprising but only sent 300, and they were withdrawn after the Battle of Sheriffmuir. His death on 19 March 1717 removed the need for an inquiry into his conduct.

- Dunans: During the 18th century Archibald Fletcher – by then 9th chief – and his son Angus added more farms to Dunans until it was a substantial estate. About 1850 a mansion was built and the great door of Achallader

Castle, made of oak from the forests of Crannach, was the door of the private chapel. Dunans House was sold in 1997, although, luckily, the Fletchers took away the great oak door of Achallader. Dunans was then briefly a hotel but was gutted by fire in 2001; two years later it was bought by Charles and Sadie Dixon-Spain, who are making major renovations.

Sources

- *The Peat Fire Flame* – Alasdair Alpin Macgregor.
- *Royal Commission on the Ancient & Historical Monuments of Scotland* – Volume 2, Argyll.
- *Septs of the Highland Clans.*
- *Sons of the Wolf* – Ronald Williams.
- Loch Awe Community website http://www.loch-awe.com/history/the-fletchers/
- *The Ancient Fletchers* – Margaret Mason. In it she states that the late Angus Fletcher of Tyndrum used to tell the story of Sir Duncan and Angus Fletcher, which he said had been passed down to him by natives of Glenorchy. http://www.spaceless.com/fletcher/flet2.htm
- *Glencoe – Myth & Reality* – Raymond Campbell Paterson.
- *The Black Book of Taymouth.*
- *Origines Parochiales.*

A tale of two Smiths

Of arms & armour – of love and war

This is no tale of Fred Smith and his son Wullie, but of the ancient trade of armourers and smiths, whom today we tend to call blacksmiths.

Cast your mind back several hundred years to the days when everything was made by hand, and the nation was in an almost constant state of war. Vikings, English, Irish, Scots – there was always a good battle to be had somewhere, and if no outsider could be found the clans resorted to fighting themselves. Fighting meant swords, dirks, axes, chain mail, arrowheads and armour as well as all the fittings for horses to protect them too. Armour

meant a skilled man, and skilled men were not only paid well but were never short of work. In the rare interludes of peace there was demand for ploughs and peat knifes for the farm, locks and latches for the house and byre. When times were prosperous the smith could beat from silver rare ornaments of beauty, brooches and buckles to adorn the Chief – or even his wife if the Chief was feeling generous. And if a wee bit of that precious metal stuck with the smith, who could blame him for prospering!

The Smith Macnab

Just south of Dalmally, on a steep and grassy hill are the remains of several houses and barns that once formed the clachan of *Barr a' Chaistealain* [The Ridge of the Castle]. Not, as one would imagine, Kilchurn Castle, but the much older Iron Age dun whose stones were robbed to build the later post-medieval farm settlement, which probably dates from the mid-fifteenth century.

A defensive farmstead, the dun was probably constructed about the first or second century AD, but may be as late as the seventh or eighth century. Still to be seen are the low remains of the walls, some six feet thick, enclosing a circular area fifteen yards across; this would originally have been roofed over to form a house, with a low tunnel entrance.

The dun and later clachan are now surrounded by forestry, but when Alasdair Alpin MacGregor visited in 1935 there were still three thatched houses and a barn. They had sweeping views of Ben Cruachan to the west, whilst to the north the River Orchy meandered through the strath to Loch Awe. Here lived the MacNabs, hereditary armourers and smiths from around 1100 until 1800 to Campbell of Glenorchy. Pennant, in 1780, wrote:

> On an eminence on the south side of this vale dwells M'Nab, a smith whose family has lived in that humble station since the year 1440, being always of the same possession.

In fact the MacNabs traced their descent, and their trade, back nearly 700 years to a certain fair lady in the train of the Saxon Princess Margaret, who had fled north from the Norman invasion of 1066 to the protection of King Malcolm of Scotland. Now Sir John MacGregor, Laird of Glenorchy, just happened to be looking for a wife, and this lady-in-waiting fitted the bill. In due course they had two sons, the elder diplomatically called Malcolm after the King and the younger called Gregory; don't ask me after whom – some rich uncle I suppose.

Gregory was destined for the Church, often the fate of the younger sons of nobles, and packed off to the sunshine of Italy for his education. His poor brother had to make

11-1 Barr a' Chaistealain looking towards Ben Cruachan

do with learning to hunt and fight and carouse, normal training to be a Chief – it was a tough life all round then. When Gregory returned he was eventually made Lay Abbot of Glendochart and Strathfillan, and his offspring were known as *Mac an Aba* – Children of the Abbot, or Abbotson in English.

Now Gregory wished to do the best for his son, and not only did he teach him to read and write, uncommon in those days, but he had him appriced to a useful, lucrative trade – as an armourer and smith. In due course MacNab, as he was now called, settled on his grandfather MacGregor's lands, at *Barr a' Chaistealain*, and there his descendants stayed for 700 odd years.

In 1309 one Angus MacNab, along with his MacGregor clansmen, made the mistake of joining MacDougall of Lorn against Robert the Bruce, and were defeated at the Pass of Brander. Once Bannockburn was won – with the help of Mel Gibson – all the MacGregor and MacNab lands were forfeit to the Campbells, who in due course cleared the glen of all carrying that name. However, so famous were the skills of the MacNabs of *Barr a' Chaist-ealain* that Campbell of Glenorchy left them in peace and made them his hereditary smiths and armourers.

About 100 years later, in 1440, Sir Colin Campbell was away at the Crusades, and his wife, Lady Margaret, as wives often do when husbands are away for a few years, decided to improve Kilchurn Castle. Admittedly it was a bit basic, but not content with new kitchen units she built a five-storey tower house with that essential extra of the time – a dungeon. The MacNabs, as smiths, were called in to do all the iron-work. Pennant commented that they were,

> employed by the Lady of Sir Duncan Campbell, who built the castle of Kilchurn when her husband was absent. Some of their [MacNab] tombs are in the churchyard of Glen Urqhie; [Orchy, i.e. Dalmally Churchyard] the oldest has a hammer and other implements of his trade cut on it.

There was at *Barr a' Chaistealain* a massive elm tree which overshadowed the smiddy, and a local superstition had it that when the last smith MacNab died, the tree would fall. And so it came to pass, for in the closing years of the eighteenth century old MacNab lay dying, the last smith, for none of his sons had followed the trade. During the night a howling gale came from the north, and in the morning the old man was dead and the great elm fallen across the smiddy door. MacNabs lived at *Barr a' Chaistealain* and in the area for some time, but after 700 years none thereafter took up their ancient trade.

The 1861 Admiralty chart of Loch Awe shows seven dwellings at *Barr a' Chaistealain*, but the smithy is marked beside the old road from Dalmally to Cladich. There it would attract much passing trade from travellers on horseback, as well as from the great herds of cattle being driven to Crieff Mart each autumn.

In the 1930's, when Alasdair Macalpin Macgregor visited the site, the MacNab's house and smithy were ruinous, but with one gable still standing. Now they are simply a heap of stones.

The Smith McCaillirinn

Which brings me to my tale of the second smith, one Duncan McCaillirinn, who originally hailed from Kintyre, but as a young man was apprenticed to the smith at Kilmartin, near the southern end of Loch Awe. This was about 1290, at the time when Edward I of England was claiming Scotland, and Wallace was defying him – as we all know from 'Braveheart', however inaccurate it is historically!

Times were troublous, and so great was the demand for armour and weapons of all kinds that young Duncan had much practice. Indeed, so adept at his trade did he become that he soon surpassed his master, who, not unnaturally, became intensely jealous of his pupil. And what is more, young Duncan was a good-looking lad and his master's wife was comely. So it came as little surprise when one morning the smith suddenly attacked young Duncan in a fit of rage.

"You not only stole my art, but my wife's heart also," he screamed, lunging at the lad with his dirk – in defending himself, the boy killed his master.

Although it was an accident, Duncan knew fine well the consequences and fled for his life up the eastern shore of Loch Awe, shortly to be pursued by the smith's brothers, strapping men all.

Now, Loch Awe is twenty-four miles long, and Kilmartin a few miles from its end, so it is no wonder that by Braevallich Duncan began to flag, and his pursuers gained on him. Seeing this, a man digging in his garden cried out to the lad:

"Son, thou hast lost the race". This spurred on young Duncan, and he rounded the head of the loch, sped through the Pass of Brander and came to the ford crossing the River Awe at Fannans. There he found the river in full spate, but with his pursuers close behind him Duncan had no choice but to throw himself into the foaming torrent. Swiftly the current bore him downstream to where bushes over-hung the water and brought him up short, concealing the lad from his pursuers.

"Have you seen a boy?" they asked of a man sitting on the bank, quietly smoking his pipe in the calm of the evening.

"Aye. Aye. He went towards Loch Etiveside". So saying, he directed them off on a fruitless search, which they eventually abandoned. The man had admired Duncan's pluck and courage, and when the men were safely gone he launched his *curragh,* rescued the lad and took him into his own home.

Duncan McCaillirinn sought the protection of Sir Alexander MacDougall, Lord of Lorn, and eventually set up a smiddy 'at the bridge of Iochdrachan, the Muckairn side of the Nant' [near Taynuilt]. His fame as a smith spread far and wide, although he had competition locally from a family called MacPheidirean (Paterson). Their forge was at *Creagan Corrach*, in Benderloch, and 'they were famous armourers, their swords being celebrated for their high finish and excellence'. An old Gaelic verse extols their skills:

Bogha a dh'iubhar Easragain,
Ite firein Locha Treige,
Saighead a bheithe an Doire-dhuinn,
Smeoirn o'n cheard MacPheidirean.

Bow of the yew of Easragan,

Muckairn

Loch Etive

Glen Orchy

Kilchurn
Castle

Fannans

Dalmally

Barr a'Chaistealain

"Aye. Aye. He went towards
Loch Etiveside"

Portsonachan

Loch Awe

Braevallich

Kilmartin

11-2 Map featuring Kilchurn Castle

Feather of the eagle of Loch Treig,
Arrow of the birch of Doire-donn,
Arrow-head from the craftsman MacPheidirean.

As explained in tale ten, Easragan is by Ardchattan Priory, on the north shore of Loch Etive; here Robert Bruce repaired after the Battle of the Pass of Brander in 1308. Loch Treig is deep in the wildness of Rannoch Moor, and any eagle living here would need strong feathers. *Doire-donn* (brown grove) is in Glen Orchy, renowned for its birch woods.

Tradition has it that in 1306 McCaillirinn and his seven sons, with the ferocity of their charge and the energy of their fighting carried the day against Robert the Bruce at the battle of Dalrigh (near Tyndrum). They were fighting for John MacDougall of Lorn, and in the combat the Bruce narrowly escaped capture by shedding his plaid and losing to the MacDougalls his brooch, which became famous as the Brooch of Lorn.

With the forfeiture of the MacDougall lands in 1308/9 and their acquisition by the Campbells, the McCaillirinns shrewdly changed their name to Campbell, and at some stage moved to Muckairn, between Connel and Taynuilt.

Four hundred years later, when Queen Anne died in 1720, Malcolm Campbell, smith at Muckairn, was so noted for his work that he was kidnapped by John MacDougall, nineteenth chief of the Clan MacDougall. The cause was the planned Jacobite rising, and MacDougall required the smith to prepare every weapon that could be mustered. Before he was set at liberty, Malcolm Campbell had to give his oath not to reveal where he had been, or what had been his task.

~

So ends my tale of two smiths, each family spanning several centuries – what stories they could have told.

Map references

- OS Landranger Sheet 50. OS Explorer 377. NN 159 266.

- *Barr a' Chaistealain* makes an excellent expotition (as Pooh would say) and there are good interpretative boards on site.

Sources

- *Myths Legend and Traditions of Western Argyll* – KW Grant.
- *Carmina Gadelica* – Alexander Campbell, Volume II.
- *Collins Encyclopaedia of Scotland* edited by John Keay and Julia Keay.
- *The Royal Commission on Ancient & Historical Monuments – Argyll* – Lorn, Volume 2 – HMSO.
- *Highways & Byways in the West Highlands* – Seton Gordon.
- *A History of Clan Campbell*, Volume 1 – Alastair Campbell of Airds.
- *Somewhere in Scotland* – Alasdair Alpin Macgregor.
- *Records of Argyll* – Lord Archibald Campbell.

The Weaver's castle

And of piracy, shipwreck & due justice

The Outer Hebrides lie off the Scottish mainland, a protective chain of islands stretching from the latitudes of Cape Wrath south to that of Fort William. In shape they resemble a kite, with Lewis and Harris the main body, whilst a string of smaller islands and islets form the tail.

Scattered in between are a myriad of skerries and rocks, some grazed by sheep, some barely above the sea which restlessly surges between the channels with each tide. Amongst these islands are snug anchorages for seafarers, as the Vikings discovered when they arrived here many years ago.

They originally came to plunder, but later to settle, and throughout the Hebrides their descendants inherited the Viking love of raiding and piracy. Nowhere was this truer than on Barra, and indeed the last Viking stronghold was reputed to be the small island of Fuday, just to the north of Barra itself.

Highland chieftains inherited from the Norsemen a love of sea-roving and piracy, and in the troubled times following the forfeiture of the Lordship of the Isles they embraced both with fervour. MacNeil of Barra and Clanranald from South Uist excelled among many a chief at supplementing their incomes from piracy; few vessels were safe from their depredations, for they roamed as far afield as Ireland. So efficient were they that in September 1613 the Clerk to the Privy Council in distant Edinburgh wrote:

The haill Iles ar in a reasonable goode estate and quietnes, except the Lewis and the Ile of Barra.

One MacNeil of Barra was so piratical that he was known as *Ruairi nan Tartair* – noisy and turbulent Roderic. He flourished at the end of the 16th and early 17th centuries and so successful was his sea-roving that he filled Kisimul Castle with the spoils of his depredations. He became so bold that he even seized ships belonging to Queen Elizabeth of England – fair game, I would have said, for a Scottish pirate! The Queen, however, thought otherwise, and complained to her fellow sovereign, James VI, who entrusted MacKenzie of Kintail to capture MacNeil. This he did by enticing *Ruairi* on board his galley for a feast; instead he was clapped in irons and brought to Edinburgh to face the King and explain his actions. There, MacNeil told the King that he was merely avenging the wrongs done to James' mother, Mary, Queen of Scots – as *everyone* will recall, Elizabeth had caused Mary's head to part company from her body. Recognising a rogue when he saw one, but appreciating the Hebrides needed strong Chiefs, James pardoned *Ruairi*, but henceforth his estates were to be held under MacKenzie of Kintail.

The lesson was obviously not learnt by his neighbour Clanranald in South Uist, for in 1636 the English ship *Susanna* was driven far to the north by gales. Her Master was Richard Seyman of Chichester and the ship was bound from France with a cargo of wines, fruit and coin for one Peter Fox of Limerick. Dismasted and her boats swept away, she sought refuge in the Sound of Barra, where she anchored in the land's shelter. There she signalled for help to the islanders, who duly arrived, but armed to the teeth; however, after much bargaining, they agreed to tow the ship to a safe anchorage, in exchange for 'a butt of sack [126 gallons of wine] and a barrel of raisins.'

However, MacNeil of Barra being at that time absent from Kisimul Castle, Clanranald had ideas of his own. The islanders having hoisted the *Susanna's* anchor and towed her safely into Castlebay Harbour, Clanranald appeared with about three hundred men and a load of empty barrels. Each day thereafter he drew off the ship's cargo of wine, together with everything else she carried, even robbing the crew of their very clothes. Finally, under threat of handing the whole crew over to the 'savages that dwell in the [Spanish] mayne' (i.e. condemning them into slavery) Clanranald forced the captain to sell him the *Susanna* for £8 sterling, when the barque was worth at least £150.

~

No one knows quite when the following tale occurred, but possibly it was in the late 16th century, in the reign of James VI, for as we saw above, Barra then was a wild, wild place. My tale concerns a weaver, unknown by name, but from his actions no doubt a descendant of *Ruairi nan Tartair* – but from which side of the blanket is unknown. Although a weaver by trade, he was banished from Barra for his many misdeeds and sent to live on the uninhabited Stack Islands. With him he took a small boat, some hens in a fishing creel, a few sheep, an old *cas chrom* (foot plough) and other implements to till the soil.

Now, the three Stack Islands lie just north of Barra, and I passed them often on my way to shelter in Eriskay harbour *Acairseid Mhor*. The Stacks are a lovely spot on a summer's day, but in winter, when the Atlantic gales hurtle across the Sound of Barra to meet the turbulent waters of the Minch, they can be a very bleak place. There is good grazing there, and from the top of the main island – *Eilean Leathan* [pronounced lee-hun and meaning Broad Island] – there is a stunning panorama north and south to the Minch, and over Barra Sound to the Atlantic beyond. Clearly the Weaver could not live on the view alone, but with what he produced from the land, a bit of fishing from his boat, and what he stole from the nearby islands, he did not fare too badly.

Among the first things he did was to sail across to Eriskay one dark but still night and carry off a small white mare, or *lair bhan* as she was called. With her he also stole a couple of panniers, for he needed to build a stronghold on his island. *Eilean Leathan* is shaped like a figure of eight, and in the centre is a small landing place, where the Weaver used to haul his boat safe above the tideline. From the landing the southern half of the island rises 150 feet to the summit, with

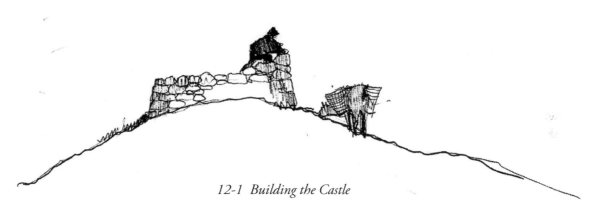

12-1 Building the Castle

only an easily defended steep and narrow path up the cliff.

Daily the Weaver and the white mare laboured up this path, carrying small rocks from the shore to build a fortress which would command the surrounding waters.

Bit by bit the walls rose, each stone strongly bound to the next with mortar made from the shell sand of neighbouring beaches, for the Weaver was determined to build himself a fortress against allcomers. But just before it was finished, the white mare collapsed at the top of the path, worn out by the rocks she had carried. The panniers on her sides spilled their loads, and to this day you can see the two small cairns on either side of the path where she fell.

The Weaver struggled on alone, and at last the castle was finished; true, it was small, about 12 feet by 10 feet, but the walls were a goodly 4 feet thick and the whole fort was well able to withstand attack. Now he needed a wife to share his lonely kingdom – and of course the chores – so after a good deal of thought he set off for Loch Eynort in South Uist in search of a bride. He sailed well before sunrise, for it being July, all the womenfolk were at the summer sheilings. The cattle had been driven to the rich hill pastures, and there all the women and young boys went for the summer, making cheese and butter for the long months of winter and to pay the laird his rent in kind.

The women were at the morning milking, each cow's hind legs hobbled by a heather rope to stop her kicking as the sweet, rich milk spurted into the wooden pail. Casting his eye over the assembled company – not easy when the girls heads were pressed into the cow's flanks – the Weaver selected a suitable lass, slung her over his shoulder, and high-tailed it for the boat and the safety of his castle. Whether she objected too much I know not, but let's give the Weaver the benefit of the doubt, and say that she came to accept her fate, for she certainly became adept at sharing his new trade – wrecking.

In those days ships used cables and hawsers for anchoring instead of chain, and vessels often sheltered in the lee of Hellisay and Gighay islands, only a few miles to the south. The Weaver and his wife used to row out in the dead of night, oars muffled, and creep up on the unsuspecting ships. With a sharp knife they would silently cut the cable, and when the vessel was wrecked on the shore they would plunder the contents – and the crew.

12-2 Cutting the cable

12-3 Due justice

Over the years three sons were born to the Weaver and his wife, and from an early age the older boys became as adept as their parents in the art of wrecking and raiding. Eventually things became so bad that the King sent a ship with orders to apprehend or destroy the Weaver and his brood. Now, on the day that the King's ship arrived the Weaver and his two older sons were fishing in the Sound, whilst his wife was ashore in the castle with the youngest boy. Seeing a boat leave the ship, and thinking it bound for the island, she ran to the top of the cliff path, where a goodly pile of stones was kept ready to repel any boarders.

The cutter, however, was after the Weaver and his sons, one of who said, "It is the King's boat".

The Weaver gazed at the boat, then chided the boy for a false alarm and that it was merely a fishing boat. But as the boat drew nearer the boy said again "It is surely one of the King's long boats".

"What though it is?" replied the Weaver. "There are only six oarsmen and, with your assistance, we shall be able to hold our own against them".

"I see," said the boy, "the breath of many rising over the gunwhales of the boat". Scarcely had he spoken than twenty men leapt up from the floorboards and each thrust out an oar.

The Weaver saw that it was useless to resist, so he and his sons bent their backs and headed for the castle as fast as they could dip the oars into the water. However, the long boat gained on them with each stroke, and eventually blockaded their way to the castle. They seized the Weaver's boat, so he and his sons leapt into the sea and swam strongly for the Eriskay shore. The boys were soon taken and killed, although the Weaver made it ashore, but with the long boat right behind him. Drawing his sword the commander landed without delay and slew the Weaver, ordering that the blood should dry on his sword as proof that the Weaver and his sons were dead. To this day the landing-place just south of *Gleann Fada* is known as *Sloc na Creiche* (The Cove of Disaster).

Meanwhile, back at the castle, the Weaver's wife did not know that utter disaster had befallen her family. She had seen the long boat return to the ship, and watched as it sailed away to the south. But then came news from Eriskay that her husband and two sons were all dead, and as news does in the islands it soon reached Loch Eynort and her father. Thus it was that her father arranged for the funeral of the Weaver and his sons, and after that he came to fetch his daughter and young grandson to leave the castle on *Eilean Leathan* to go to live with him in South Uist.

Shortly after the widow and her only remaining son had left the island the King's ship returned and blew apart the castle with gunpowder. And ever since that day no one has lived on *Eilean Leathan* or in the castle, which, however, is still called *Caisteal a' Breabhadair* – The Weaver's Castle.

And in 'The Weaver's Son' I will recount the tale of what happened to John, the one surviving son.

Map references

- OS Landranger sheet 31. OS Explorer sheets 452 & 453:

  Weavers Castle NF 786 072.

  Sloc na Creiche NF 783 088.

Historical notes

- This tale is based mainly on two original sources:

  Firstly, the manuscript papers of Father Allan MacDonald, now in the Carmichael-Watson collection at the University of Edinburgh under MS 58B. Father Allan MacDonald was the Parish priest of South Uist and Eriskay from 1884 for ten years until ill-health dictated his appointment to Eriskay alone until his death in 1905. Although not a native Gaelic speaker he was deeply interested in the language, its poetry and it folklore, recording much in a series of notebooks.

  His friend, Alexander Carmichael, was a Gaelic-speaking collector of folklore who was based in Barra and South Uist as an exciseman from 1864-1882. Dr Donald William Stewart is the Gaelic researcher on the Carmichael Watson collection and confirmed that the MS at the University was compiled by Father Allan MacDonald in about 1893.

The second version is the book published by Dr John Lorne Campbell, *Tales from Barra Told by the Coddy*. The Coddy was born in 1876, so was six when Carmichael left Barra, although doubtless he had heard around the fireside many of the tales that Father Allan and Carmichael recorded.

- Neither source explains why MacNeil of Barra would sanction the building of a small castle on one of his islands. Mary Miers, in *The Western Seaboard – An Illustrated Architectural Guide* provides the most likely account, in that it was '… once a stronghold of the MacNeils. Later it was the home of the notorious pirate wrecker *Breabadair Stache*…'

- Weaver's Castle is almost identical in size and construction to *Caisteal Bheagam*, near Howmore, South Uist – Ronald Alansoun of 'Yland Bigram' appears on record in 1505. So it is possible that Weaver's Castle was originally built by the MacNeills of Barra in the early 16th century. They already possessed Castle Calvay to guard the entrance to Loch Boisdale and their South Uist lands, with Kisimul castle guarding Castlebay. What more logical, in that age of vital seapower, than to build Weaver's Castle to guard the sheltered anchorage of *Ottir Mhor* between Barra and South Uist?

- Father Allan writes that the builder of the castle was a stranger from the mainland, fleeing justice; that his wife was a weaver from Kildonan on South Uist; and that she married him willingly.

- The Coddy's version recounts four sons to the Weaver and his wife, Father Allan has three. The Coddy has the Widow leaving the castle with her one remaining son, which I think the most likely outcome. Father Allan wrote that she stayed on: 'The King's boat sailed round the castle but spared the life of the widow and the child at her knee' – little did they know that her 'store was filled with the plunder of the ships wrecked'!

- An obscure volume entitled *A Royalist family Irish and French (1689=1789) and Prince Charles Edward* contains the captain's journal of the French frigate which conveyed Bonnie Prince Charlie to Scotland in the fateful summer of 1745. The frigate – more a sloop armed for war really, as she only had 18 guns and a crew of 67 – was named '*Dutillet* of Nantes' in Captain Dupre's journal and *Doutelle* in contemporary English accounts. But as she was named after one Monsieur du Teillay, Commissaire de la Marine at Nantes, *Le du Teillay* is the accepted version. In his journal Dupre notes for Monday 2nd August 1745 [23rd July in the Julian calendar]:

> We have agreed to change our route and to seek a port which lies between the island of Barra and the island of Uist which is fairly big and from which it is only possible to leave by the West. (This port can be recognised by a square tower, which served formerly for fire [a beacon of the time] demolished at the top. It forms the north side of the entrance.) Having a pilot we went there to anchor.

The 'port' is *An-t-Acarsaid Mhor* which lies between Barra and South Uist, and the 'square tower' can only be the Weaver's Castle. This is the only reference that I have found to the castle being used as a beacon, but on the 1654 Blaeu map of South Uist there is a symbol on the Stack Islands which is clearly a tower with a light beacon. Whether the castle was used as a beacon before or after the Weaver's demise we shall never know!

Sources

- *Tales from Barra Told by the Coddy* – printed privately by JL Campbell. John Campbell says the ruins show signs of having been demolished by gunpowder.
- Personal letter, July 2001, from Father Calum Mac-Lennan, parish priest on Eriskay, who identified for me Sloc na Creiche. He wrote: "Your story echoes well the one I've grown up with – I've marked the spot where the Weaver met his end".
- Carmichael-Watson MS 58B, ff 55r-59v, University of Edinburgh.
- *West Coast of Scotland Pilot* – Admiralty Hydrographic Department.
- RCAHMS *The Outer Hebrides, Skye and the Small Isles*, 1928.
- *West Over Sea* – D D C Pochin Mould.
- *Summer Days among the Western Isles* – Alasdair Alpin Macgregor.
- *Scottish Lighthouses* – Sharma Krauskopf.
- *A Royalist family Irish and French (1689-1789) and Prince Charles Edward* – translated from the French by AG Murray MacGregor.
- *The Western Seaboard – An Illustrated Architectural Guide* – Mary Miers.

The Weaver's son

Of his life at sea – and of retribution

I have told in tale twelve of how the Weaver and his two oldest sons met their death at the hands of the commander of the King's long boat; and of how the Weaver's wife left the castle on *Eilean Leathan*; and of how her own father took his daughter and his young grandson to live with him at Loch Eynort, in South Uist.

Now the old man loved his grandson dearly, and by the time the boy was twelve he was a great help on the croft, caring for the cows and sheep and horses. The hens, of course, were his mother's responsibility, for hens were women's work, and thus not fitting for a man to do! Yet although young John was happy enough, it disturbed him to see his mother weeping each day, and although he continually asked, she would not tell him the cause of her distress.

Finally, when he had turned fourteen years of age, his mother told him the dreadful fate that had befallen his father and brothers. Young John took a long, deep breath, then said, "I am going to sea, and I shall never stop until I meet the man who killed my father and my brothers".

At this his mother was much afraid, for she knew in her heart that John intended to kill the commander of the long boat, and she did not wish to lose her last remaining son. But John was determined, and as the months went by he daily made up his mind to go.

We tend to forget in these days of the motor-car and steamers how easy transport is, but in those days the only regular ferry was from Lochmaddy, in North Uist, to Dunvegan, on the north end of Skye. So bidding his mother and grandfather a most fond farewell, young John set out on the first stage of his long journey to Greenock, for he had heard that was where all the ships were to be found.

First he had to walk the length of South Uist, crossing the ford to Benbecula, and then the ford to North Uist. Arriving at Lochmaddy he found the boat did not sail for another two days, but by making himself useful to the ferryman he not only received his board and lodging, but also a free passage across the Minch to Dunvegan. There he helped on a croft for a few days, and so grateful was the crofter that he set John on his way across Skye with a few coins from his own meagre hoard.

Arriving at Kyle the boy crossed to the mainland, and there he stayed for a week, working for an old ship's carpenter, who told him many tales of the sea.

"Aye," said he, "mony's the time I've sailed frae Greenock. Ye'll have nae trouble findin' a ship there".

And so the journey went, John MacNeil working where he could, and then travelling on. Finally, over a year later, he arrived at Greenock and stood on the quayside staring at all the ships with their lofty masts. The captain of one of the ships, noting that John had been there the previous day, called down to him in English:

"Do you want to go to sea, boy?" To which John, having very little English, did not answer. So the captain repeated the question, but this time in Gaelic, for he himself came from Arran.

"Yes, I want to go to sea," replied John.

"Come on board then," said the captain. And John did.

Then the captain asked John where he came from, and the boy said that his father was from Barra, but that he himself was born on the Stack Islands. The captain then asked his name, and the boy replied: "My name is John MacNeil". Then the two MacNeils shook hands – for the captain too was a MacNeil – and ever since that time they were the best of friends.

Now, the ship was due to sail with a mixed cargo

13-1 Captain MacNeil greets John at Greenock

of goods to South America and round Cape Horn to Vancouver Island, where she was to load timber, especially the tall masts for which that part of the world was famous. Young John was at first rather lost on this strange ship, but the captain having taken a liking to him he was fairly and kindly treated by the others in the crew. Indeed, seeing how quickly John learnt the skills of seamanship, the captain resolved to teach the boy his alphabet; and by the end of the two-year voyage John could both read and write.

So fond had he become of the boy, and having no family of his own, Captain MacNeil sent John to school. And when he himself left on his next voyage the lad was left behind to continue his education and take his Second Mate's exams, at which he succeeded. And so the years passed, John next taking his First Officer's ticket, and then his Masters, all the while sailing with his good friend, Captain MacNeil. And all the time John listened for news of the commander who had slain his father and brothers, but not a word did he hear, so that he began to despair of ever finding the man.

At last Captain MacNeil said to John: "I shall soon be retiring, and I have spoken to the owners of the ship, and you shall have command of her". And when that day finally came, you can imagine with what tears did the two part, for the captain had been like a father to John. But part they must, for the old captain had to go ashore for the last time, and the new captain had to take his ship to sea for yet another long voyage.

John's quest appeared to be fruitless, until one day, when his ship was in London, he was supping at an inn when he heard some old seamen discussing their past exploits – as old seamen are wont to do. Suddenly one old veteran stood up and described how, many years ago, he had slain a notorious ship-wrecker on one of the islands off the West Coast of Scotland. "And what's more," he boasted, "I still have my sword with the dried blood on it as proof of those I killed".

This statement was greeted with much acclaim, for, truth to say, no one can admire those who deliberately wreck ships and endanger the lives of seamen. But John MacNeil, fired with the thought of an end to his long quest, went up to the veteran and roundly congratulated him. So pleased was the old man that he invited John round for a meal the next day, and he duly presented himself at the house. A fine spread was laid out for him, and several bottles of good wine, but John declared that he would not eat until he had seen the famous sword.

So the old commander took him into the parlour, and from a cupboard drew forth the sword from its scabbard; there on the blade was the dried blood of the Weaver and his sons. Now, John had thought to kill the old commander with his own sword, but seeing the blood of his father and brothers on the blade he decided not to. Instead, he struck the old commander such a blow on the head that he never recovered. John immediately returned to Scotland, leaving his ship and her cargo where they lay.

Coming eventually to Loch Eynort, he spied his mother sitting at the cottage door, busy spinning wool at her wheel.

"Oh sir!" cried she, seeing his captain's uniform, "Have you seen ought of my son, John MacNeil?"

You can imagine with what joy mother and son were reunited after so many years apart, and how much they had to tell each other. And so John stayed in South Uist

13-2 Retribution

for two years or so, until the murder of the old commander was forgotten. Then he sailed as a captain again, but this time from Liverpool, where his descendants are to be found to this very day.

Map references

- OS Landranger sheet 31. OS Explorer sheets 452 & 453:

  Weaver's Castle NF 786072

Historical notes

- As with *The Weaver's Castle*, there are two original sources: the Carmichael Watson archive at the University of Edinburgh, and the version as told by The Coddy in *Tales of Barra*.
- Alexander Carmichael was a Gaelic-speaking collector of folklore who was based in Barra and South Uist as an exciseman from 1864-1882. The Coddy was born in 1876, so was six when Carmichael left Barra, although doubtless he had heard around the fireside many of the tales that Carmichael recorded. Father Alan McDonald recorded, about 1893, a similar version to that of Carmichael.
- Carmichael's version of this story has John killing the commander of the long boat at Dunvegan after a short search. As it involves witches and the second sight, I prefer the Coddy's version above!

Sources

- *Tales from Barra* Told by the Coddy – printed privately by J L Campbell, 1960, pp. 83-91.
- Carmichael-Watson MS 58B, ff 59v and 134r-139v, University of Edinburgh.

HMS Dartmouth

An English ship in Scottish waters, Jacobite support for one king against another
& the wreck of the Dartmouth with heavy loss of life

MS Dartmouth was wrecked in the Sound of Mull during a great storm on the night of 9 October 1690, with the loss of all on board 'bar five men and a boy'. Although the Dartmouth's log, not surprisingly, is missing, there are several letters extant from her Captain, Edward Pottinger. His complaints over poor provisioning and tardy payment echo similar comments from Naval Officers in the centuries to follow! I handled several of his letters, giving me a tangible link over three centuries with the affair – quotations from his letters are in *italics*.

But what was an English man-of-war doing in these waters, Scotland being then an independent nation and justifiably touchy about the presence of English ships in her territorial waters? This was exacerbated by the accession of William and Mary, for the new sovereigns did not quite appreciate that they ruled two independent nations, and tended to be rather high handed in their dealings over matters Scottish.

For the answer we'll need to step back two years from the wreck and loss of so much life.

~

James II ascended the English throne on the death of his brother, Charles II, in February 1685, and his reign began auspiciously enough. But his adoption of the Roman Catholic faith and the Declaration of Indulgence produced internal religious dissension; in late 1688 William of Orange was invited by the English Parliament to assume the throne.

James, as Duke of York, had for many years worked closely with Samuel Pepys, Secretary to the Admiralty, in building and improving the ships of the Navy; it was now that this fleet must be ready and able to prevent William's landing. Pepys made herculean efforts to man and victual the fleet at a time of year thought not wise to prosecute a war at sea; but having forged the weapon, Pepys was to see it fail to perform the very task for which it was created. The Admiral, Lord Dartmouth, prevaricated over sailing until the fleet was fully equipped, although James and Pepys urged on him the necessity of intercepting William. Dartmouth admitted 'it was as fine a winter fleet as ever had been', but having delayed over the equipping of his ships he now found them trapped at the mouth of the Thames with contrary winds. By the time he extricated himself from the sands, the English fleet were unable to intercept William, and he landed without opposition at Torbay on 5 November 1688. James, deserted by his army, fled to France on 11 December: Pepys had the grace to resign his office, but Dartmouth, when he heard William was landed, wrote at once to put the services of the fleet at the Dutchman's command.

Thus was the Glorious Revolution inaugurated without a blow, although the Scots delayed making a decision, for James was after all a Stuart king. But only in Ireland and the Highlands and Islands, with their mainly Catholic populations, was there any real support for James.

~

On 12 March 1689 King James, convoyed by a French fleet, landed in Ireland and set up his court in Dublin. Two days later the Convention Parliament of Scotland declared for William and Mary; Viscount Dundee, however, left Edinburgh to raise the Highlands for James. To prevent the Jacobites in Ireland assisting Dundee and to give aid to those Protestants beleaguered behind the walls of Londonderry and Enniskillen, it was vital for the Convention to control the Irish and Western seas. Within a week they had chartered two small ships and outfitted them as frigates, the Pelican (18 guns and 120 men) and the Janet (12 guns and 80 men):

> two frigates … to cruise on the west coast of this kingdom … and to employ Captain William Hamilton and Captain John Brown, who are to command the said frigates, to look after fit ships and seamen, with power to the said persons to make bargain thereabout and to report.

They were ordered to

> cruise on the western coasts from the Point of Cornwall to the Isle of Skye, and to fight and sink all ships belonging to the late King James; and the seaports of England are requested to furnish him with victuals should he put in to any of them.

But so scarce were the munitions of war that Captains Hamilton and Brown were authorised

> to seize and make use of any cannon which may be fit for the service of the said two frigates, wherever the same can conveniently be had, and that they give receipt to the owners to the end that the hire damage or value thereof may be repaid by the public.

All in all a pretty tough assignment!

~

Also in March – for King William – General Hugh Mackay of Scourie sailed to Leith with 'little more than a thousand foot', but these were veterans of the Scots Brigade who had fought in the Dutch wars. General Mackay was appointed Commander-in-Chief of the Government forces and set about raising more troops, and establishing provisions and supply lines to the west coast and Highlands. He had an excellent grasp of the necessity for sea power, but had to fight a lengthy battle to obtain the ships and supplies he required.

After the indecisive engagement of 1 May at Bantry Bay between the English and French fleets, Captain Rooke, commanding the Deptford, was sent north with a small squadron to assist in keeping command of the seas between Ireland and Scotland.

By July, a further 14 ketches and hoys (of between 40-50 men and 2-12 guns each) were added to the Irish Squadron from the English Navy. In August, HMS Swallow – a 4th rate of 48 guns and 230 men – joined the Irish Squadron, and seven ships were ordered to convoy ordnance stores to Londonderry. It is a measure of Pepys' success in establishing a sound Navy that the Board was able to meet the needs of the Irish Squadron, for ships were stationed as far apart as Iceland, Newfoundland, Virginia, New England and Gibraltar. The herring and mackerel fleets, and the North Sea convoys all required protection, and there was the ever present threat of the French Fleet.

~

On 11 June the Privy Council considered 'what expense will be necessary for a new outrig of the two frigates,' and on the 20th the order was given

> to furnish such a quantity of biscuit and small beer with pease and brandy wine as may sufficiently furnish and provide the two frigates under the command of Captain Hamilton and Captain Brown until Lammas next … and to buy two barrels of small powder … for the use of the said two frigates … and to deliver … the salt beef taken from on board the French ship [captured at Kilberrie] … in such quantity as will be necessary for furnishing the two frigates till Lammas next.

However, in July 1689 the Scots frigates Pelican and Janet met with three French ships on passage to Duart Castle; heavily outgunned they were eventually captured by the French after a bloody battle. A graphic account of the engagement was given in the *London Gazette* of 2nd of August 1689:

On Wednesday the 10th of July, Captain Hamilton commanding the *Pelican* carrying 18 guns and 120 men, and Captain Brown of the *Janet* frigate carrying 12 guns and 80 men cruising between the Mull of Kintyre and Carrickfergus Lough happened to discover at sea to the southward three sail of ships … carrying the English flag and colours … which led them into the mistake of believing them to be English and friends; but they did no sooner perceive their error, than they found it impossible to retreat, they being three French men of war, having on board a battalion of 400 men of Colonel Porsil's regiment of foot, that was going to join Dundee, the biggest of them carying 36 guns, the second 30 and the third 24 guns. And so to action they fell immediately, and fought it with all the gallantry and resolution imaginable with their guns above an hour. Captain Brown's main mast was shot down when they came and lay aboard him, in which action his right arm was shot off with a cannon ball; yet notwithstanding … he continued giving directions and orders to his men until he received seven musket bullets in his body, the last of which killed him dead. And being overpowered by the enemy's men … after great slaughter … Captain Brown's ship was taken. Captain Hamilton … had the misfortune to be thrice boarded by the enemy … his forcastle and steerage being torn open by the violence and frequency of the enemy's shot … as his last effort gave orders to his gunner to go down to the hold and blow up the ship … but a cannon bullet at random shot came and dispatcht him: and so his ship fell into enemy hands.

The Scots Navy had for the time being ceased to exist.

~

The death of Viscount Dundee at Killiecrankie, the relief of Londonderry and the defeat of Brigadier Cannon at Dunkeld all eased the military situation for William during the summer of 1689. But Maclean of Duart, on the

Isle of Mull, was one of King James' most stalwart supporters, with Duart Castle strategically placed to control the Sound of Mull and the Firth of Lorn. It threatened supply routes to both of the Hanoverian garrisons at Dunstaffnage and Inverlochy, and with his many men and boats Maclean was not easy to subdue. And as long as James continued to rule in Dublin and draw support from the Highlands strong policing was necessary to control the narrow western seas; an English squadron remained on station until normal campaigning ceased for the winter months.

General Mackay had subdued the north and east of Scotland, and although few Highland chiefs had accepted the terms of the Indemnity he was confident of eventual success. He wrote on 10 September that:

> I am of opinion that the neck of this rebellion is broken, if all succour from Ireland be hindered. … tomorrow the term [of indemnity] is out … and ther is none of the chief Highlandes have made their application yet, but it is no great hazard … they can soon and easily be subdued nixt yeare … Colonel Canan is in no reputation or esteeme by them, for he and Dunfermeling [Lord Dunfermline] doe nothing but drink acquavity, as I am informed…

And the Privy Council reported the next day that 'The army is marched southward, and the fleet under Captain Rouck is sailed that same way'.

~

In December the Privy Council petitioned the King that

> the greatest part of the rebels be in the isles … and do come over and join as called. Three frigates may destroy their boats and transport parties (of soldiers) to the several isles … to subdue them.

General Mackay was of like mind, but 'received no return to his propositions and frequent letters'.

~

14-1 Drawing after Van de Velde: HMS Dartmouth

Amongst the Irish squadron was HMS Dartmouth, a fifth rate of 36 guns, and with a complement of 120. At 80ft length, 25ft beam, and 12ft draught she was a light and manoeuvrable sailer, ideal for West Coast waters. She had been built in 1655 with a major refit in 1678, and seen service in the Channel, Lisbon, Tangier, the Mediterranean, Virginia and the Leeward Islands. Dartmouth had over-wintered at Plymouth,

our ballast being so bad, stinking and all of a quagmire, and sandy so that it stoaks [blocks] *the limbers, that the water has no course to the pump.*

With the start of the campaigning season in March William prepared to cross to Ireland and breathe new life into his forces there. To subdue the Islands – and there being no longer a Scots Navy – orders were issued for the establishment of a small squadron of English ships to be stationed on the West Coast of Scotland. On 19 March 1690, Captain Edward Pottinger relinquished command of HM Sloop Fanfan and took command of both the Dartmouth and the squadron. With him he had HM Sloops Lark and Fanfan, together with five merchant ships to transport some 900 soldiers under the command of one Major Ferguson. The Lamb, a small ship of 20 guns, was also hired, for Maclean of Duart, quite naturally, was taking his toll of ships supplying the new garrison at Fort William.

The Dartmouth's log was lost with the ship, but Fanfan's survives; together with Captain Pottinger's letters we can piece together the squadron's movements. They sailed to Greenock in late March, but as Pottinger explained to the Admiralty, during the night

a sudden gaell fell upon us; to the loss of our long boat: her stem towed out … the officers assure me shee was a very old boat;

In April the Privy Council informed Captain Pottinger that they

have ordained the present magistrates of Glasgow … to give credit to yow for six weeks provisiones for the use of the two friggots and soap [sloop] under your command sent down to cruize on their coasts … and that ye order … the kyndes and quantities of the provisiones yee will stand in nee[d] off for that tyme

The never ending problem of manning the ships also had to be solved; 20 seamen of Aberdeen, 8 of Edinburgh, 7 of Burntisland, 8 of Culross, 6 of Linlithgow, were sent to Captain Pottinger.

The squadron's orders from General Mackay were explicit:

> … to make a diversion, allarme the rebells coasts, cut their communications with the Islanders and to take away or burn all their boats and birlinns. The Major … shall use with all the rigour of military executions such as shall continue obstinate in their rebellion, with this proviso, that women and children be not touched or wronged in their persons.

During the summer they did just that:

Gigha: 'destroyed all ye rebells houses Come and Cattle'.

Jura: 'ye Laird here has gone to Edinburgh to give himself up'.

Mull: 'seeing a parcel of houses neare ye shore which my men burnt'.

Eigg: 'burnt all ye houses and destroyed ye cattle meeting with no opposition'.

Canna: 'orderd all ye houses burnt and ye cattle destroyed.' Loch Nevis: 'burnt broke or destroyed four small boats and bought off a, large birlinne'.

Skye: 'staved and burnt nine birlings and boats and a new vessel, with the prettyest house in the Highlands of Scotland … reducing all to flames and ashes'.

~

On 19 June Captain Pottinger reported to the Navy Office:

In Dewart road (Isle of Mull)
May it please yor. honrs. Since my being upon this station amongst these islands, have with the Lark, ffanfan and Lambe a hired shipp; Majr Ferguson his men, ships and boats; done the best service wee were capable of by burning and destroying the severall Islands and houses, boats, cattle etc of such as are actuall in rebellion. To be particular would bee too tedious to yor hons tho upon some islands the souldiers have scarce a beast, nor a hutt to shelter them … nor in all this burning and destroying was there above l2 men lost … 3 whereof belonging to the Dartmouth by stragling from their boats beyond order; and a fourth tho intercepted from the boats, secured himselfe, but discovered too or three days afterwards: who most barbarous by those villains was hanged: soe that 1/3 of this loss ffell of our side by their own folly.

The cheife of this disorderly Clann hath submitted

… as also to my Lord Seafort, who with others follow: tho the mackClains, MacCamerons, Glengarie, Loughwhaber and many more continue as obstinate as Jews, which in good tyme I hope shall be reduct, from this I desist. …And if a Letter be directed to mee to bee forwarded by the Postmaster of Edinburgh it may come to my hands. tho our being here is as far from communication as if in the East indies; neither can I send the ffanfans books and acctts., nor the Dartmouths conforme[ing] to Instructions, for which I crave pardon, ever acknowledging my

Yor honrs most obedient, most obliged, ffaithfull humble servt Edward Pottinger

General Mackay, establishing a garrison at Inverlochy, later to be named Fort William, was also beset with problems:

… I pray … the garrison be sufficiently provided of money and provisions with all diligence. I have wryt to Arckinlas [Ardkinglas, chamberlain

to the Earl of Argyll] to send butter, cheese and what other provisions they can … our men have nothing but meale and water, with now and then a little acquavitie … If the meale from Glascow and other partes cum not, the garison will be very speedily reduced to great necessitie … for the partys I had out met with no catle within 20 miles … for neither the meale of Glasgow or Souther-land [Sutherland] is cum as yet, nor yet the barck which I order'd out of Cathnesse [Caithness] with 400 bolls, nor have we any notice of the two ships with the plancks, canon and ammunition. I wish the canon and ammonition were cum lest some enemy ships might com to in commode the garison before it be well cover'd towards the sea, which will take tyme … the frigats provisions drawes to an end …

In Ireland, on July 1, uncle and nephew met at the River Boyne, and by evening William was the victor. For James the adventure was over, and with it all sensible hopes of regaining his throne.

Log of the Fanfan Sloop, Eleventh of July:

> … to Dewart, here Rydeing ye Larke, I had ye good Newes of King Williams victory in Ireland and demonstrated our Joy by drinking their Majesties health and fireing of Gunns etc. Ye Dartmouth and Lamb sayled today a Cruizing.

In London it was reported:

> we hear that Sir Donald Mackdonnel has capitulated; he is the chief of the Highland clans; the rest, for the most part, live by theft and violence.

The Earl of Argyll was ordered to raise a regiment and reduce those still in rebellion 'to their Majestie's obedience and authority'. Such a chance for legitimate clan warfare was too good to be missed, and Argyll eventually gained most of Maclean of Duart's lands.

Captain Pottinger and the Dartmouth had had a busy summer:

being scarce 48 hours in one place without motion our ships with the Major … burning houses, breaking boats and wasting the substance of such as were in actual rebellion.

He was not enamoured of his command:

for our being here is as far from communication as if in the East Indies I conclude I am moared here to this miserable melancholy station, where its scarce possible either Credit or Profit can be expected.

At the end of July the Dartmouth returned to Greenock for provisions:

… the extreme want of provisions in being wholly out of bread beer pork pease and cheese brought me here of ye 26th instant … I got out my guns and ballast with what else was necessary; after clearing the ground, layed her ashore and found only the stirrop under the fore foot soe scuffed as to catch our cables or bouy ropes which we broke off, and smoothed as well

as we could scouring the lining of the stemm, scraping washing and scrubbing her as clean as the place and tyme allowed us; she is now again afloat: our guns powder ballast etc aboard, our topmast aloft and bent all in readiness attending our provisions and further orders:

I have inclosed … my ffanfans muster books as also mine and my servants Ticketts to Mr William Browne my agent … [and] most humbly pray those ticketts may be paid as soon as conveniently your honours can: since I have had great oppurtunities to advance moneys for their Majesties service; and have a considerable ffamily to provide for…

Log of the Fanfan sloop, at anchor off Greenock, 27 August l690:

This morning ye Dartmouth sailed for ye Sound of Mull. Capt Pottinger, the Commander, sent his Lieut in my abscence and tooke away two brass guns from on board ye Fanfan. [short range anti-personnel breech loading swivel guns, often made of brass and sometimes called murderers].

Sir Cloudesley Shovell in HMS Monk commanded the Irish Squadron of over thirty ships and was thus was able to contain any incursions from Ireland to Scotland, as well as any threat from the French fleet.

King James' flight had taken the heart out of the Rising, and Captain Pottinger found the clans beginning to succumb.

The Egg men submitted, surrendering their arms, taking the oath of allegiance I left them with their sustenance; the same to ye Island of Canna. Sir Donald obliged himselfe forthwith to send his overtures of submission to this govuornment.

Captain Pottinger had consulted with and received orders from Colonel Hill at Inverlochy, and on 2 September 1690 wrote to the Navy Office.

… my staying here is not found necessary, soe that

I conceive, I may leave this coast in a fortnight or 3 weekes at most, thence I return to Grenock road … and now also our best bower cable, with often anchoring, and in deep waters, and more than one cable is soo extremely worn, as not to be trusted and much thereof cut away: the Boatswain and Carpenter assures me all their stores run out … I have purchased a Long boat to make a shift with all, but only for a shift, our pinnace with continual rowing and night service soe much shaken as either a new boat or great repair will be wanting … I have only to add that this station hath been soe unprofitable as where ever I shall be appointed, Yr orders shall be most cheerfull[y] received and faithfully put in practice by

Yoy Honrs most obedt very much obliged humble Servt Edward Pottinger

However, Pottinger's longed-for release was not to be, for he was ordered to assist the Earl of Argyll in subduing Mull.

… and the said Earl to give such orders and directions as he shall find necessary to Captain Pottinger, and ordains Captain Pottinger so long as he is on the sea coasts and Captain commander of the Scots frigate to give ready obedience to his orders.

Having called at Fort William, *'and conscious that garrison having noe more occasion for mee'*, Captain Pottinger and the squadron cruised among the islands. In early October the Dartmouth was anchored with the Lark in Scallastle Bay, north-west of Duart Castle, and Captain Pottinger penned his last letter to the Admiralty:

aboard ye Dartmouth Scallastle Bay
in ye Sound of Mull
October 4th: 90

… In this trip I had the good luck to Surprise the Island of Egg: whose people formerly escaped us … the Egg men submitted, surrendering their armes, taking the oath of allegiance I left them with their substance: the same to ye Island of Canna. Thence

I ranged alongst Sr Donald McDonalds coast … upon firing some neighbouring houses and corne soe alarmed Sr Donald as to send [him] aboard … he upon parole of honour obliged himselfe forthwith to send his overtures of submission to this govournment. [he continues by describing the lack of stores] … not an ounce of butter aboard, nor pease … noe pork, nor 10 days beef: our men being three days without flesh … Upon my being surprized with a new order to attend this station and the Earl of Argylls instructions for subduing Mull theres only onboard about 2000lb of bread for present releife: I humbly pray that mony's may be ordered my purse at Glasgow without loss of tyme for soo much provisions as shall be thought fitt to carry us thence, where we shall be appointed to be fitted for our winter station; I hope in less than all this month the Island may be subdued, soo that the needful may be directed to Greenock.

But a great gale blew up:

For two days it blew very hard, and the ship's anchors

aboard the Dartmouth Scallast & bay in ye Sound of Mull Octob: 4: 9⁹

May it please yor honrs.

364

according to his grace my Lord high comission⁹ order, I returned to Dewart road
thence to the [...] of [...]

14-2 Selections from Captain Pottinger's last letter to the Admiralty

[...] subdued, so that the needfull may be directed to Grenock.
most humbly craving yor hon⁹ pardon from

Yor. hon⁹. most obed.t very much obliged humb: Serv.t

[...]

Edward Pottinger

held during that time; but on the third day the wind was so violent that some of the cables gave way, (about 1800 on October 9), and she drifted, pulling the anchors after her. And away she went, stern foremost, until she struck the Knight's Point in Morvern, across the Sound. The waves beat on her until she went to pieces there, to the great rejoicing of the Macleans.

The Dartmouth was wrecked on the opposite shore three miles away, on *Eilean Rubha an Ridire*, a rocky islet only a few hundred yards off a safe shore. Captain Pottinger and all but six of his crew – five men and a boy – perished.

The gale which wrecked the Dartmouth was widespread, as the Fanfan Sloop – one hundred miles away in Greenock – recorded in her log:

9th October
… about 6 in ye evening it blew Extreame hard wee lett goe our sheet Anchor[.] it continued a very Violent Storme of Winde insomuch that wee often feard ye Sloope would have overset …

wee narrowely escaped being lost several shipps in Greenock … were oversett after midnight ye Storme abated. (margin note) In this storme ye Dartmouth was lost in ye Sound of Mull.

18th October
We had brought ye Unhappy News of ye Dartmouth being lost ye 9th Oct in Callastle Bay only 5 men and a Boy saved and ye Larke puld there and Cutt her main mast by ye Board.

[It would appear the Lark attempted to salvage what could be saved]

25th October
… came to Greenock ye 6 men that were savd from ye Dartmouth, and went for Glasgow in Order for London …

Epilogue

Plagued by shortages of men, supplies, support and money, Captain Pottinger in the Dartmouth showed much skill navigating in difficult and unfamiliar waters. He played a major part in subduing the Islands, and although pockets of rebellion flickered during 1691, the Massacre of Glencoe put a final end to resistance – but only for a few years.

However, the New Year opened with a reminder of the previous year's tragedy.

> *1st January 1691 Petition to the Privy Council*
> … by Thomas, brother of Captain Edward Pottinger, detailing that in March 1688 at Culraine he [EP] levied a company at his own expense, and beat off the Irish he then went to London, and was appointed Captain of the Fanfan Sloop, and at the siege of Carrickfergus distinguished himself he was then appointed to the Dartmouth: when commander of the said ship he with his men and the said ship were lost.

The Privy Council recommended his widow and child to the King's bounty, but in March Whitehall ducked a decision and referred it to the Lords Commissioners for Irish Affairs. I have been unable to find out what happened to his widow and '*considerable ffamily to provide for…*'

~

The wreck of HMS Dartmouth is now protected, one of only a handful in the Highlands. A major marine archaeological excavation was carried out by St Andrew's University, and much of historical value uncovered.

Map references

- OS Landranger 49 & Explorer 375:

  Duart Castle NM 749 354

  Scallastle Bay anchorage NM 695 353

  Eilean Rubha an Ridire NM 724 405

Sources

- *The Old Scots Navy 1689-1710* – Navy Records Society 1912.
- National Maritime Museum: drawing and dimensions of HMS Dartmouth.
- *Letters of John Graham of Claverhouse* – Andrew Murray Scott. *Scottish History Society Miscellany XI* 1991.
- *Records of the Privy Council* – Register House, Edinburgh.
- *Memoirs of the Scots War* by Major General Mackay. Bannatyne Club.
- Maclean of Duart's letters – *The Melville Papers.* Register House, Edinburgh.
- Admiralty Records at The Public Record Office, London.
- Captain Pottinger's letters. Captains Logs of HM Ships Deptford, Fanfan & Pelican. Masters Log of HMS Dover. Ship movements and stations. List Books 1673-1691.
- State Papers Domestic – William and Mary.

- Clan Donald Lands Trust, Armadale, Isle of Skye.
- *The International Journal of Archaeology and Under-water Exploration*: The Dartmouth, a British frigate wrecked off Mull, 1690: Adnams (1974), McBride (1976), Martin (1978).

Three stories of Eilean Donan Castle

Before we get to the stories you'll have to wade through a bit of boring old history, but I assure you it's worth it!

Probably the most photographed castle in Scotland – and certainly on the most tins of shortbread – Eilean Donan Castle enjoys a dramatic location perched on its island at the meeting of Lochs Long, Duich and Alsh. The Five Sisters of Kintail tower over the lonely road to Inverness and the east down Glen Shiel, whilst Skye fills the western seaboard.

It was to counter the threat from Norsemen, then in possession of Skye and the Outer Isles, that King Alexander II built the castle sometime about 1230, but his was not the first on the island. A vitrified fort had stood there from early times, and the island itself was named for St Donan, massacred by pirates on the Isle of Eigg, along with fifty of his followers in 617 AD.

Alexander III gave the castle in 1266 to Colin Fitzgerald, a son of the Earl of Desmond, in recognition of Colin's services at the battle of Largs, three years before. Fitzgerald is thought to be the ancestor of Clan Mackenzie, whose chiefs became a great power in the land, Lords of Kintail and Earls of Seaforth. Although there is no record of Mackenzies as such at Eilean Donan until the 15th century, they attracted to themselves as bodyguards the 'Wild Clan Macrae', who became known as 'Mackenzie's shirt-of-mail'. So assiduous in their duties were the Macraes that in 1520 they were rewarded with the office of Hereditary Constable of Eilean Donan, although others seem to have carried out the post at times.

Now, having bored you with history, I'll get on with my stories. The first is one version of how the castle came to be built – I think it's a better tale than the facts! The second is historically accurate, if a wee bit embroidered in the telling. The third is completely accurate following much research.

A Scots Dick Whittington & how Eilean Donan came to be built

In days of old there was a belief that if an infant when weaned took his first drink from a raven's skull, on reaching man's estate he would thereby gain supernatural powers. Now, there lived on the shores of Loch Duich a petty chieftain who was determined that his son should possess these powers, and he made certain that the first drink the infant took when weaned was from the skull of a raven.

The years passed, and the boy grew into manhood – I've forgotten his name, but let's call him Angus. One day the starlings in the thatch were making such a racket that the chief could not hear the wireless, so he turned to his son and asked: "Whit the bloody hell are they starlins jabberin aboot?"

So the boy listened to the birds, then replied: "Actually, pater, they are discussing the fact that one day you will be waiting on me at your own table".

Not surprisingly, this so enraged his father that Angus thought it best to make himself scarce for a while, so he bundled some clothes into a rucksack, bid farewell to his mother, and set out up Glen Shiel for Inverness. There he found a ship bound for France, and after many adventures he learnt that the King was so pestered by the squabbling of the numerous sparrows in the palace that he could not sleep at night.

"I can sort that for you, O King", said Angus, for he was a pretty polite sort of chap, and although not much used to chatting with Kings, he *had* been brought up proper. So he listened to the sparrows squabbling and bickering, and it turned out they were arguing over who should be first at the crumbs fallen from the King's table.

"Look", said Angus, when he had listened to all their arguments in turn, "why don't you make up a rota? Each family goes first on certain days, then you'll all get a fair turn".

"Oh", replied the sparrows, "we never thought of that". (Pretty thick birds, sparrows!). So they worked out a rota, everything was at last peaceful, and the King was able to sleep again at nights. In fact, he was so delighted that he gave Angus a ship, fully equipped and manned, and himself came down to the dockside to wave farewell to our hero.

The years passed, and Angus with his ship sailed to many exotic places, until he finally landed in a country where another King had a palace overrun by rats. The King was so fed up with this plague and the destruction they were causing that he had offered a hogshead full of gold coins to anyone who would rid him of the problem. So Angus went back to his ship, collected the ship's cat – who was snoozing beside the galley fire – and returned to the palace with her tucked under his arm. Let loose there she soon made short work of the rats, and the delighted King presented Angus with the hogshead of gold and the cat got a gold collar studded with gems.

"Stuff that for a lark", mewed the cat, "Faaar too heavy to wear". But, of course, only Angus could understand her, and once back at the ship he undid the collar and gave it to the cabin-boy, whose cat she really was.

"Thanks guv", exclaimed the delighted boy, as well he might.

By now ten years had passed, and Angus decided he would like to see his old Mum again. So he headed the ship north, sailed up the Irish Sea, on through Kyle Rhea with a fine following wind, and finally came to anchor in

15-1 Angus & his hogshead of gold

him the birth-mark on his shoulder, and then the two were completely reconciled.

And as for Angus, so wise were his decisions – and so great his wealth – that King Alexander commanded him to build a castle on Eilean Donan to check the predations of the Norsemen from the islands.

Or so they say!

the channel between Totaig and the rock outcrop called Eilean Donan – or St Donan's Isle.

His ship was so magnificently carved and gilded, with sails of the finest canvas that his father – as the local chief – sent a ghillie with an invitation for the owner of the vessel to come and dine. The chief did not recognise his own son, but so impressed was he at his great show of wealth that he himself waited on Angus, so making come true the starling's prophecy. When the truth was out his father at first would not believe it was his son, until Angus showed

How Duncan Macrae & wee Jimmy saved the castle from Donald Gruamach Macdonald

Which brings me to my second tale, which is this. In 1539 the Mackenzies were absent from the castle, maybe at a party somewhere, maybe shopping in Inverness, or more likely doing a bit of cattle lifting against the winter. Wherever they were, they left the castle guarded by only three men and a boy, which was a bit stupid, knowing their neighbours. For as soon as he heard this, *Donald Gruamach* (Macdonald) 4th of Sleat – who lived just round the corner, at Dunscaith Castle on Skye – rounded up 400 men and with fifty galleys set out to seize Eilean Donan. Setting sail from Dunscaith *Donald Gruamach* caught the flood tide through Kyle Rhea, and in no time at all was knocking on the castle door demanding surrender.

A chap called John Dubh Matheson of Fearnaig was Constable at *Eilean Donan* just then, but he must have been a bit dim, for the silly man stood by an open window and was promptly killed by an arrow. One down, three left. Of those three, one was the watchman, and not much of a fighter; one was an old, old man – Duncan Macrae – but who in his youth had been a famed archer; and one was a young stable-lad called Wee Jimmy. Now Jimmy's *real* name was Ferdinand, after his father, a Hooray-Henry who had come up from London for the Skye Balls, led his mother astray in the hay-loft, and then scooted back to London – as they are wont to do. But ever since wee Ferdinand was sent protesting to Dornie Primary he had been so teased at his name that he changed it to Jimmy, and Wee Jimmy he will remain in our story.

Reckoning it would be an easy fight, *Donald Gruamach* landed from his galley below the castle and sussed out where best to attack. Seeing this, Duncan Macrae attempted to draw his bow and fire an arrow at the chief on the rocks below; but Duncan was just too old and too weak to even bend the bow, so he turned to the lad.

"See you Wee Jummy. Away up here and draw this bow, whilst I aim the arrow at yon muckle Macdonald". So Wee Jimmy leapt up to an arrow-slit window and drew the great bow at Duncan's bidding, whilst the old man fitted his last arrow, whose barb was from the smith MacNab.

*15-2 Duncan &
Wee Jimmy firing the
arrow at Donald Gorm*

Duncan aimed his arrow straight for the heart *of Donald Gruamach*, but just as he released it the old man had a fit of the coughs, for the castle was damp and draughty and not at all good for his chest. So although Jimmy had drawn the bow to its full extent, the arrow flew low and instead of piercing Donald through the heart as destined, it hit his ankle.

"Bother", exclaimed Duncan, but I suspect he used far worse language than that, for it was his last arrow

Down on the rocks *Donald Gruamach* regarded the arrow sticking out of his ankle as one regards a midge bite, and promptly pulled it out. Silly man, for the barb severed an artery, and blood gushed out all over his shoes.

"Oh dear", said he, for the shoes were new, and he would get stick from his Mum when they returned to Dunscaith. Not knowing that the arrow was the defender's last, the Macdonalds hastily bundled their chief into a galley and rowed as hard as they could out of range. However, it soon became very apparent that there was nothing they could do to save the life of *Donald Gruamach*, and as it is bad luck to die at sea, they abandoned the attack and headed for home. But by now a strong westerly wind was blowing from Kyle against them, and hard as they rowed they made little headway, and the chief's life was ebbing fast. So they headed for the nearest land, a small drying reef, where they erected a hut as best they could for the dying man; and there, before long, *Donald Gruamach* did just that.

Thus died *Donald Gruamach* of Sleat:

among pipers his name will always be known

15-3 And there died Donald Gruamach

because of the beautiful composition in *ceol mor* which bears his name' – *Donald Gruamach's Lament on the Death of his Brother*.

And ever since that day the reef has been known as *Larach Tigh Mhic Dhomhnuill* – The Site of Donald's House, although house is rather a grand word for what was only a temporary shelter. But then, he was, after all, a chief, and chiefs are grander than us mere mortals!

Of the Jacobite Rising of 1719, the battle of Glenshiel & the destruction of Eilean Donan Castle by gunpowder

This is my last story of Eilean Donan, about the little-known Jacobite Rising of 1719, the battle at Bridge of Shiel and the destruction of castle, blown apart by Spanish gunpowder.

Following the failure of the '15, The Chevalier (also known as The Old Pretender, son of King James II) did not give up the attempt to restore the Stuart dynasty, although his efforts were somewhat thwarted by the death of King Louis XIV of France. He turned next to Charles XII of Sweden, who had long wished to invade Great Britain, and who saw support for The Chevalier as a means to this end. But as with most Jacobite plans, this too came to naught, and in the end it was Philip V of Spain who came up trumps at the instigation of his minister, Cardinal Alberoni.

In a two-pronged attack, the Duke of Ormonde was destined to invade England in the West Country, supplied by Spain with ships, 5,000 troops, and arms for 30,000 English Jacobites. The 10th Earl Marischal, his brother James Keith, the young Marquis of Tullibardine and other survivors of the '15 Rising were to head the Scottish attack, later joined by William Mackenzie, 5th Earl of Seaforth and other clan chiefs.

The Earl Marischal sailed from San Sebastian on the 2nd of March 1719, headed for Stornoway on the Isle of Lewis. Embarked in his two frigates were 307 Spanish troops, 2000 muskets, and a considerable quantity of money, stores and ammunition. Meanwhile, James Keith had been active in France, and on March 19th he, Tullibardine, Clanranald, Lochiel and other Jacobites set sail in a small ship of barely twenty-five tons from the mouth of the Seine. They too were headed for Stornoway, and having narrowly avoided capture by English men-of-war landed there on the 4th of April, only to find no sign of the Earl Marischal.

An anxious few days followed before the frigates arrived, and there then occurred the first of many interminable and indecisive councils of war, at which the splits in command began to appear. Marischal, supposedly the commander, was keen to land on the mainland and immediately march on Inverness, then only garrisoned by 300 troops. But Tullibardine suddenly produced his commission as Lieutenant-General, over-ruled Marischal, and advised caution until they heard news of the Duke of Ormonde and the main landing in England.

Finally a decision was made, pilots were engaged, and they sailed across the Minch to land in Loch Alsh on 13th April, much delayed by storms. The following day arrived from France Lord George Murray, Tullibardine's younger brother, and it was decided to make Eilean Donan Castle the Jacobite base. Stores, gunpowder and ammunition were landed from the ships, forty-five Spanish troops garrisoned the castle, and word was sent to the clans to be ready to rise immediately. The main body camped nearby, and they were soon joined by Clanranald, Lochiel, MacDougall of Lorn and Rob Roy Macgregor, a fine gathering of some 1,100 men. All was in readiness, but the days, which should have been spent in marching on Inverness, were wasted in lengthy and pointless discussion. As James Keith later wrote:

'The same demon who had inspired them with the design of staying in Lewis, hindered them from accepting this proposition. We were all in the dark what could be the meaning of these dilatory proceedings'.

Tullibardine wished to re-embark the whole force for Spain, but Marischal ordered the frigates to sea in early May.

Meanwhile, the government had not been idle, for London had known of the plans for some time. Indeed, as Lord Stair so presciently wrote:

I am not worried about these few rebels who have landed in Scotland, they will soon die of hunger in the mountains, and if some of the Spaniards manage to escape, that will discourage others from going to Scotland.

Off the Lizard Admiral Sir John Norris despatched the 50 gun ships *Assistance* (Captain Holland) and *Worcester* (Captain Boyle) to sail west of Ireland to search for the Spanish ships. At the same time he sent the 50 gun *Dartmouth* (Captain Eaton), along with the sloops *Enterprise* (40 guns, Captain Herdman) and *Flamborough* (24 guns, Captain Hildesley) to sweep up through the Irish Sea. At Stornoway they learnt of the Spanish frigates, and Captain Holland also engaged pilots; Henry Gray, Roderick McCleod and John Campbell, all for the princely fee of £1-8s-6d – and perhaps some persuasion from the point of a cutlass? On the 6th May *Worcester, Enterprise* and *Flamborough* sailed south about Skye 'to the Castle of Donnain,' whilst the *Assistance* and *Dartmouth* went to the north of Skye in search of the Spanish frigates, finally anchoring in Loch Kishorn.

About the 9th of May disastrous news from Edinburgh reached Tullibardine at Eilean Donan – the Spanish ships with the Duke of Ormonde had been shattered by storms off Cape Finisterre, and the invasion of England was cancelled. He was warned to re-embark the Spanish forces and disperse his men with all haste. But it was too late for the Spanish, for the Earl Marischal had ordered the frigates to sea; and even as Tullibardine read his dispatches the three English ships under Captain Boyle sailed into Loch Alsh, flying Spanish colours. The Spanish soldiers, seeing their own flags, flocked to the shore, 'little black men with long black coloured hair … in white uniforms with yellow'.

At 9am on the 10th of May Captain Boyle of the *Worcester* sent a Lieutenant ashore under flag of truce to demand the castle's surrender, but the boat was fired upon. Being of shallower draught, the sloops *Enterprise* and *Flamborough* had anchored close under the castle walls, and immediately began a bombardment at very short range. As Captain Boyle reported to the Admiralty:

> at 8 in the evening we made a great Discharge of our Cannon upon the Castle, and under that cover I sent … our Boats Man'd and Armed a shore under the foot of the Castle, which they attack'd and took after a small resistance…

He made prisoner 'an Irish captain, a Spanish lieutenant, a sergeant, one Scotch rebel and 39 Spanish soldiers.'

Having been incorrectly informed by a deserter that the main body of Jacobites was 4,700 strong, and fearing the castle could be re-captured, he decided to 'blow it up without loss of time.'

From the arsenal was sent off to the ships – to be divided among the crews as lawful prizes –

343 Barrels of Powder, and 52 Barrels Musquet Shot, two hundredweight each with some baggs of meal, likewise burnt several barns, etc., where they had a quantity of Corn for use of their Camp.

And with the remains of the Spanish gunpowder, Captain Herdman and his landing party demolished the castle so thoroughly that over two hundred years elapsed before it was rebuilt.

The *Flamborough* sailed up Loch Duich in search of the magazine in Strath Croe:

> about 3 Leagues further up the Lake, and … upon his [Captain Hildesley] first appearing the Rebels set fire to a great quantity of Powder and other Ammunition, by the success of which they are Depriv'd of the greatest part of their Ammunition'.

As indeed they were, for with the loss of both their arsenals the Jacobites were in dire straits, although worse was to follow. News arrived that Major-General Wightman – a

15-4 Eilean Donan Castle after being blown up

veteran of Sherriffmuir – had left Inverness for Kintail with a force 1,000 strong, along with over 100 dragoons and a battery of four light bronze mortars.

For twelve days the ships roamed the area, mounting vigilant patrols, burning and destroying at will; for as Captain Holland reported on 21st May:

> This blow (at Eilean Donan) has put them upon the wing, for they have dislodged their camp and marched to the head of Loch Carron … we often have small encounters between their parties and our boats.

As news of the disasters spread out to the country, the clans refused to rise, but still Tullibardine failed to give the order for his men to disperse to their homelands. They were about to be trapped.

Nearly a month after the castle and their ammunition was destroyed – long after they should have dispersed – the Jacobites took up a strong defensive position in the gorge referred to by Tullibardine as Glenshielbeg but whose local Gaelic name is *Lub-innis-na-seangan*, or 'the bend of the river at the island of ants.' Here, the towering heights of *Sgurr na Ciste-Duibhe*,

> juts into the glen … [which] … contracts into a narrow gorge, down which the Shiel, at this point a roaring torrent, runs in a deep rocky channel, between steep declivities covered with heather, bracken, and scattered birches. Above the pass the glen opens out into a little strath.

It was a perfect defensive position, ideally suited to the warfare of the clansmen, who further improved it by a series of entrenchments as well as blocking the rough track that wound through the gorge. To the south were the slopes of *Sgurr a Chuillinn,* and Lord George Murray commanded this right wing, whilst Tullibardine led the main force on the left wing to the north. This totalled some 1,000 men, largely the Earl of Seaforth's Mackenzies placed high on the steep slopes, and 200 Spaniards lower down near the gorge. The defences were 'impregnable provided they were directed with any tactical intelligence and flexibility,' but this proved to be sadly lacking.

Battle was joined between 5 and 6pm on the 10th May, coincidentally the birthday of James Stuart. General Wightman stationed his mortars on the road, and shelled Lord George Murray's right wing, followed by three fierce assaults, which were, however, repulsed. Murray held out for two hours, but the mortars had set the heather afire, and as he received no support from across the gorge Murray was forced to retire.

General Wightman now concentrated his attack on the left wing, but before Lord George could reinforce this, Mackenzie was badly wounded, his men lost heart, and they withdrew uphill carrying their chief with them. The Spaniards fought bravely, but seeing the Highlanders fleeing, they did likewise, and all were pursued up the slopes of *Sgurr na Ciste-Duibhe* by the Hanoverian troops, sweating and panting in their heavy red coats and packs.

By nightfall it was over, but the pass by which the Spanish troops escaped is still known as *Bealach nan Spainnteach*, although they surrendered to Wightman next day. As prisoners-of-war they were taken to Inverness, and then to Edinburgh, from where they were eventually repatriated in October of that year, 274 of them in all.

Lacking ammunition and food, demoralised and defeated, the Jacobite chiefs gave the clansmen orders to disperse as best they could. 'Everybody … took the road he liked best,' i.e. they headed for home. The leaders of the Rising concealed themselves in the wilds of Knoydart and Glengarry until they could take ship for France and exile. Their clansmen suffered worse, for General Wightman was 'burning the houses of the Guilty and preserving those of the Honest.' 'Twas ever thus.

～

In the Battle at Bridge of Shiel casualties were light on both sides, and only one English Officer was killed, a Captain Downes; he was buried on the field of battle, but for some reason his burial place was known locally as 'the Dutch Colonel's Grave.'

On moonlit nights, especially in June, 'The Colonel's Ghost' is still said to haunt the glen!

Map references

- OS Landranger 33. OS Explorer 413:

  Eilean Donan NG 881 258.

  Larach Tigh Mhic Dhomhnuill NG 852 253.

- OS Landranger 33. OS Explorer 414:

  Bridge of Shiel/*Lub-innis-na-seangan* NG 990 132.

Historical notes

- THE AFTERMATH: The Earl Marischal forfeited his title, and was the last ever to hold it, although he and his brother, James Keith, later pursued outstanding military and diplomatic careers with Frederick the Great of Prussia.

  William Mackenzie, Earl of Seaforth, lost lands and titles, never to be restored; but he was pardoned by George I in 1726 and died peacefully in Scotland fourteen years later. For Mackenzie's grandson a new earldom of Seaforth was created and the old allowed to lapse. The new earl raised the famous Seaforth Highlanders but the title died with him in 1781 – all heirs were to the old title, not the new.

  The Marquis of Tullibardine, already outlawed for his part in the '15, forfeit the right to inherit the Dukedom of Atholl; he also was pardoned, but was out in the '45, and died in the Tower a year later.

Lord George Murray commanded the Jacobite army in the '45, but after Culloden fled abroad, never to return.

And Rob Roy? Well, Liam Neeson doesn't actually show it in his surprisingly accurate film, but Rob Roy too was pardoned after submitting to General Wade in 1725, and died nine years later after a turbulent life.

• THE DUTCH OFFICER: Boswell, in his Journal of a Tour to the Hebrides with Samuel Johnson, 1773 visited the site of the battle with Dr Johnson on their way to Glenelg. He later refers to Captain MacLeod of Balmeanach as 'a Dutch officer', and the editors have footnoted this as follows: 'i.e. an officer of the Scots Brigade in Holland'. Possibly Captain Downes was also so employed.

• EILEAN DONAN CASTLE: It lay in ruins until 1912, when a twenty year restoration – including a new bridge to the mainland – began under the MacRae family, as hereditary keepers. It was not to everyone's liking however,

for that doughty writer MEM Donaldson made her views extremely firmly known in print:

> … one can only marvel at a taste which takes any satisfaction from turning a picturesque ruin into … a permanent blot on the landscape.

About 2012, stonemasons were working to weatherproof the walls by replacing the lime and concrete coating applied to the castle in the 1950s. They uncovered 2 iron cannonballs from the ships, 7" in diameter, embedded in the masonry, some 30 feet above the ground.

Sources

- *Wanderings in the West Highlands* – MEM Donaldson.
- *Somewhere in Scotland* – Alasdair Alpin Macgregor.
- *Inglorious Rebellion* – Christopher Sinclair-Stevenson.
- *Scotland and the Sea* – J Smout.
- *Ships of the '45* – John S Graham.
- *The Companion Guide to the West Highlands* – WH Murray.
- *West Coast Cruising* – John MacClintock.
- *The Reader's Encyclopaedia* – William Rose Benet.
- *Proceedings of the Society Of Antiquaries Of Scotland*, January 12, 1885. [Plan of] the Battle of Glenshiel, 10th June 1719 – Note upon an unpublished document in the possession of His Grace the Duke of Marlborough by AH Millar, FSA Scot.
- *Burke's Peerage, Baronetage & Knightage and Scottish Clan Chiefs* – 107th Edition.

The strange but true story of Lady Grange

This tale has been taken from over 200 pages of my historical research and copies of original documents so is as accurate as I can make it. I've let the original letters tell the tale as much as possible, for nothing beats a contemporary view; such quotes are in *italics*.

Lady Grange was abducted in 1732 by her husband and Lord Lovat when she threatened to denounce them for their Jacobite leanings. With the connivance of others they confined her first near Stirling, then conveyed her, by force, north through the Highlands to Loch Hourn; from thence she was shipped, like so much cargo, firstly to Heisker, then St Kilda, Assynt, Harris, Uist and at the last to Skye, where she died of madness in 1745.

Such are the bare facts of this strange tale, but to which none of her family or friends raised objections – they preferred to believe her ensconced in some comfortable lodging for her own protection from madness. In reality she was immured without any physical or mental comforts, and, to a woman of her class, in utter destitution and isolation. Even when news of her imprisonment on St Kilda finally reached Edinburgh in December 1740, Grange and Lovat were able to remove the unfortunate woman elsewhere and keep her captive until her death.

The main evidence we have is from two letters by Lady Grange smuggled off St Kilda, reputedly in a ball of wool carried by the minister's daughter. One, dated St Kilda, 20th January 1738, is in her own hand; the second is a very detailed 'Journal' of her abduction, and was mostly dictated to the minister there, Roderick MacLennan; only the final lines are in her own hand. These arrived in Edinburgh in early December 1740, whilst other letters or documents were destroyed by Lord Grange and an Earl of Mar, for Grange was of that family. Throughout her letters Lady Grange was meticulous at recording names and relationships of those involved in her abduction, for she clearly hoped they would at some stage be brought to task – they were not. Lord Grange wrote in the third person but only a few letters survive, for as he often instructed, *'This letter is too free not to be burnt, and then it cannot accidentally fall into other hands'.*

Chapter One – The principals

Lord Grange was a law lord and Jacobite sympathiser, although outwardly he supported the Hanoverian regime to ensure his own preferment. But when his termagent of a wife threatened to denounce him and the others Grange had to ensure her silence – and their heads. So he simply abducted the lady – sequestered is the modern euphemism!

Grange is described as:

> a complex figure, politically and personally … He intrigued ceaselessly and was regarded as useful but unreliable by political colleagues.

James Erskine made rapid advancement in the legal profession; in 1707, at the age of 28, he was raised to the bench of the Court of Session and took the title of Lord Grange. But:

> The truth was that the man had neither learning

nor ability. He was no lawyer, and was a bad speaker. He had been raised on the shoulders of his brother, the Earl of Mar…

Outwardly a Whig, he harboured, but concealed, Jacobite sympathies – in June 1745 he advised the Pretender that 'there never was and never can be such a favourable opportunity to attempt your Majesty's restoration'. Truly the man was backing both horses.

Rachel Cheisly, later Lady Grange

This then was the man who married, in about 1707, Rachel Cheisly, a beauty and wit, the principal of our tale. She was the 'daughter of Cheisly of Dalry, who shot the Lord President, Sir George Lockhart, in revenge for deciding against him in a lawsuit'.

Dalry made no attempt to escape; he was tried the next day and duly hanged the day after. His right hand was cut off, the offending pistol hung round his neck and his body condemned to be hung in chains. Friends retrieved it during the night and buried him at Dalry – many years later, when alterations were being done to the house, a skeleton of a man was found, minus one hand but with the remains of a pistol closeby!

Rachel was about ten at the time, so the event was bound to have a deep impression on her and may well explain some of her later actions.

This lady been very beautiful, but of a violent temper. She had, it was said, been debauched by her husband before marriage.

By all accounts, Lady Grange had inherited a touch of her father's madness, which coupled with a violent temper and a fondness for alcohol did not make for the most peaceful of marriages – but then her husband was certainly no saint.

In Mr Erskine's annual visits to London he had attached himself to a mistress, a handsome Scotchwoman, Fanny Lindsay, who kept a coffee-house about the bottom of the Haymarket. This had come to his lady's ears, and did not make her less outrageous.

However, the couple jogged on well enough for twenty odd years, producing four sons and four daughters. Lady Grange was not especially fond of her children, whom she referred to as the 'dammed Erskine brats'. They, in turn, had little affection for her, and a certain fear – it is hardly surprising that they were later indifferent to her 'sequestration', and raised no enquiries. Lady Grange's versions of the marriage breakdown was

That after I had lived near twenty five years in great love and peace, he all of a sudden took a dislike to my person, and such a hatred that he could not live with me, nor so much as to stay in his house;

Lord Grange later wrote to her kinsman and legal agent, Thomas Hope of Rankeillor, that she

abused all in the family … and committed outrages, so that at length I was forced to have a watch in my house, and especially at night time, as if it had been in the frontier of an enemyes country, or to be spoiled by robbers.

These and other insults and persecutions on me and my family, and nearest friends, were not only for a short time, but a considerable tract.

To his cousin Grange referred to his wife as *'that plague of his life [who] has encumbered him…'*

With two such mercurial temperaments discord was inevitable, eventually breaking into open warfare. Matters became so bad that friends – including Lady Grange's sister and Thomas Hope of Rankeillor – considered a separation necessary for the sake of the family. There were faults on both sides, but in 1730 Lady Grange reluctantly signed a letter of separation; in it she agreed that

if you'll allow me a hundred pounds Str: [sterling] yearly … and if you'll drop the Process of Separation you have raised against me … then I will retire and live by my self for five years … nor sett my Foot within your Doors in Town or Country…'

Thes Letter I have writt and subscribed with my own

hand at Edinburgh the twenty seven day of July one thousand seven hunder and thirty years.

I am, your
Unfortunate tho obediente Wife
Rachell Erskine.

Lady Grange lived for some months outside Edinburgh, but bored of country life

I took a chamber in a private house near to my lord's lodging, that I might have the pleasure to see the house that he was in, and to see him and my children when going out and in.

Events were not quite as straightforward as the lady portrayed, for she '*shamelessly cried up to the windows injurious reproaches, and would not go away, though entreated.*' One Sunday she followed her daughter and '*fell upon her with violent scolding and curses … Thus she became a disgrace to herself, her husband, and her children, and especially a ruin to her daughters*'.

LADY GRANGE IN EDINBURGH.   313

ORIGINAL LETTER OF SEPARATION, &c., RACHELL CHIESLY
TO JAMES ERSKINE OF GRANGE.

27TH JULY, 1730.

MY DEAR,—Since you are angry with me & will not live with me I promise that if you'l allow me a hundred pounds Str : yearly and pay it at two Terms in the year, in full of all I can ask or crave of you during the time I retire, and if you'l drop the Process of Separation you have raised against me befor the Commisars of Edinburgh then I will retire and live by my self for five years from the date hereof and shall not trouble you nor sett my Foot within your Doors in Town or Country and I also expect you'l [give] me such Household furniture Linnings & Plate as you think fitt for my service and use & I will instantly on your acceptance hereof retire from your House and fulfill what is above on Honour. This Letter I have writt and subscribed with my own hand at Edinburgh the twentyseven day of July one thousand seven hunder & thirty years.

I am, Your

Unfortunate tho obediente Wife
Rachell Erskine.

To
JAMES ERSKINE OF GRANGE.

16-1 Deed of separation

In an age when a good marriage was vital for daughters, the latter comment bore great weight with families. Even Lady Grange's friends and relations who had arranged the separation appear to have regarded her as impossible, and that her seclusion was desirable for the sake of the family.

As Lord Grange later wrote, '*These were things that could not be redressed in a court of justice, and we had not then a madhouse*'. He also wrote, in 1741, to Thomas Hope of Rankeilor that

> *it was incumbent on the relations and friends of the family, for the sake of … the person who made all the disturbance, to wish that proper and necessary measures might be taken to prevent it for the future…*

Laudable and understandable reasoning, but not exactly what happened later. Somewhere between the reasoned arguments and the reality occurred a gross miscarriage of justice.

Simon Fraser, 11th Lord Lovat

This slippery but ingenious rogue was the probable instigator of the whole plot. He has been more favourably described as 'the last and oldest of the great Celtic-Scottish chiefs'.

Machiavellian Lord Lovat certainly was, but there is more to this complex and much-derided character, for from his youth his enemies were voracious in their attacks.

As Master of Lovat he carried away the Dowager Lady Lovat to his island fastness in the River Beauly and there forcibly married her. The tale is told of a local priest being 'persuaded' to conduct the ceremony, the pipes played at their loudest to drown the lady's denials of the vows. Those same pipes drowned any further objections as the Master's retainer slit the Dowager's stays with his dirk preparatory to consummation of the marriage. After three months the lady was returned to her family – it is said with some reluctance – but for this act Simon was outlawed, fled in 1703 to France and became a Jacobite spy.

In the '15 he changed sides and led his clan for the Government, thus, eventually, earning a pardon and the much-coveted title with the Lovat estates. However,

Lovat's primary focus was always for his own benefit, and to this effect he would swing to the prevailing wind and he was – finally – out in the '45. Lovat was indebted to Grange for legal advice in gaining his estates, and the two were obviously close friends. Lovat, 'According to his Machiavellian talents, appears as the director of their enterprise'.

~

Two further people were closely involved in the continuing 'sequestration', if not in the actual abduction itself. The first was Norman MacLeod, 22nd Chief of MacLeod, and the other was Sir Alexander Macdonald 14th of Sleat.

Whether or not they were true Jacobites is debatable, for in an age when mere suspicion of being Jacobite laid a person open to charges of treason, few committed their innermost thoughts and convictions to paper. They may well have been doing what many, many similar families were doing – keeping both options open.

Chapter Two – The plot

There is some doubt as to how deeply Grange was involved in Jacobite affairs at this time, but certainly Walpole distrusted him. That Lady Grange was a thorough nuisance to her husband, children and family is clear; but whether her evidence was conjectural or factual and whether she posed a risk to certain Jacobite sympathisers we have no firm proof. The Lords Grange and Lovat clearly felt she was a risk, and persuaded others that action was needed. Lord Grange:

You will remember with what lying impudence she threatened Lord Grange and many of his friends with accusations of high treason and other capital crimes.

In 1732:

The Stuarts were a dynasty but recently dethroned, struggling to overthrow the dominant power. [But]

There are now few or none who feel what it was to be a Jacobite, when that name incurred the peril of the gibbet and the axe.

The tipping-point came in January 1732. On the eve of his departure for the south Grange heard that his wife also intended to visit London and work against him. Grange was confident that in Edinburgh the situation was contained, but in London,

What effect her lies may have, where she is not so well known ... one cannot certainly know: but if proper measures be not fallen on against it, this creature may prove troublesome. At any rate, this wholle affair will require a great deal of diligence, caution and address.

The die was cast – Lady Grange had to be 'sequestered'.

Grange secretly cancelled his wife's coach seat and the plot swung into effect. Lady Grange had taken rooms next to her husband's house *'the house belonging to Margaret Maclean, a Highland woman'*. Mistress Maclean must have been privy to the plot, for she sent her servants to bed an hour and a half before usual.

... upon the 22nd January 1732, after eleven o'clock at night ... then rushed in some Highland men, whom I had seen frequently attending my Lord Lovat, ... who threw me down upon the floor in a barbarous manner, and I cried out murther. Then they stopt my mouth, and dang out several of my teeth, and I bled; and abused my face most pitifully with their hard rude hands, till there was no skin on my face all below my eyes; for I was always putting out the cloaths as fast as put in ... and I defended myself with my hands, and beat with my heels upon the loft, in hopes the people below would hear. ... they had wrestled so long with me, that it was all I could breath, and then they carried me downstairs as if they had a corps.

Blindfolded and tied, she was by now powerless to resist such force; bundled into a waiting sedan chair she was sat upon the knee of the occupant, who held her tightly with his arms, although:

> *I made all the struggle I could. The chair carried me off very fast, and took me without the ports; [city gates] and when they opened the chair, and taken the cloth off my head to let me get air, I perceived, it being clear moon light, that I was a little way from Multer's Hill, [now St James' Square] and that the man on whose knee I sat was one Alexander Foster of Carssbonny, who had there six or seven horses and men with them, who said all these were his servants, though I knew some of them to be Lord Lovat's.*

Alexander Foster mounted one of the horses and Lady Grange was tied behind him with a cloth *'that I might not leope off'*, and she was gagged and blindfolded. They rode all that *'frosty, cold, bitter night'*, Foster refusing to stop even when the lady begged him to do so to relieve a stitch in her side from being so constrained. *'… it being Saturday we met no body'*, and at dawn, cold and weary, they were a little beyond Linlithgow. Gratefully the party stopped at Muiravonside, after some 20 miles of night-time travelling.

> *When he saw that day was approaching, he [Foster] took me into a house which belongs to John Macleod, who is an advocate, whose servant had known of my coming, and met me with candles in their hands at the far end of the entry … so that they knew of my coming … he presently took me up stairs to a very good bed-room, which had a fire, and good linnings [linen] on the bed, which I looked to, and found Mr Macleod's name on them'*

John MacLeod was a highly successful advocate, an active Jacobite agent during the '15 and a Privy Councillor to Prince Charles in the '45; however, he was not attainted, and died in his own bed. No doubt, as a careful lawyer, he took pains to be absent from his house during Lady Grange's stay, for no mention is made by her of him being there. To the servants Lady Grange explained *'whose wife I was, and that I was stolen'* – all to no avail. A man was mounted guard within her bedroom all that Sunday,

*for which reason I would not throw off my cloaths
for as weary and cold as I was, Sandy Fraser was so
barbarous and cruel.*

About seven that night Lady Grange was again forcibly
mounted on a horse and tied as before, travelling south
of Falkirk,

*and through the Tore Wood, which way I knew all,
having travelled it before … he [Foster] brought me
streight to Wester Pomeise, [now Steuarthall]. He
took me through a laigh [low] vault, and then into a
room of[f] the vault, the windows of the room being
nailed with thick boards, and no light in the room;
but in a little closet, a little slitt … and a very ugly
bed without a roof, a timber chair with the half of
a bottom in it; and there I was kept a close prisoner
for thirteen or fourteen weeks, not having liberty as
much as go without doors; and two doors lockt on
me, cross bars on the outside'.*

Confined in what was little better than a dungeon, the
tenant farmer's wife and two servants looked after Lady
Grange.

*They kept me so long close prisoner, that it endan-
gered my health, and I grew sick, and Andrew told
Mr Foster he would allow me to go out, and that
he would not have a hand in my death; and then I
was allowed to go to the high rooms, and to go to the
court to get the air much against Mr Foster's will.*

Lady Grange:

*give them some thing to tell the ministers of Stirlin
Hamilton and Erskine that I was prisonr in Pomeise
but all in vain. I was their near seven moneth…*

With Lady Grange gone, her husband got on with his life
in Edinburgh. Her friends and family seemed content to
let the abduction pass, and assumed – or found it more
convenient to assume – that she was firmly but comfortably held somewhere. For as her legal agent wrote eight
years later:

16-2 Wester Polmaise – Lady Grange was held in the tower, at the far left.

after she was carried off and being assured she was well entertained and cared for, I thought it best not to move in that affair. And now this is the first time I have heard from her'.

Chapter Three – Journey to the Highlands

The initial abduction had been put into place in some haste; time was needed to arrange the permanent confinement of Lady Grange in some more isolated part of the country, but her efforts to alert the outside world made this ever more urgent. In August Lovat's page came with three other men.

Lady Grange:

> *I had kept my bed all that day* [15th] *with grief and sorrow Peter and James Fraser tho I was naked took me up by force they set me on a horse behind Mr Foster I fainted dead with grief as they set me on the horse, And:* [Andrew] *Leishman rode that nights journy with me, when ever I cri'd they came to stope my mouth, they rode to the highlands with me our guide a Servant of Sir Alexander Macdonald Rondall Macdonald…*

They travelled by Stirling Bridge, but as Lady Grange

wrote *'after that I knew no more of the way'*. North they went, the road lit by moonlight, and at dawn they sheltered in a house.

The next night [16th and 17th]:

> *they set my Lord Lovat's footman, James Fraser, before me, and tied me to him, that I might not leap off; and rode all night with me, and brought me …*
> *I knew not how far into the Highlands.*

And so the abduction continued, travelling at night and sheltering by day. If Lady Grange attempted to cry out at the few houses they passed, *'then they offered to stop my mouth'*. Even if she attracted attention, her captors were armed with the excuse that she was a madwoman, with whom they were returning home after a visit to a healing pool. As the distance increased from Stirling the captors felt more confident, for on Friday 17th, '*it being far in the Highlands, by four in the afternoon they set me on a horse again, and rode all night'*.

She was lodged the next day in a barn:

> *Upon Saturday … [at] night they set me on a horse again, and carried me among the Highland hills, and rode till it was near morning, and laid me down on the grass, being very weary; and they rode all the Sabbath; the side of a hill, and the way was so bad, that it was not rideable, [Corrieyairack Pass] for they carried me in their arms; we were at an open shills [sheiling] all that night, and the next day the [River Tarff] waters were so high, that we could not cross till it was near night, then they got me on horse and carried me to a place called Milltown … I was never in bed all the time we came from Pomeise.*

Milltown I believe was Newtown, three miles south-west of Fort Augustus, on Lovat's land – where better to hide an abducted woman than close to the bustle of a military fort then building.

After being a captive for eight months, and forced to ride at night to she knew not what fate, Lady Grange must have been physically and mentally exhausted. She was to have two weeks much-needed respite, for:

With their rude hands they had hurt one of my breasts. I was kept there sixteen days, and all the company left me, but James Watson's herd. This was on my Lord Lovat's ground.

Glad though she was for the rest, poor Lady Grange's journeys were by no means over.

Chapter Four – Voyage to the Heisker Islands

Lady Grange:

[Alexander] *Grant came on the … September* [probably the 6th] *and set me on a horse by force, at night, and put me in a boat, which was in a loch,* [Oich] *about a mile from Milltown. They crossed the loch with me, and James Fraser left me there some nights without, and some nights in byres. After we crossed the loch, and again the 9th of the month* [September] *we came to a loch-side on Glengarie's ground.*

They had travelled through the heartland of MacDonnell of Glengarry to the shores of Loch Hourn, a sea loch thrusting deep into the mainland. Alexander Macdonald – tenant of the Heisker Islands, which belonged to his kinsman, Sir Alexander Macdonald of Sleat – was waiting at Kinlochournhead with a sloop to convey her the 120 miles of open sea to Heisker.

They dragged me by force, and I cried bitterly out; they were all Highlanders, and nobody understood me; and took me into a sloop, of which Alexander Macdonald is master ... who told me ... he was ordered to take me home to his own isle, and keep me there till further orders. I told him I was stolen out of Edinburgh, and brought there by force, and it was contrary to the laws what they were doing.

Although certainly against her will, Lady Grange had become something of a local celebrity, but her ending comment is one of infinite pathos.

We lay long on the loch for want of wind, and young Scoto's son and his father's brother came into the sloop the time that the sloop lay in the loch. They came with design to see me, but not to relieve me.

On the 19th September:

there came in a son of Dornicks, called John Macleod, and William Toling, [Tolme] *who lives on Macleod's ground ... and Rory Macdonald, brother to Castleton, and they all understanding the language, I told them all my misfortunes; and William Toling said he was at Edinburgh the time I was stolen, and promised he would tell Renkiller* [Thomas Hope of Rankeillor] *where I was to be taken.*

It seems incredible to me that none of these 'gentlemen' offered any sympathy or assistance to Lady Grange – even Tolme, who promised to pass a message, did nothing. Perhaps it is merely a sign of the power and influence wielded by the likes of Lovat, MacLeod and Macdonald, for, 'Each clan was so devoted to its chief that any measure directed by him was little examined, never disputed, or betrayed'.

Some years later, having kept silent, William Tolme was MacLeod's factor – what a coincidence!

They cleared the mouth of Loch Hourn on the 19th of September, and were eleven days crossing the Minch and navigating the tricky, rock-strewn channels of the Sound of Harris to the Heisker Islands.

We were storm-stay'd by the way, and we were in hazard of being lost before we came to Hesker, which was a poor miserable island. Upon the 30th day of the month we came there.

The Heisker or Monach Islands lie some eight miles west of North Uist – five low-lying islands, the three main ones connected by sandy spits at low water. At that time it had about 70 inhabitants and Lady Grange correctly observed that *'It was but a small island, none in it but cottars, and his servants'.* Now sheep graze the islands, inhabited only during the summer by a few lobster fishermen.

The Monachs must have seemed to Lady Grange the uttermost ends of the world:

'I was in the island Hesker ten months before I got bread, [only oatcakes] and suffered much cold and hunger, and many hardships and barbarous usage. I was in that strait almost I wanted stockings, shoes, and many other necessarys. And Macdonald said he had no orders to give me any meat but what they eated themselves; but had no orders for cloaths [clothes]. After I was near a year in his custody, he said he would go and tell them from whom he got me, that he thought it was a sin to keep me, and that he would let me away, and that he had writ twice or thrice about what necessarys I wanted, but got no answer.

True to his word, Alexander Macdonald went to see his Chief to plead for some leniency, but returned with a flea in his ear:

he was bidden to treat me harshly, and do nothing but was his pleasure, and to cross me in every thing. Though he got me bread, I was much more hardly dealt with than he had done the first year…'

He was forbidden to let Lady Grange go until he had further orders, or to allow her to write to her friends, or *'tell me the place of the world I was in. I was many months there before I knew whose ground I was on'.*

She tried to get a message to the minister of North Uist, *'one Mr John Maclean … to come and see me and pray for the distress of my family'* but that Christian man demurred

She also tried to escape, for we have just the one sentence, full of pathos: '*I sent a man for a boat and he ran away with my money.*'

With Alexander Macdonald a reluctant jailer, and his Chief '*sorry he had meddled in such an affair and did not know how to get out of it*', matters came to a head. Alexander was summoned to Uist in May 1734 to meet with his Chief, together with the Captain of Clanranald and Roderick MacLeod WS, whose sister was married to the Captain.

> ... *on the 14 of Jun: John Macleod and his Brother Normand came with their Galley to the Huskyre for me they were very rude and hurte me sore. Oh alas much have I suffer'd often my skin mead black and blew ... Alexander Macdonald told me he knew not where I was going to, and John Macleod said he was taking me to the Orkney islands. ... He was in such terror that it should be known that I was in his custody ...*

By this meticulous recording of names and relationships Lady Grange clearly hoped that those involved in her abduction would at some stage be brought to task – none ever were.

~

Whilst she was immured on Heisker, in Edinburgh her husband gave scarce a thought to his hapless wife – unless it was one of gratitude that his life was more peaceful without her! With his brother, the Earl of Mar, dead, and the 7th Earl childless and ineffective, Lord Grange was now the heir. He still cherished political ambitions, saying that '*the interests of the family of Mar depends on it*', and was duly elected an MP. However, he was not a success, and when the news broke in 1740 of Lady Grange's incarceration her husband was a bitter and disappointed man, already failing in influence.

Chapter Five –
St Kilda: on the edge of the world

Sir Alexander Macdonald of Sleat had finally managed to rid himself of his costly, unwanted, and for her part – most unwilling, guest. He had persuaded his close friend Norman MacLeod of MacLeod to accept custody for Lady Grange, for 'MacLeod was incapable of refusing a request'. MacLeod owned the St Kilda archipelago, 100 miles west of the mainland, 38 miles north-west of Heisker, and thither Lady Grange was bound. In 1734 they were as remote from Britain as was Mongolia, and probably less well understood. There were about 70 inhabitants living in primitive conditions, but generally without want in good years. They had 1000 small sheep, 40 cows and 10 ponies on Hirta – the one inhabited island – with more sheep on Soay and Boreray. The St Kildans grew oats and barley on the poor soil, but these crops were only gained by intensive labour and manuring, tasks usually carried out by the women and children. For fuel they burnt turf, carted down from the hill by pony in wicker panniers, for there was no peat or trees on any of the islands.

However, the main harvest was from the seabirds nesting in countless numbers on the cliffs – the eggs and bodies all provided a bounteous food source. They were either salted or stored in the cleits – ingenious dry stone structures which filtered moisture from the wind and air-dried the food stored within. Each fulmar also provided nearly a pint of oil, which was used in the *crusie* lamps, for medicinal purposes, and as part-payment of rent, as were feathers from all the birds. The men were superb cragsmen, using 180-foot long ropes of plaited cowhide to lower themselves down the cliffs; to protect the ropes from chafing on rocks they were enclosed in sheepskin, and each rope was handed down from father to eldest son. For the more accessible cliffs 60-foot ropes of plaited horsehair were lighter and easier to handle.

Fish were caught from the rocks, or in calm weather from the one boat possessed by the St Kildans, for there were few safe landing places; in winter the boat was drawn up well ashore and filled with stones and turf to prevent its being blown away. Nor was there any safe anchorage for visiting vessels:

16-3 Hirta, the main island of St Kilda

This bay is so open … [and] … must be, in my opinion, an unsafe road for vessels of any burden before the latter end of April and after the middle of August.

The islands were tacked [leased] to Macleod's kinsman, known as the Steward of St Kilda; he was usually based on Pabbay, a highly fertile island in the Sound of Harris. To recoup his rent – and, no doubt, make a handsome profit – the Steward taxed the St Kildans heavily. There was thus little incentive for them to produce more than needed for their subsistence and basic rent. And yet:

… in the balance of unprejudiced reason, the St Kildians possess as great a share of true substantial happiness, as any equal number of men elsewhere.

~

To these islands – in ways more remote than many a foreign outpost – Lady Grange was destined.

… they took me to St Kilda. John Macleod is call'd Stewart of the Island he left me in a few days, no body lives in it but the poor natives it is a viled nasty stinking poor Isle. I was in great miserie in the Husker but I'm ten times worse and worse here … He left me in a very miserable condition, but had no provisions for me but what the island afforded, and nobody to wait of me that understood me, but one ill-natured man [Finlay McDonald] *who understood a little English, and explained to others what I wanted; and he was not only ill-natured, but half-witted, and one day drew out his durk to kill me.*

The lady forbore to explain that she was attempting to belabour Finlay with a candlestick at the time – he only avoided the beating by 'taking to his heels before she could have at him'!

Her two-roomed cottage – normally used by the Steward on his annual visit – is said by some [albeit biased] accounts to have been well furnished and that Lady Grange had ample provisions and was comfortably clothed – including 3 silk gowns [on St Kilda?!].

She is reported to have had:

a cottage of two small apartments, tolerably well furnished, and a girl to wait upon her, and provided with a sufficiency of good food and clothing. Of educated persons the island contained not one, except for a short time a Highland Presbyterian clergyman, named Roderick MacLennan. There was hardly even a person capable of speaking or understanding the English language within reach. No books, no intelligence from the world in which she had once lived. Only once a year did a steward come to collect the rent paid in kind by the poor people; and by him the lady was regularly furnished with a store of such articles, foreign to the place, as she needed… Thus she had no lack of the common necessaries of life; she only wanted society and freedom.

How true this is we don't know, but Lady Grange thought otherwise, for Thomas Hope wrote:

of the wretchedness of the lodging – an earthen maist floor – rain and snow coming thro' walls and roof, and thence an necessity to scoop out the water, and take the snow by handfuls from behind the bed.

Robert Chambers, who saw many original documents, now missing, affirmed that

She was kind to the peasantry, giving them from her own stores; and sometimes had the women come and dance before her; but her temper and habits were not such as to gain their esteem. Often she drank too much; and when anyone near her committed the slightest mistake, she would fly into a furious passion, and even resort to violence.

Given her reputation for drunkenness in Edinburgh her husband may well have wished Lady Grange would drink herself to death. Indeed,

upon the third night after her establishment on St Kilda, she was found lying beside the rum cask, in a condition which obliged the steward and his servants to lift her from the ground, and carry her to bed.

After what she had endured, who can blame the poor woman!

For better or worse, with silk gowns and tea service or not, Lady Grange was to be immured on St Kilda for six and a half years. It seems hard on the islanders to be taxed so heavily for her upkeep, but the Steward had so decreed, and they dared not gainsay him.

A chance of rescue must have seemed possible with the arrival in the summer of 1734, shortly after herself, of the newly ordained Minister for St Kilda, Roderick MacLenann and his wife Katherine.

> *… a minister and his wife came to the island, to whom I am exceeding much obliged; and had it not been for the care he and she took, I had died for want of meat, for there were no provisions sent me but two pecks of flour, and what the place can afford, such as milk and a little barley knocked, and that forced them by threatenings, for the people is very poor, and much oppressed. I have nobody to serve me but a little Highland girl and the minister and his wife must explain to her. He is a serious and devout man, and very painfull [painstaking] and what time he can spare from his business he is so good as to come see me. I am not sure whose hands this may come to, but if I be dead, I beg my friends may be kind to reward this minister and his wife, for he hath helped to preserve my life, and made it comfortable the time I lived.*

As Lady Grange wrote to Thomas Hope:

> '*When he went from this island* [probably to attend a Presbytery meeting on Harris] *he resolved to go to Edinburgh …* [and] *I gave him a bill on you and two others of my friends, that they might know where I was; but his life being threatened he left this island, and he was after hindered either to go to Edinburgh, or to write to any body about me … he is in such fear of his life, and his uncle's. Some other of the ministers*

were angry at him for the care and concern he had taken of me. I am not sure who of my kin and friends is dead, or who is alive; but I beg whosoever hands this first comes to, to cause write it over in a fair hands, and to shew it to all my friends'.

Lady Grange tried to bribe the Steward with a promise of three thousand marks [nearly seven years the Minister's salary] if he would convey her to any place from whence she could reach Edinburgh, but he refused. One year a vessel called for water, and as soon as she heard of it Lady Grange sent the minister's wife to tell the crew of her situation – Mrs MacLennan got there too late.

Roderick MacLennan was at odds with the Steward from the first, for the latter resented providing sustenance for the Minister. MacLennan complained that the:

Laird of MacLeod had refused to assist him with the provision of a house and cow's grass, and that his Steward of the Isle gives him no Encouragement.

The Minister was also not popular with the islanders, and later events showed that poor MacLennan was out of his depth as a Minister. One account likens him to:

one of those illiterate and wretched catechists to whom, in the remote Highlands and Isles, the instruction of the people had been committed after the banishment of the ancient clergy.

In spite of all these difficulties the MacLennans survived five years before they abandoned St Kilda and its inhabitants, in July 1739:

being much Discouragement [discouraged] by the harsh Treatment his Family met with from the Steward in so much that he intends not again to return thither, and Craves to be Employed by the Society Elsewhere.

Aware that the Minister planned to lodge complaints against him, John MacLeod, Steward of St Kilda set out to destroy the Minister's reputation, gathering statements from the St Kildans 'touching several Immoralitys, where-of Mr McLennan is said to have been guilty when there'.

Other powerful forces joined in, alleging:

> certain malicious and vile practices whereof Mr Roderick MacLennan late Minister there had been guilty which are vouched by Documents in the hands of Mr John MacLeod, Advocate.

MacLennan was powerless; wary of the allegations against him, the SPCK chose not to re-employ him although the case dragged on until June 1742, when it was quietly dropped.

~

The MacLennans carried away with them painful memories of their time on St Kilda; but for Lady Grange their daughter carried away, hidden in a ball of wool, letters to her kinsman, Thomas Hope of Rankeillor. They were to take over a year to reach their destination.

Chapter Six – The kidnapping made public

MacLennan's family had brought to Edinburgh more than his complaints to the Society. The Minister had once been *'in such fear of his life'* that he refused to deliver letters from Lady Grange, but his wife, I think, was of sterner stuff. It would appear that Mrs MacLennan realised the powerful forces ranged against her husband, and how parlous was their situation. She now had little to lose by delivering the letters – probably without the knowledge of her husband – and possibly much to gain, for Lady Grange had written:

> *I beg my friends may be kind to reward this minister and his wife, for he hath helped to preserve my life, and made it comfortable the time I lived.*

Seventeen months after leaving St Kilda the letters from Lady Grange were delivered – and with devastating effect.

~

The letters arrived at the house of Thomas Hope of Rankeillor [Lady Grange's legal agent] on 11 December 1740, '... *left att my House ... by an unknown hand*'. Lady Grange had instructed, '*I beg whosoever the hands this comes first to, to cause write it over in a fair hand, and to shew it to all my friends*'.

Manuscript copies of were quickly made and distributed around Edinburgh, soon awash with gossip.

This place is again filled with the story of Lady Grange at Present an Inhabitant of the Island of St Kilda, from where she has found means to get Letters conveyed to some of her friends here particularly to Rankeilor with Accounts of the way of her being seized in the night time while in bed in Edinr by persons in Disguise.

Lord Grange immediately went on the offensive and complained to Thomas Hope that:

strange storyes were spread all over the town of Edinburgh, and made the talk of coffee houses and tea tables, and sent, as I have ground to apprehend, to several other places of Great Britain.

But Rankeillor staunchly replied

... these letters were delivered into my house open, days after others had got theirs, and as to the narrative of her case, it was copied by those into whose hands it first came before I saw it so that I could not answer for that, or hinder its being made the publick talk of tea tables or coffee houses...

At the foot of one letter Lady Grange had marked '*To the Solicitor*'; this was Charles Erskine of Tinwald, in Lady Grange's absence promoted to Lord Advocate.

St Kilda, Jan. 20, 1738
Sir, ... I have the Honour to be your Relation and I know you have much interest [influence] *with Lord Grange ... you know I'm not guilty of any crime except that of loveing my husband to much, he knowes very well he was my idol and now God*

has made him a rode [rod] *to scourgeth me … but if friends cannot prevaile with Ld Greange let me have the benefit of the law[.] it is impossible for me to write or you to imagine all the miserie and sorrow and hungre and cold and hardships of all kindes that I have suffer'd since I was stolen …*

Whatever her faults, one cannot not help be touched by the pathos in these words. After a lengthy detailing of her abduction, journeys and imprisonment Lady Grange concludes:

the Society sent a minister here I have given him a much fuller account then this and he wrat it down. You may be sure I have much more to tell then this, When this comes to you if you hear I'm alive do me justes and relieve me, I beg you make all hast but if you hear I'm dead do what you think right befor God.

Thomas Hope received the letters on 11th December 1740, and attempted to deliver the one above addressed 'To the Solicitor'. The letter is a masterpiece of diplomacy and tact, offering Lord Grange a way out, accepting in advance the Lord Advocate's advice, but at the same stating firmly that if Lady Grange is not released then he will have no hesitation in taking 'all legall steps'.

My Lord,
… the affair is concerning poor Lady Grange, I in-close you a Letter from her of an old date, and shall shew you on[e] to myself of the same date … She [Lady Grange] *left a Factory* [power of attorney] *for me with my wife, a little before her intended Journey to London* [in January 1732]. *I told her I would never use it till I heard she was at a distance from her husband so as she could not disturb him. … She bids me apply to your Lod/ first, and indeed I wauld have don it whether or not for your advice is so tender* [discreet] *ane affair, and if it cannot be compromised among friends, that I should call for her money and take all legall steps to relieve her. She has been so harshly and barbarously used, that I dar say her Husband knows nothing of it, for his friends*

from him I suppose alway assured me all care was taken of her … I think in duty I cant with stand this call, but most follow out a course to restore her to a seeming liberty and a comfortable life: And it shall be don with that caution and moderation as your Lops/ shall direct, and Grange and his friends could wish; though she has mett with such cruelty and barbarity as ever a Chrystian did, and more than any almost is able to bear. I am sure I never thought she could be alive under such hardships …
I shall have the honour to wait on you, as I have of being
Sir
Your most obet humble Servant
Edenr. Saturday 13th Dec', 1740

Rankeillor seems to have consulted with his lawyers, then in early January 1741 proposed to Lord Grange that his wife should be quietly set at liberty, without recourse to the law. That he and her other relations would advise her strongly not to molest her husband or children; and that she should live with relations in Aberdeenshire. As with the Lord Advocate, he also appears to have backed up these very reasonable proposals with a threat of legal action if the lady was not set at liberty.

Lord Grange, in character, obviously considered that attack was the best form of defence; at no time in a lengthy reply does he refer to Lady Grange by name or as his wife, but invariably calls her 'that person'. Nor does he make any mention of what had happened to her in the eight years since her abduction – callousness that is hard to imagine. He strongly vindicated himself and accused Rankeillor of a:

want of consideration and judgement … very injurious to me and my children, and all interested in them, and to several others who deserve more regard and respect; and the welfare of the person you say you have so much concern for could not have prompted a considerate man to take such a course.

Grange continued with a long account of all his wife's faults, that he had tried his best in an impossible situation, and that Hope and her other relations had agreed that a separation was in the best interests of all concerned. But he then goes on to shoot himself in the foot:

> … [the family] *would not but desire that that person should alwise be treated, not only with humanity, but with all the care and tendernes that she would let it be possible to use towards her. … and that the person has alwise been under such direction and care as they could trust themselves, and family, … and that ane allowance plentifully sufficient for all the comfortable accommodation of life has been duly paid, and … if they had suspected it to have been otherwise, they would have been more careful and earnest to redress it than any others would be.*

This last is a neat sideswipe at Hope, and others, as to why no one had made any complaint of it until now, even though the actual abduction was well known. Lady Grange's exact whereabouts may have been uncertain, but as Thomas Hope wrote to the Lord Advocate, all *'were assured she was well entertained and cared for'*.

Having tried vindication and veiled threats – *'One cannot doubt but that this is a serious thing to many more than me'* – Grange now makes an appeal for the sake if the family:

> … *Judicial proceedings must bring these and other facts into publick records, open to the perusal of the present age and posterity, for if one be attacked, he must plead and prove what is proper for his defence, though otherwise very improper to be mentioned.*

As to Hope's specific proposals, Grange completely ignores the one that his wife should be set at liberty, for to admit she had been imprisoned leaves him and the others involved open to charges of abduction and imprisonment.

~

The accusations had also reached Skye, for Sir Alexander Macdonald wrote to his lawyer and friend denying involvement of himself or Macleod.

> … *As to the story of My Lady Grange whiche you*

say mak's so much Clamour, I'me surprised how My Name shou'd be mention'd ine it as I never had any acquaintence of Her Nay never saw her that I know of … As to My Nighbour McLeod Every body that Knows him Know's his Passion is not for keeping Old Women.

Thomas Hope clearly had no wish to start legal proceedings for the release of Lady Grange, for that would have meant washing the Erskine's dirty linen in public. But from the tone of Grange's letter it was more than apparent that his lordship would use every legal obstruction he could to prevent his wife's release. Rankeilor did in fact start proceedings, but Grange, with his legal connections, managed to block them. Having failed diplomatically, Hope chartered a ship to Lady Grange.

Chapter Seven – A rescue attempt & the final years

On 12th February 1741 Thomas Hope chartered the sloop *Arabella* to proceed with Captain William Gregory to St Kilda and from there to rescue Lady Grange. Speed was crucial, for now that the lady's place of imprisonment was made public her captors would be sure to move her.

Thomas Hope penned a letter to MacLeod of MacLeod – a masterpiece of diplomacy to a powerful man, coupled with the threat, albeit unwilling on his part, to have recourse to the law as a last resort. The outside is addressed '*To The Honble The Laird of McLeod att his house of Dunnvegin in Skye*':

Sir,
In December last I received letters from the unfortunate Lady Grange dated at St Kelda January 1738 – describing her miserable condition and praying me to obtain her reliefe. This was Communicate to Mr Erskine of Grange att London and some of his

friends here, who both exprest their great unwillingness that any application should be made to a Court of Justice for her deliverance by a legal authority, nor indeed was that needfull, unless she should be detained where she was, or carryed some where else by force; I therefore have sent the bearer Captain William Gregory with his sloop Arabella in order to bring her away from St Kilda, and directed him, in case she should not be found there, though still alive, to repair furthwith to you and deliver this. ... to give the bearer your protection and assistance to discover where that unfortunate Lady is, and to bring her away with him ... if the bearer should not succeed, there will then remain no other remidy for me to pursue, but to trye ... the Laws ... But this I hope you will have the goodness to prevent, from the good character I hear of you, and for the sake and quiet of all Concerned, which I so wish and labour for. I am with all respect

Edinburgh, 14 February 1741.

When Captain Gregory reached St Kilda he found Lady Grange already taken elsewhere; he wrote to the Chief of MacLeod:

To the Honble the Laird of McLeod at present in or near Inverness

Sir,

According to orders and instructions from Mr Hope of Rankieller I went to the Island of St Kilda to enquire for the unfortunate Lady Grange but being well informed that she was removed from that place some time agoe, and likeway informed of the place of her present abode, It being in a place I can not goe conveniently with my vessel, my supt [supplementary] order was to waite upon [you] at Dunvegan and deliver the inclosed, but being well informed you was not at home I came here to Lorn where I am obliged to remain till I receive your answer which I humbly entreat by the Bearer hereof, and according to the answer I shall receive from you must take my resolution according to my instructions from my employer.

'Lorn' is probably Cardingmill Bay, near Oban.

Within five days Captain Gregory's letter was at Inverness, and MacLeod had penned a very circumspect reply:

Sir,
My return last night brought me yours of 28 letter
dated at Lorne alongst with a letter from Rankillar,
wherein you are pleased to tell me you have searched
St Kilda for unfortunate Lady Grange, that she was
not there, but that you've had information where
she is, you'll please on receipt of this lett me know
the particulars of your information, and in what
manner you think I can be of any service to you. I
shall then be able to judge what is proper for me to
do consonant with the Rules of Justice and Honour.

Discovering the Chief was in Inverness Hope despatched a further letter to him there; MacLeod kept the bearer waiting ten days before he replied. On receiving it Hope ordered Captain Gregory to continue at the Oban anchorage until further orders, but little more is heard of Gregory and the *Arabella*.

Knowing Lady Grange was taken elsewhere, Thomas Hope raised an action citing Lady Grange's letters, but powerful friends of Grange in the judiciary ensured its failure, for:

none of her children, or any friends acquainted with her former scandals, would interfere in her case … all of these tacitly acknowledged the justification of Lord Grange in the furore of his lady, and none offered any extenuation of her blame, or gave any countenance to the proceedings of her agent.

Lord Grange, in character, continued strongly to deny any wrongdoing; he instructed John Macleod, his lawyer:

I wish there may be proof of [it] *because all along*
I have been informed it is true viz that that person
has continued and still continues in the same courses
and disposition of fury, passion … Revenge, Lain
and Desire of strong drink, attempted threatenings
of Mischief etc. These have been and continue to be

reasons of confinement, which will be a main part of the future conferences, and will also be such if the Don after all will bring it before a Court'.

The sloop *Arabella* had found Lady Grange already gone from St Kilda – probably to Assynt, Harris and then Skye. By 1741 she had become indifferent to her fate, and, 'latterly she became gloomy and solitary, confined herself entirely in the day, and went abroad only at night'.

According to a Skye tradition she thus made little resistance when carried on board a vessel at St Kilda to avoid discovery by Captain Gregory. Being still winter the weather was atrocious, and:

As she was several days on board this small sloop, confined to a miserable hole of a cabin, in a boisterous sea, with a contrary wind, she suffered greatly from continued sickness; and when she arrived at Assint on the north-west coast of Sutherland, she was so weak that she was carried from the shore to the house of a shepherd where she was to remain. She remained in this place for several months, being allowed every freedom she desired, as she did not seem to have any wish to leave it, or wander far from the hut where she resided.

No doubt Lady Grange was at last resigned to being immured, and if her mind was indeed going she probably cared not where she was, as long as she was fed and comfortable. On one of her journeys it was said:

the person who had the management of the boat having beside him a rope, with a running noose at one end and a heavy stone at the other, intending according to his orders to fix the noose around the prisoner's neck and confine her immediately to the deep should the sloop of war come in sight.

It seems likely that for a year Lady Grange was transported between these places like so muchjetsam if the tale of the noosed rope is to be believed. One report says:

By that time her reason had given way, and she

These are to enform you that the first in this ffamilie departed this life about 3 of the Cloak fryday last being the tenth instant: which puts me to no small trouble in thir hard times when I cannot get any sort of Eatables to Buy, yet I will doe en it what I cann, and Seeing You are from the Countrey, & the principal men of your name saving watterstein & a few emore that can be of no use upon this Occasion

16-4 Letter from Rory MacNeill to Macleod of Macleod

wandered over Skye in a state of idiocy, supported by the charity of the people, until at length she was overcome by misery and disease and closed her chequered life at Idrigal, in Waternish…'

Mad she may well have been, but she was not destitute; Charles MacSween kept her on Skye from March to September 1742, and then handed her over to Rory Mac-Neill, a minor tacksman at Trumpan, and here 'that unfortunate Lady' would at last find peace. Rory MacNeill's letter below, reporting her death, shows a genuine compassion for his guest, and his accounts to MacLeod of MacLeod show she was well cared for – not before time.

Debit the Laird of MacLeod To Rorie McNiell

To Lady Grange board for one year	
& due the 5th current	£30.00.00
Necessaries provided for her	3.00.11½
Dunvegan 2d August 1744	

This when the salary of the St Kilda minister was £25 per annum!

Trumpan may ye 12ᵗʰ
1745

Honble Sir,
These are to inform you that the first in this familie departed this life about three of the Cloak fryday last – being the tenth instant. Which puts me to no small trouble in this hard times when I cannot get any sort of Eatables to buy, yet I will doe an if what I can … seeing you left me no written orders where or how to burie her in caice she should happen to die in this hous but I hope to see her decently interred Wednesday next.

I am as ever
Honble sir
Your most humble & obedient humble Servt
Rory Mac Neill

Her elaborate public internment, as befitted one of Lady Grange's rank, was in Duirinish churchyard, by Dunvegan, wherein are buried several MacLeod Chiefs. In fact, that coffin contained only turf and stones, for the actual body of Lady Grange had been quietly buried in the quiet of Trumpan churchyard, close to where she died. 'That unfortunate Lady' was finally at peace, and no longer a threat to her husband and her friends.

At Dunvegan, on 6th August 1745, Rory MacNeill's account with MacLeod of MacLeod was *'filled and cleared twixt us'*:

Debit MacLeod

To ane particular Acct. off expenses	
in Lady Grange's Internment:	£30.15.05
Do. her &c for Nine Moneths:	£22.10.00
	£53.05.05

On hearing of his wife's death, Lord Grange wrote from Westminster on June 1st 1745 – without one word of sympathy or regret – to his informant:

I most heartily thank you, my dear friend, for the timely notice you gave me of the death of that person. It would be a ridiculous untruth to pretend grief for it; but as it brings to my mind a train of various things for many years back, it gives me concern. Her retaining wit and facetiousness to the last surprises me. These qualities none found in her, no more than common-sense or good-nature, before she went to these parts; and of the reverse of all which, if she had not been irrecoverably possest, in an extraordinarily and insufferable degree, after many years' fruitless endeavours to reclaim her, she had never seen these parts. I long for the particulars of her death, which, you are pleased to tell me, I am to have by the next post.

The case of Lady Grange may yet have excited the chattering classes of the day, but with Bonnie Prince Charlie landing and the subsequent Rising, folk had other things on their minds. For Grange, however, it dragged on legally for another six years as Lady Grange left her estate to Mrs Hope and her three daughters. Thomas Hope now pressed their claim against Grange and a decreet was duly obtained, but after going to arbitration the matter was finally settled in 1751. Mrs Hope and her daughters renounced their claim against Lord Grange; he in turn repaid Thomas Hope all 'his advances in the account of Mrs Rachael Chiesly'.

Robert Chambers commented in 1824 that Lord Grange:

> does not appear to have ever felt a moment's compunction at leaving the mother of his children to pine and fret herself to death in a half-savage wilderness'. He justifies the sequestration 'as a step required by prudence and decency; and in shewing that the gross necessaries of life were afforded to his wife, seems to have considered that his whole duty towards her was discharged. Such an insensibility could not be peculiar to one man; it indicates the temper of a class and an age.

Writing in 1943 RC MacLeod comments fairly that:

Kind ladies' hearts may melt, and tongues wax warm in sympathy with the unhappy lady and her sorrowful times; … but, if Lady Grange had succeeded in bringing the wrath of the Hanoverian authorities down on some Jacobite-minded gentlemen, a few distressed widows and fatherless boys might have brooded on the memory of Lady Grange with little complacency.

On the whole we are constrained, willy-nilly, to concede there must have been pressing reasons for getting the lady lodged where she could do no harm. One cannot believe that such prominent men as those named could have embarked on such an unlawful business on account of some mere domestic troubles.

Surely the last words must come from Lady Grange herself:

… it is impossible for me to write or for you to imagine all the misserie and sorrow and hunger and cold and hardships of all kinds that I have suffered since I was stolen … I never read or heard of any Wife whatever was her crime so cruely and barbarously treatt as I have been.

Epilogue

So, our tale is told. Lady Grange at last found peace in Trumpan churchyard, overlooking the Minch. A fitting place for the end of a turbulent life.

But what did Fate have in store for the other players?

Lord Grange

At the time of his wife's abduction Lord Grange was already in financial trouble; Alexander Carlyle sums up the end of this odious man so succinctly and accurately that I cannot better it:

In 1748, Lord Grange was so much reduced in London that he accepted of two guineas from Robert Keith, then living with Field Marshall Lord Stair. By my lord's application he got a pension of £200. On his wife's death he married his old mistress, Fanny Lindsay [in about December 1745] and brought her down to Preston, where he still had the house and about 50 acres of land.

Lord Prestongrange's lady and my mother were the only two ladies who called on her, having been wheedled into it by the old gentleman, who to his other talents added a very irresistible form of flattery. Fanny took pet at not being visited, and made him return to London again, where in a year he died in obscurity, not being then so much thought of as to be despised or hated.

Lord Lovat

Having finally decided for Bonnie Prince Charlie, Lovat was arrested, escaped and fled to the fastness of an island in Loch Morar. In June 1746 he was finally captured 'lying on two feather beds not far from the side of the lake'. The last peer to be condemned for treason, he was found guilty by unanimous vote of all the peers assembled. On his way to the Tower the London mob were jubilant at the end of this old Jacobite. His coach tried to force a way through the crowds, and an old woman stepped forward.

"You'll get that nasty head of yours chopped off, you ugly old Scotch dog," she screamed through the open window.

"I believe I shall, you ugly old English bitch," retorted Lovat, witty to the end.

He met his death 'with exemplary dignity' – in his eighties, and after an eventful life, including three wives, he surely had little more to look forward to.

Norman MacLeod of MacLeod

Norman MacLeod was active on behalf of the government during the '45, but received scant reward. Having lost the trust of his friends in the North, nor gained the gratitude of those in the South, he returned to Scotland in 1756 but not to live at Dunvegan. Although still titular Chief, Culloden had meant the end of the old clan system and he was now merely a landlord, and retired to an estate near Edinburgh with its attractions. HHeavily indebted, racked by gout, sore eyes and his stomach, deserted by his friends and despised by many of his clansmen, Norman MacLeod, 'The Red Man', 22nd Chief of MacLeod, died in 1772.

As Canon MacLeod summed up his ancestor, 'If he did not abduct Lady Grange, he certainly treated her with great cruelty'.

Sir Alexander Macdonald of Sleat

Although Sir Alexander took no part in the '45, he was zealous on behalf of those of his kinsmen who had and frequently remonstrated with Cumberland at the excesses of his troops. When meeting with Cumberland for the first time, the Duke greeted him arrogantly.

'So, here comes the great rebel of the Isles'.

'If, Sir, I had been a rebel, you would never have crossed the Spey' replied the Chief boldly.

Both Sir Alexander and his wife did all in their power to assist the Prince in his escape and instructed their clansmen to do likewise. If he had not actually joined the Rising, Sir Alexander was sufficiently loyal to the cause to ensure the Prince escaped. Perhaps his last shreds of loyalty to the Hanoverian government that had restored his estates after the '15 were blown away by Cumberland's inaccurate and insensitive greeting.

Sir Alexander Macdonald, 7th Baronet and 14th Chief, died of pleurisy at Glenelg on 23 November 1746, on his way to London to plead for certain of his captured kinsmen.

Roderick MacLennan

The Minister delivered the letters from Lady Grange in December 1740 but now faced powerful adversaries; MacLeod of MacLeod could not deny that the lady had been kept on his island in poor conditions, and he thus sought to discredit the MacLennans as witnesses. In this he succeeded:

> Whatever the truth, Roderick MacLennan never really recovered his credibility as a missionary, and the unfortunate coincidence of his stay on St Kilda with the 'imprisonment' there of Lady Grange blighted his life thereafter'.

MacLennan was in Tongue, Sutherland, in 1743 but biased Presbytery there found him 'unacceptable to the People, useless in his Station, and that there is a necessity of removing him to Some other Place'.

In Thurso his 'performances were Satisfying to all the Hearers' but in Wick he was of no use as 'he cannot Speake the English Language so as to be well understood by the people'. Two years later he was appointed to the small island of Stroma, in the Pentland Firth, where he took the tack of a small farm. In 1751 he was adjudged 'with all his other Defects very Negligent and Lazie'; three years later he was 'as diligent and Active as can be Expected'. But in 1756 he was 'under an Indisposition that unfits him for teaching or being otherwise useful in this Station'.

The SSPCK, neglecting his years of service, however unsatisfactory, decided that Roderick MacLennan should be dismissed at the end of April 1757. The Presbytery of Caithness:

> He is still bad and disordered in his mind. He has been long in the Service, and will in all probability in a short time hence be in a miserable Condition, destitute of Bread for him and his Family.

Poor 'Mr Rorie', incompetent as a minister, maligned by his enemies but kind to Lady Grange, was in these few words confined to oblivion.

Sources

My primary source has been the published transcripts of the two letters dictated and/or written by Lady Grange from St Kilda. Secondary sources are of varying accuracy but were all cross-checked. The first published reference I can find to this strange affair is in *Boswell's Journal of a Tour to the Hebrides,* where he wrote at Raasay House in 1773 that, 'The true story of this Lady, which happened in this century, is as frightfully romantic as if it had been the fiction of a gloomy fancy'.

Samuel Johnson merely added wryly that, 'If MacLeod would let it be known that he had such a place for naughty ladies, he might make it a very profitable island'.

Primary sources & original documents

- The Edinburgh Magazine, November 1817 – *An Account of the Misfortunes of Mrs Erskine of Grange, Commonly called Lady Grange* This is the first widely published account of the affair, and contains a transcript of a manuscript copy of Lady Grange's letter, partly dictated to the Minister of St Kilda, Roderick MacLennan, but completed by Lady Grange after MacLennan left the island about August 1739.
- *Traditions of Edinburgh* by Robert Chambers. Published 1824 and revised 1865, pp 231-242.
- *Chambers Edinburgh Journal New Series, 7th March 1846 – The Story of Lady Grange.* William and Robert Chambers viewed several original papers, which now appear to be missing.
- *Letters of Lord Grange* – Miscellany of the Spalding Club Volume III, 1846. Several of these letters relate directly to Lady Grange, although most concern the Mar family.
- Tales of The Century or Sketches of The Romance of History between 1746-1846. By John Sobieski Stuart and Charles Edward Stuart. Published by James Marshall, Edinburgh 1847. On page 296 it states:

> This account is completed from two copies of the Narrative of Lady Grange, and documents and papers connected with her case, now in our possession. Where tradition has added any other notices their authority is marked in the margin.

However, as the brothers were almost certainly impostors – whose real name was Allen – their account must be read with caution; that said, they did appear to have seen several other contemporary documents connected with Lady Grange.

- The Proceedings of the Society of Antiquaries for Scotland – *An Episode in the life of Mrs Rachel Erskine, Lady Grange.* The author, David Laing, was a former secretary of the Society, and at the time he possessed the original letter from Lady Grange dated St Kilda, Jan. 20, 1738.
- *Chambers' Journal*, No. 551, July 18th, 1874 – *Story of Lady Grange.*
- *History* Volume XVI, April 1931 – *The Strange Story of Lady Grange* by R W Seton-Watson. An accurate summary of events, and Seton-Watson possessed the original letter, dated 14 February 1741, from Thomas Hope of Rankeillor to Norman MacLeod of MacLeod, informing him he had chartered Captain William Gregory of the sloop *Arabella* to proceed to St Kilda and relieve Lady Grange.

- Dunvegan Castle Archives: Dunvegan Vol 2/4/149-153.
- National Records of Scotland: NRAS3273/362. NRAS3273/366/1.
- National Library of Scotland: NLS: GB233/MS.3142; folio 21-22.

Secondary sources

- *Historical Memoirs of Rob Roy … Including Original Notices Regarding the Mysterious History of Lady Grange* by K Maclean. A highly fanciful account, inaccurate in many instances. Unfortunately it is often quoted elsewhere.
- *History and Traditions of the Isle of Skye* by Alexander Cameron, 1871.
- *Epistle from Lady Grange to Edward D Esq. Written during her confinement in the island of St Kilda*, 1799.
- *The Chiefs of Clan MacLeod* by Alick Morrison.
- *The MacLeods – Their History and Traditions* by The Rev. Canon R C Macleod of MacLeod. 1929.
- *The MacLeods – The History of a Clan* by I F Grant. 1981.
- *Lady Grange – A new Reading of her Story, introducing*

Lord Dun, by R C MacLeod. Clan MacLeod Magazine, 1943.

- *Lord Lovat of the '45* by Moray MacLaren. 1957.
- *Autobiography of Alexander Carlyle of Inveresk 1722-1805* – edited by John Hill Burton. 1910.
- *St Kilda – Church, Visitors and 'Natives'* by Michael Robson. 2005.
- *History of St Kilda by Reverend Kenneth Macaulay, 1764.*
- *St Kilda and Other Hebridean Outliers* by Frances Thompson. 1970.
- *Buildings of St Kilda* by Geoffrey P Stell and Mary Harman. RCAHMS 1988.
- *Clan Donald* by Donald J Macdonald of Castleton. 1978.
- *The Clan Ranald of Knoydart & Glengarry* by Norman H Macdonald FSA Scot. 1979.
- *Ancient Castles and Mansions of Stirling Nobility* by J S Fleming FSA (Scotland). 1902.
- *Stirlingshire Volume 2* – RCAHMS 1963.
- *Boswell's Journal of a Tour to The Hebrides with Samuel Johnson 1773.*
- *The Life and Letters of Duncan Forbes of Culloden, 1685-1747,* by George Menary. 1936.

- *Wade in Scotland* by J B Salmond. 1934.
- *The Military Roads in Scotland* by William Taylor. 1976.
- *Kilcumein and Fort Augustus* by Dom Odo Blundell. 1914.
- *A map of the King's Roads, Made by his Excellency General Wade in the Highlands of Scotland.* Thomas Willdey, 1746 [NLS shelfmark: Newman 1152(1)].
- Scottish History Society Miscellany XII – Fifth series, volume 7, 1994.
- There is an excellent CD of the High Court of Admiralty Scotland Records 1627-1750 by Sue Mowat and Eric J Graham.
- *The Hunt for Rob Roy: The Man and the Myths* by David Stevenson. 2004.
- Rob Roy MacGregor: His Life and Times by W H Murray. 1984

Ardsheal's Cave

*Of Charles Stewart of Ardsheal, his duel with Rob Roy, defeat at Culloden,
a perilous escape, exile & a happy ending for his son*

This is a tale of Charles Stewart, 5th of Ardsheal, and how he escaped to safety – with many hair-raising incidents – after the Jacobite Rising of 1745. Being tall and excessively large he was known as 'Big Charles' and when younger was a fine swordsman; he fought – and won – a duel with Rob Roy, and the full story will emerge later in our tale.

Ardsheal [spelt on some old maps Ardshiel] is in one of the most beautiful parts of Appin, that area between Loch Creran in the south and Loch Leven to the north. Nowhere in Appin is more than a few miles from the sea at Loch Linnhe, but it is largely mountainous land, with but a few good bits of arable scattered amongst the lower ground.

~

In 1732 Charles Stewart of Ardsheal was desirous of a wife, and duly paid his attentions to the elder daughter of John Haldane of Lanrick and Ruskie, near Callander. The lady, however, refused him, for her heart was already engaged to one Dundas of Mann, and as one old memoir continues:

… as he was retiring from the unsatisfactory

interview, he met, on the staircase of Lanrick Castle, the fair Isabel, who, in addition to her other charms, had the housekeeper's keys suspended from her girdle. The Laird must have had an eye for domestic economy as well as female beauty; for he immediately conceived the idea that she would make the better wife of the two sisters, and made her a proposal upon the spot. The young lady, however, required rather more time for deliberation, and he was obliged to submit to a period of suspense'.

Charles and Isabel were married that year, when she was nineteen, and by the time of this tale they had five children. In 1739 Ardsheal received his commission as Colonel, signed in France by the exiled James VIII.

At Duror Charles Stewart had a shop, in common with many another laird of the time, for it was they who possessed the means to finance the stock, and the shop provided all the necessities of life that his clansmen could not grow or make for themselves. It was actually run by his half-brother, James of the Glens, who was later to be wrongfully hanged for the murder of Campbell of Glenure, the tale of which was later immortalised by Robert Louis Stevenson in *Kidnapped*. Goods for the shop were purchased from a merchant in Leith called the Muileartach, who will feature again in our tale.

Bonnie Prince Charlie raised his standard at Glenfinnan on 19th August 1745 and duly summoned the clans. However, the Chief of the Appin Stewarts, Robert, 8th of Appin, was old and infirm, and his only son, Dugald, was summoned back from school in Edinburgh to lead the clan in support of the Prince. Dugald, whose mother was a Campbell, clearly had a more practical grasp of the political situation, for he replied without hesitation:

> I would rather spend the inheritance of Appin on the gay women of Edinburgh than risk it being lost striving for the Crown for the Prince, what I know cannot be done.

Dugald then beat a hasty retreat back to school in Edinburgh!

His father, naturally, was furious, and threatened to

disinherit Dugald – 'the son of the Campbell woman' as he called him – but the clan said they would kill Robert if he did so. The Chief then suggested that he appoint his son-in-law, Robert MacLachan of Strathlachlan, to lead the clan; but they would have none of it, saying they would only follow a Stewart, and that if MacLachan came anywhere near they would tear him to pieces. And this to one of their own, let alone to the English! Dismayed by his clan's intransigence Robert Stewart next suggested he appoint as Colonel his kinsman, Charles Stewart of Ardsheal. Whether he feared his great bulk would make him unwieldy in battle, or whether, like young Dugald Stewart, he considered the Rising a forlorn hope we do not know, but Ardsheal was initially reluctant to accept. His wife, however, had other ideas.

"If you, Charles, are not willing to become Commander of the men of Appin", said Lady Ardsheal, "stay at home and take care of the house and I myself will go and become their Commander".

Stinging words, to which Ardsheal had no choice but to accept command of the Appin Stewarts. He handed over management of the estate to James of the Glens and off he went to join the Rising, supported by 300 Stewarts – nearly one third of whom would not return to Appin. The standard bearers of the clan were the Carmichaels, and a wise man predicted than nine Donalds would fall protecting the standard – as we shall see later, the prophecy was duly enacted in all its grim detail.

The tale of the '45 Rising is too well known to bear repeating here, other than in outline. The gradual gathering of the clans, or at least some of them, for many clans were unwilling to rise again. Success at Prestonpans, when the Hanoverian army of Sir John Cope was routed; the capture of Edinburgh Castle and the heady reception of the Prince in the city – at least by some. The long march into England, receiving little of the expected support on the way; the bickering counsels-of-war at Derby, with the Prince keen to march on London, but short of men, money and arms. The fateful, and ultimately fatal, decision to return to Scotland; the long retreat north, the clansmen drifting away home to gather in the harvest, for if they did not their families would surely starve that winter. Success at Falkirk in January 1746, followed by retreat to Inverness in the depths of a bitter winter.

In February 1746 Ardsheal returned home to raise more men, but it all culminated with disaster at Culloden on the 16th of April that year. Division at the top was fatal, for the Prince and his commanders should have known their guerrilla troops were incapable of winning on a set battlefield against the cannon and disciplined regiments of the Hanoverian army. The Stewarts, as ever, fought bravely, and the Appin Banner – of light blue silk with a yellow saltire – was first carried into the battle by Donald Carmichael, and was stained by his blood when he fell. True to the prophecy, eight other Donalds, including a MacColl, fell protecting the flag, and it was left to the 18 year-old Donald Livingstone to save it. Tearing the cloth from its pole he wrapped it round his body, and, although badly wounded, he found a horse and delivered the standard to Appin himself. The Appin Banner still exists, and is now in the Museum of Scotland, Edinburgh

After such a crushing defeat there was little option for Ardsheal – and many another Highland laird – but to flee to the safety of France. But before he did so he resolved to see his wife and family once more, traditionally returning home astride a huge white stallion, nicknamed *Macphail* after a local strongman. Due to his great bulk no horse could for long carry the weight of Ardsheal until he purchased *Macphail* from the Muileartach in Leith; this gallant steed carried Ardsheal first to battle, then to escape, and finally to safety.

The new roads built by General Wade down the Great Glen enabled the faithful *Macphail* to carry Ardsheal swiftly home, but the Hanoverian troops were in pursuit. Conscious that they and retribution were close, Ardsheal ordered all of value in the house to be buried or hidden. Reunited briefly with his wife – long enough to conceive their sixth child – Ardsheal took to the precipitous slopes of *Sgurr Dhearg*, sheltering in the Red Pass Cave, high above Ballachulish. With him were his cousin, Alexander Stewart of Invernahyle, and MacColl of Glen Stockdale. As the three fugitives sheltered in that cold, small cave I have no doubt the duel with Rob Roy was retold – so I shall do the same. No written records exist, only traditions, but I have researched all the different versions and think this one is the most probable.

~

The dispute was, as so often, concerning land over which the MacGregors claimed influence. Rob Roy's lease on the farm Inverlochlarig Beg expired in 1732, and although he assumed it would be renewed it was in fact granted to John McLaren, whose wife was Beatrice Stewart, sister to Invernahyle. John MacLaren was wise enough not to try to evict Rob Roy, but in 1734 he did attempt to gain possession of another farm he had leased, probably Drumlich, adjoining Rob Roy's farm. Sir Walter Scott did much to establish the myths surrounding Rob Roy, but as he wrote in his volume *Rob Roy*:

> The MacGregors of Rob Roy's tribe claimed a right to it by ancient occupancy, and declared they would oppose to the uttermost the settlement of any person upon the farm not of their own name.

Rob Roy mustered his followers, a pretty rough lot, even for those times; the McLarens had fewer men, so appealed to their relations, the Stewarts of Appin. That summer Appin arrived with two hundred men, and this time the

17-1 Ardsheal's Cave

MacGregors were outnumbered. They met at Kirkton of Balquidder, and Rob Roy agreed with Appin that it was pointless they should fight; both clans were staunch Jacobites, and enough of their blood had already been shed at Killiecrankie and Sheriffmuir. No more should be shed over a minor domestic issue, so Rob Roy offered himself in single combat to determine the issue.

Ardsheal was chosen to represent the Stewarts, although some accounts say it was Invernahyle. Charles was much younger than Rob Roy at 63 and as they fought it was obvious that Rob's day had passed. When Ardsheal drew blood from Rob's shoulder, the latter dropped his sword-tip to the ground, for this was a duel of honour, not to the death.

"You are the first ever to draw blood from me with the sword," he congratulated Ardsheal. The latter replied that only age and suppleness had enabled him to do so. I have seen the Andrea Ferrara sword used by Ardsheal in this duel, still in the possession of his direct ancestor, Kenneth Stewart, latterly resident laird of Coll for fifty years. Indeed, family tradition has it that bad luck will visit the family if they ever part with the sword.

Some accounts have Rob Roy throwing his own sword into Loch Voil in disgust at it having failed him. Certainly he never drew it again, for he did not recover from the wound and by October Rob kept to the house. By winter he took to his bed, and died on the 28th of December that same year.

The dispute was not over though; in March 1736 Rob Roy's youngest son, Robert, came to Drumlich where John McLaren was ploughing;

> … and without any provocation, as the Baron was holding the pleugh, shott him behind his back, of which wound he dyed that night.

~

Red Pass Cave proved to be too small and inhospitable for the three occupants, so they moved to another cave in Glen Stockdale before Ardsheal found refuge for some weeks in a cave close to his house and family. Now known as Ardsheal's Cave or Stewart's Cave it is sited well up a deep gash in the side of *Beinn 'a Bheithir*, known as *Eas-nan-con*. It is a precipitous scramble up, especially for one of Ardsheal's size, but the cave was probably well hidden by the waterfall that cascaded in front of it before the adjacent quarry diverted some of the burn.

By May the Hanoverian troops were thick on the ground, scouring the countryside for rebels, and all the Ardsheal cattle were driven off. However, on the 24th the Commander of the West Highland Forces – Major-General John Campbell of Mamore, later 4th Duke of Argyll – took pity on Lady Ardsheal and wrote:

Madam – Your misfortune, and the unhappy situation Ardshiel has brought you and your innocent children into, by his being so deeply concerned in this unjust and unnatural rebellion, makes my heart aik. I know the King to be compassionate and merciful. I know the brave Duke, under whose command and orders I act, to have as much humanity as any many on earth; from which, and my own natural inclination, I have taken the liberty of ordering back your milk cows, 6 wedders, and as many lambs; the men who pretend a right to them shall be paid. I have taken the freedom at the same time of ordering two bolls of meal, [280 lbs] out of my own stores to be left here for you, which I desire you to accept for the use of your self and your little ones; and if what I write can have any weight, I most earnestly entreat you to bring up your children to be good subjects to His Majesty. I wish your husband, by surrendering himself to the Duke of Cumberland, had given me an opportunity of recommending him to His Majesty's mercy. I feel for you, and am, Madam, your most obedient and humble servant.
(Signed) John Campbell

Starvation was averted, and as the search for rebels lessened Ardsheal slipped down from the cave to see his wife and family. Suddenly a whistle of alarm was heard, and he hurriedly burrowed under a pile of hay, whilst his lady threw a blanket over him, sat down and played with her daughter – thrusting open the barn door the soldiers observed this domestic scene and withdrew. Thinking himself safe, Ardsheal retired with his wife to the garden, but again there sounded the alarm whistle and he had no choice but to hide by burrowing on the ground amongst the cabbages.

On another occasion he only evaded capture by squeezing between a precipice and a huge rock on the seashore, called the *Caigionn*. A half-witted retainer who had also been at Culloden, by name Donald MacColl, managed to succour his laird by pretending to cut hazels for basket-making from the banks above the rock; in time the watching soldiers became used to the fool at his work and ignored him. Whenever their attention was elsewhere 'Black Donald' would slip Ardsheal the food and water hidden amongst his capacious clothes.

Eventually word of the cave in *Eas-nan-con* reached the notorious Captain Caroline Scott at Fort William, and he immediately and secretly set out to capture Ardsheal. He crossed the Ballachulish ferry, and divided his forces to create a pincer movement, the major part going with him by the coast road. The rest took the old road east of *Beinn 'a Bheithir,* which climbs up *Gleann an Fhiodh* from Larach to Glen Creran, and is a superb walk nowadays. However, I doubt the Redcoats had time to admire the views, sweltering in their uniforms and packs as they climbed the road, then branched off at the watershed over rough ground to Glen Duror.

Crossing the ferry with 60 men had taken time, and a panting messenger managed to warn Ardsheal of the troops approaching by the coast road – what he did not know about were the troops coming down Glen Duror. He hastily slid and slithered down the slope from his cave and mounted the waiting *Macphail* to head up Glen Duror with twelve men, not realising he was heading straight into the trap engineered by Captain Scott. Another scout then warned of the danger; Ardsheal dismounted, *Macphail* was led to hiding in the trees and the men hid behind a large boulder close by the road. Charles Stewart clasped his great broadsword, 'The Turk', vowing to sell his freedom dearly; but the troops passed on the other side of the rock, and once clear they remounted and made all haste up the glen.

Their route lay south-east up Glen Duror, then over the saddle below *Fraochie* and down into Glen Creran; at first the lowering mist covered their movements from the searching troops, but then the sun broke through and they were discovered. By now they were at the summit

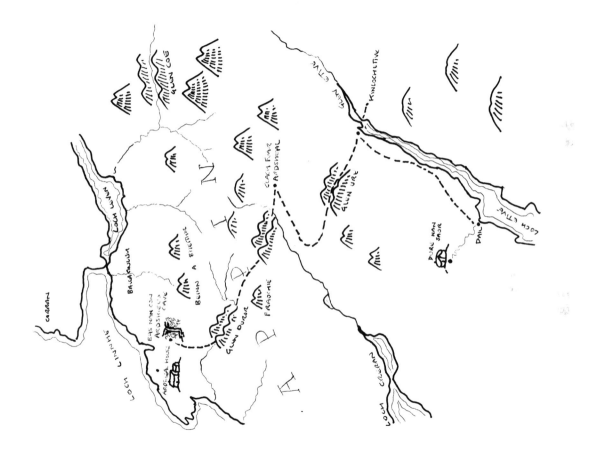

GLEN COE

GLEN ETIVE

KINLOCHETIVE

LOCH ETIVE

DAIL

CLACH FARR
ARDSHEAL

GLEN URE

DURE NAN SAOR

LOCH LEVEN

BALLACHULISH

BEINN A BHEITHIR

N

A

P

P

I

N

CARRAN

EAS NAN CON
ARDSHEAL'S
CAVE

GLEN DUROR

FRAOCHIE

ARDSHEAL HOUSE

LOCH LINNHE

LOCH CRERAN

17-2 *Route of Ardsheal's escape*

with the troops far below, but *Macphail* was exhausted, for his great weight, coupled with that of his rider, caused him constantly to sink in the peaty ground. Steam rose in clouds from his heaving flanks as he laboured upwards, until Ardsheal was finally forced to abandon his trusty mount, although he also was exhausted. Two men seized a branch, one at each end, and with this behind the laird they propelled him onwards. Luckily, before too long the going became downhill and although still very rough the woodlands hid the party from the pursuing Redcoats. They found a hiding place well up Glen Creran, now known as *Clach Fear Ardsheal* – Ardsheal's Rock; it is a great boulder split in three, and by building up the gaps with stone and turfs Charles Stewart's men were able to make a shelter large enough for six men.

This was Stewart country but they were still not safe, so after a few days rest they toiled up Glen Ure and over the pass to Loch Etive. *Beinn Fhionnlaidh* and *Beinn Sguliard* towered above them on either side as they crossed the watershed and then slid down the steep brae into the head of Loch Etive. At Kinlochetive the Redcoats were close on their heels, and the farmer there was drying grain – seeing their plight he drew the fire from the kiln and Ardsheal hid within; the farmer made an inner wall of wet turfs, grain and straw being piled at the entrance and the fire replaced. The Redcoats searched every house and hiding place over the next two days, and eventually one soldier, more observant than the rest, came to the kiln. He lit his pipe at the fire and observed to the farmer:

"You have kept the corn very long on the kiln."

"There have been one or two quantities of corn dried since you have come," replied the farmer.

"Oh no! I understand how it is", said the soldier, "although the Captain does not. But we are away tomorrow, and you may take the corn off the kiln. I think that it is dry enough".

From this the farmer understood that the soldier was sympathetic to Ardsheal, although obliged to do his duty. The troops, failing in their search, assumed the fugitives had pressed on and they hastened up Glen Etive.

Ardsheal went the opposite way, down Loch Etive to a man called MacIntyre in a hamlet known as *Doire nan Saor*, some hundreds of feet above the present-day Dail. Here he stayed for some time, but his presence was discovered, some say from the frequent trips MacIntyre made to Oban for provisions, over and above what his own family would require. MacConachy of Inverawe went to the hamlet and said to MacIntyre, "Look that you keep no rebels about you; for if you should be found out you shall be made to suffer for it". So saying he took out a large sum of money and gave it to MacIntyre.

"Be kind to wayfarers" he observed, and took his leave.

Thus was Ardsheal able to reach Edinburgh, where he had seldom been and so assumed would not be recognised; but walking down a street one day he saw several people staring at him and one remarked in Gaelic, "It's a fine day this for cows and milkmaids in Duror".

Ardsheal took the hint, and fled the city for Peterhead, which he reached in late September; there he posed as a wine merchant and took ship for Flanders.

He assumed he was safe, but Redcoats in Flanders had posted patrols to intercept any fugitives and some officers saw Ardsheal at an inn where he had met the ever-faithful merchant, Muileartach. However, they were not entirely certain as to his identity, and by dint of Ardsheal and the merchant alternately calling for drink the officers were soon in a drunken stupor. The city gates, however, were barred without a pass, so the Muileartach sent a message to his wife outside the walls that he was desperately ill with colic, to come instantly with her maid, and to bring a spare set of women's clothes. Weeping disconsolately, the wife was granted two passes on her way into the city, where Ardsheal changed clothes with the maid and climbed into the coach.

"What about the boy?" he asked, recalling he had a servant boy with him.

"I shall care for him" replied the Muileartach, "and when you send word I shall send him to you".

So saying the merchant told the coachman to drive on, and the disconsolate wife and her unduly large maid presented their passes at the gate and were waived through. Safely past the walls the merchant's wife ordered the horses to be whipped up to make good their escape; at the first stage she had four fresh horses harnessed, and by dawn they were fifteen miles from Flanders. In the city the officers dared not admit that they had let Ardsheal slip through their hands, so no pursuit was mounted, and Charles Stewart reached safety in France.

As for the serving boy, it was seven years before he saw Ardsheal again; he then remained with him in exile until Charles' death, when he returned to Appin and was known as 'Red Allan'. There he settled and raised a family, and is said to have possessed a gold medallion, with the head of Ardsheal on one side and Prince Charles on the other.

~

The ferocity with which the Duke of Cumberland punished the Highlands is much recorded, resulting in his well-earned nickname of 'Butcher Cumberland'. Some of his officers were more understanding of the political and social backlash that would inevitably occur from such harsh treatment, but others were not – including Captain Caroline Frederick Scott:

> A blunt, harsh, practical man, of inflexible courage and equally inflexible heart, he was of a type congenial to Cumberland and, however little General Campbell may have liked him, obviously an ideal commander for a tight corner.

Cumberland had appointed Scott to command the Fort William garrison in March 1746 and it is clear from the latter's subsequent actions that he resented General Campbell's action in sheltering Lady Ardsheal. She was surviving as best she could, protected from the worst depredations visited on her clan by the letter from General Campbell. He, however, was closely involved that summer in chasing the Prince by sea and land throughout the islands; taking advantage of the General's absence, Captain Scott returned to Ardsheal in August, driving off the few cattle and horses left. On August 25th the pregnant Lady Ardsheal wrote again to General Campbell, by then at Inveraray, suffering badly from rheumatism but winding down the Government forces. Her letter is somewhat disjointed, as one would expect in such trying circumstances; it is full of pathos, and the frequent references to '*my poor Children*' are clearly aimed at the General's kindness – who can blame her?

> *Sir – Tho' I doubt not the uncommon usage I had from Captn Scot has come to your ears yet my desperate Situation from it is such that it puts me under*

a necessity of troubling you with this letter … his treatment of me really was such that it's only my own and my poor Childrens being the unhappy instruments of his Cruelty could make me believe that any man especially bred in a Civilized Country and good Company could be so free of Compassion or any thing at all of the Gentleman [could] descend to such a low degree of meanness as he did…

… he wou'd not allow me when at Ardsheall so much as the smallest of my potts to dress a little Victualls for my children nor spoon or knife or fork or bed to lye on or even a blanket but one for myself and one for each of my children … [he] carry'd off the little butter and Cheese I had made of the few cattle ye was pleased to indulge me with … excepting about half a pound of fresh butter for the Children and about two bolls of meal…

No doubt cautious of the wrath of his commanding officer, Captain Scott observed the General's letter strictly, for Lady Ardsheal wrote that he carried off cattle and horses *'tho I told him you knew I had them but happen'd not to be included in your letter'.*

Lady Ardsheal was obliged to buy back her own cattle and also rescue her children's teacher, *'one Mr William Cumine'* whom Captain Scott had imprisoned in Fort William,

after robbing him of his purse where there was a gold ring and some little cess then 40 shillings of money and all his Cloaths except what was on his back and his whole books and the Children's

The letter went on to detail Scott's harsh treatment of *'the poor Tennents'* and that they had been so *'burn'd and harried'* that they could pay no rent. She then asked the General for:

a protection for the Towne of Ardsheall and one of the shealling … to enable me to maintain myself and my little ones … and your Certificate of how I've been used…

However, she must have doubted her ability to manage with no rents, few cattle and no barns to keep them in, for she further asked,

> *[and] in case I may judge it more convenient for my-self and Children to remove to some part of the Low Country* [i.e. near her family in Stirling] *where I can have opportunity of their Education that ye grant me and them a pass'.*

In spite of her many ordeals Lady Ardsheal's spirit was clearly undimmed, for she signed the letter and added at the foot '*PS. Excuse ye coarseness of my paper, my good friend Capt Scott having left me non better.*'

By October it was known to the Government that Charles Stewart had safely escaped to France, and with Major-General Campbell of Mamore now in London, the troops returned to Ardsheal in December. This time they were not so compassionate, for thatched barns were burnt, cattle driven off – including the vital milk cows – fruit trees felled, and the slates and timbers of Ardsheal House carted away before it was burnt on the night of 15th/16th December. With snow falling, the heavily pregnant Lady Ardsheal took shelter with her children in a hut; next night she gave birth to her sixth child, Anne. Knowing she could no longer survive at Ardsheal, she and the children set out three days later for Stirling, battling through the cold and snow. There she left them with relations whilst she joined her husband in France, for the Ardsheal estates were forfeited. Charles Stewart, 5th of Ardsheal, never saw Appin again, and died an exile in France in 1757.

~

There is a happy sequel to our tale, for Duncan – Charles and Isabel's third son – emigrated to America after finishing his education at Stirling. He realised that as the younger son of a forfeited estate there were few prospects for him in Scotland, but in Boston he eventually became Town Chamberlain and Collector of Taxes, having also married, in 1767, the Governor's daughter, Anne Erving. When, in 1769, Duncan's surviving elder brother, Alexander, and his cousin, Dugald of Appin – he who had refused to lead

Clan Stewart in the '45 – both died, Duncan became 6th of Ardsheal and 10th of Appin.

During the American War of Independence Duncan remained a Crown officer, in spite of the danger. In the Dewar Manuscripts there is a splendid tale of Anne stealing the town jail keys from under her father's pillow, Duncan having drunk him under the table. The object was to free two British officers condemned to be tarred, feathered and set alight; they duly escaped on a convenient ship on the point of sailing for England. Duncan, naturally, was suspected, and he too had to make his escape, again by a ship on the point of sailing.

There is an element of truth in this tale, for in 1778 Duncan Stewart arranged the exchange of Colonel [later Major General Sir] Archibald Campbell, who had been captured three years earlier in Boston harbour, on his way to command the 2nd Battalion of the 71st Fraser's Highlanders. Sadly, for him, the gallant Colonel's intelligence was faulty, for his ship put into Boston not realising it was in enemy hands; he was treated harshly in captivity, the colonists believing their own prisoners were being ill-treated by the British. They must have regretted the exchange, for in the following year Colonel Campbell took Savannah, one of the few British successes in the war. He was later rewarded for his service with the Governorships of Jamaica in 1781-4 and Madras in 1788-9; there he amassed a considerable fortune, enabling him to buy the estate of Inverneill, just south of Lochgilphead.

About this time Duncan Stewart returned to London to try to regain his estates. The Duke of Argyll, Lord Howe, Commander in Chief in America, and Colonel Archibald Campbell [whose exchange Duncan had negotiated] all supported his case, citing his faithful support for the Crown. However, the estate had been let by the Commissioners for Forfeited Estates to one Peter Campbell, who had rebuilt the burnt-out shell of the house. Following compensation to him Duncan Stewart finally regained his family estate in 1785, and Anne came from Boston to join her husband. Duncan died in 1793; his grandson, Charles, 8th of Ardsheal and 12th of Appin, who never married, sold the estate in 1844.

Map references

- OS Landrangers 49 & 50. Os Explorers 384 & 377:

  Ardsheal's Cave NM 008 563.

  Clach Fear Ardsheal NM 078 512.

Sources

- *The Isles of the Sea* – Fitzroy Maclean.
- *Society for West Highland & Island Historical Research* – Notes and Queries XXIII p 18 and XXIV p 27.
- *Further Wanderings, Mainly in Argyll* – MEM Donaldson.
- *The Stewart Society Magazine*, Volume XIII pp 121-129.
- *Duncan Stewart VI of Ardsheal* by Robin H Stewart.
- *The Stewart Society Magazine*, Volume XIV pp 38-43.
- *Drumlich* by Robert Stewart.
- *The Dewar Manuscripts* – John Dewar for George Douglas, Duke of Argyll.
- *The Hunt for Rob Roy: The Man and the Myths* – David Stevenson.
- *Rob Roy MacGregor: His Life and Times* – W H Murray.
- *Rob Roy's Country* – Mary McGrigor.
- *History of Clan Campbell*, volume III – Alastair Campbell of Airds.
- *Argyll in the '45* – Sir James Ferguson.
- *Records of Argyll* – Lord Archibald Campbell.

• *Scottish Field*, June 1996 – Mary McGrigor. Quoting
  a letter among the papers of Governor Trumbull in
  Connecticut State Library.

The wreck of the paddle steamer Stirling in 1828

And how Sgeir Mhic ic Alasdair got its name

Built in 1814, the Paddle Steamer Stirling was one of the first steam vessels built on the east coast of Scotland – indeed there is a strong argument that she was in fact *the* first. Be that as it may, it was a bare two years after Henry Bell had built the PS Comet and in 1812 began the first commercially successful steamboat service in Europe, on the River Clyde between Glasgow and Greenock. In September of that year Comet made a round trip between Glasgow and Oban, taking four days. And in the early summer of 1813 she transited the Forth and Clyde Canal to make an excursion to Leith before returning to the Clyde.

Comet's arrival on the Forth convinced local opinion of the viability of steamships for those waters and inspired a group of businessmen to build the PS Stirling. She was launched from the Kincardine on Forth yard of John Gray in 1814, and while still very small was significantly bigger than the Comet. At 68 feet long she had a beam of 15 feet 2 inches, a useful 7ft depth in the hold, and measured at just over 69 tons. She had a single mast; a quarter deck raised by a mere l foot 4 inches, and was embellished with a figurehead of a Highlandman.

To reduce risk, ownership of a ship is split into 64 shares, and the Stirling was owned by 37 individuals, allocated one or more shares. They comprised 23 Stirling merchants, along with one each from Edinburgh and Glasgow; 2 soap-boilers; a wright and two butchers, all from Stirling; two tanners from St Ninians and one from Bannockburn; Henry Bell, owner of the Comet; an Alloa wright; John Gray, her Kincardine builder; and John Henderson, the first master. A fairly motley selection!

The *Edinburgh Evening Courant* for Monday, 11 July 1814 carried the following advertisement:

CHEAP EASY AND SAFE CONVEYANCE
THE
STIRLING STEAMBOAT

Elegantly and commodiously fitted up for the accommodation of passengers commenced sailing betwixt Stirling 81 Leith on Tuesday last and will continue to sail from Stirling every Monday, Wednesday and Friday, and from Leith every Tuesday, Thursday and Saturday while the weather permits. The hours of sailing will be determined by the time of the tides. She performs the voyage in seven hours and passengers are taken in and put out at Alloa, Kincardine &c. fare from Stirling to Leith – best Cabin 6s 6d. Second Cabin 4s 6d.

These fares equate to £20 and £14 respectively [in 2014] and in fact passengers for the intermediate ports were landed in shore boats as there were, as yet, no suitable piers. Operating largely in a fairly sheltered portion of the Forth estuary, the service faced some tricky tidal streams and an awkward meandering section of the river, difficult for sailing vessels to negotiate. The local road system of the period was largely inadequate, yet demand existed to link Stirling – at the lowest bridging point of the estuary – with Leith, the major port of the district. An ideal niche for a steamship.

All was not plain sailing though, for in July 1819 the Stirling suffered an explosion of her cast-iron boiler, due to failure of a safety valve. Nine people were injured, but the low pressures then in use did not lead to the inevitable destruction of the vessel. By 1820 other steam vessels were in service on the Forth and she was transferred to the Caledonian Canal. Although the canal was not yet fully completed the Stirling sailed between Inverness and Fort Augustus, while the Comet II handled the southern portion of the route from Fort William to Glasgow via the Crinan Canal. After the Caledonian Canal was fully opened in 1822 the Stirling began to operate a through service between Glasgow and Inverness, alternating with the Comet II; first on a fortnightly basis, but by 1826 weekly.

In 1825 the Stirling was lengthened by 11 feet, a fairly common occurrence at the time; however, ship technology was advancing rapidly and – even after a refit – at 14 years old she was an ageing vessel and was reckoned 'a very small boat, and of no great power'. By the beginning of 1828 she was probably living on borrowed time.

~

On Thursday, 17 January 1828 the Stirling left Fort William on a typical winter's day of south-easterly gales with heavy showers of sleet. Under the command of Captain Maclean, she carried about thirty passengers, of whom the most prominent was Colonel Alasdair Ranaldson Macdonnel of Glengarry, fifteenth chief of his clan, and two of his daughters.

Glengarry himself was every inch the

ancient clan chief imprisoned in modern circumstances. A man of feudal habits, he came to grief in a commercial world. Always arrayed in the tartan, whether in his own glen or in Auld Reekie, he went about the world with a body-guard of clansmen whom he called his 'tail'.

A man of fiery temper, he kept open house and ignored bank-books; raised and commanded the Glengarry Fencibles, recruits being drawn from his Glengarry estates, under threat of eviction if persuasion did not work; and welcomed George IV to Edinburgh with a lordly gesture. However,

Macdonnel's romantic attachment to the customs and costumes of Gaelic culture did not stop him evicting his tenants to clear his lands for sheep farming. Although Scott wrote of Glengarry in his misleading hagiography "He is a kind of Quixote in our age, having retained, in their full extent, the whole feelings of clanship and chieftainship, elsewhere so long abandoned", under his authority timber was felled for sale, the cleared land was leased to sheep farmers and many of his clansmen were forced from the land by increasing rents and evictions. He continued the evictions to make way for sheep farmers which his mother began when his father was chieftain, and most of the clan was forced to emigrate to British North America, as part of what was later known as the Highland Clearances. Robert Burns wrote a satirical poem about Glengarry in the Address of Beelzebub.

Aged twenty-four, at a ball in Inverness, Glengarry quarrelled with Flora MacDonald's grandson, Lieutenant Norman Macleod. Tempers flared, Glengarry struck Macleod with his cane, Macleod drew his dirk and issued a challenge – a duel on the links at Fort George. On the appointed morning Glengarry's seconds tried to reach a settlement with an apology, but Glengarry refused to surrender his cane, which Macleod demanded. The die was set, Macleod was shot, and the young man died a month later from his wound. His mother – known as 'Major Anne' by her friends – was the widow of Major Macleod of Stein, in Skye, and when informed of her son's death at the hands of Glengarry she exclaimed, 'Good thou art my son! Better the hero's death than the craven's life; the brave dies but once, the coward many times'.

Glengarry was duly tried for murder, which infuriated him at the impertinence of being put on trial. He was arraigned before three Law Lords and a jury of fifteen landowners, with the prosecution led by the Lord Advocate, assisted by the Solicitor General. Luckily for Glengarry, his defence was led by 'the finest advocate at the Scottish bar', Henry Erskine. For although the presiding judges held that 'by the law of Scotland, killing in a duel was murder … [and] That a person tried for killing in a duel must either be found guilty of murder or acquitted'. The sympathetic jury found Glengarry 'Not Guilty'. This was totally unexpected to all but Glengarry, and was largely due to the eloquence of his counsel. Not everyone was pleased at the verdict however; when Glengarry was deer coursing in Skye some years later, his hotel was surrounded by angry followers of Lieutenant Norman Macleod demanding him dead or alive. Glengarry had to steal out of the back of the building and hurry off the island, and his ghillies were warned that if he ever returned to Skye he would not leave alive. His deerhounds suffered more harshly, their ears being cropped and their tails docked as a warning to Glengarry.

Later, Glengarry picked a quarrel with a Fort William doctor and his 'tail' beat up the poor man, for which Glengarry was fined £2,000. This then was the somewhat unpleasant but larger than life man who boarded the paddle steamer for Glasgow – typically he was due there to pursue a court case!

The Stirling left the shelter of Banavie and made her slow way down Loch Linnhe against the gale, for the south-easterly wind funnelling up the loch raised short, steep waves against the last of the ebb. Off Druimarbin – barely two miles south of Fort William – she began to get into trouble, for the weather was 'uncommonly bad'. Without power the wind took charge of the Stirling and set her down on the Ardgour, or western, shore; the crew attempted to anchor, but whether from the force of wind, or because the loch shelves steeply, they were unsuccessful. At noon she drove ashore, within twenty minutes of low water.

Inverscaddle Bay is about one mile across, and consists mainly of salt marsh with a few channels formed by the River Scaddle. At low water springs it is largely dry, and it was just at this state that the Stirling drove ashore on one of the few rocks in the bay. The vessel had 'rather a heavy cargo with a great deal of baggage', but was not insured.

The rock the Stirling struck is barely two hundred feet long, and at high water only dries to two feet; at the time of the wreck there was at least fourteen feet dry, but several hundred yards from shore. Mr Macdougall, the tenant farmer at Inverscaddle Farm half a mile away, exaggerated somewhat when he wrote to *The Times* that the wreck occurred 'under my house' – but which of us do not exaggerate!

Two passengers, named Gunn and Noon, together with a crewman, jumped onto the rock and were thus able to save most of the passengers and crew, who were

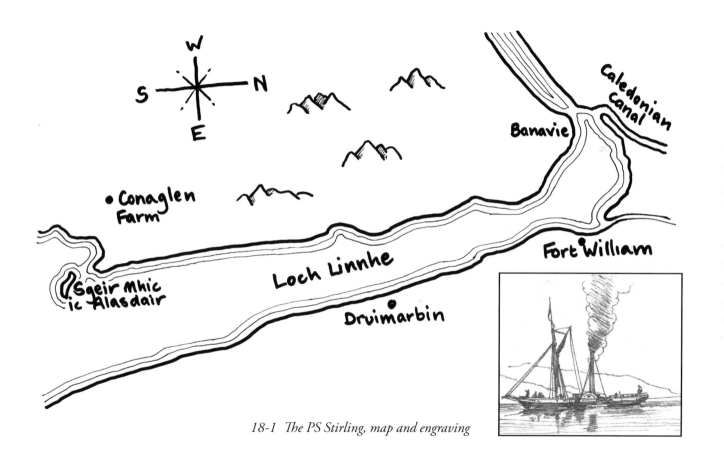

18-1 *The PS Stirling, map and engraving*

'dragged ashore with ropes'. A Mrs Macdonald from Fort William 'greatly contributed to the safety of several passengers by her activity and uncommon presence of mind'. There the survivors huddled against the howling wind and frequent showers of sleet in what little shelter the rock provided.

Glengarry's English butler, named Dubble, was drowned when he fell or jumped over the weather rail, but his body was recovered some twenty minutes later. Glengarry himself waited until both his daughters were safe, then jumped from the gunwale onto the rock but missed his footing. He was 'much hurt in the face and head on rocks', and although carried ashore to the farmhouse he died that evening about 8 pm, before medical help could arrive.

James Fraser, a painter from Inverness, had two daughters on board; the elder got safely ashore, but called out that her sister was trapped in the cabin. By this time the ship was rapidly breaking to pieces, but the pilot re-entered the flooded cabin and with great difficulty rescued the child. He passed her safely ashore, then with Captain Maclean was last to leave the doomed ship.

Battered by the waves, the Stirling was soon a total wreck, and the pieces slid off the rock into deeper water. As for the survivors, they were cared for at Inverscaddle Farm, the last portions of which were demolished in 1883 during the building of the present Conaglen House.

Sir Walter Scott was a great friend of Glengarry – whom he considered 'lived 100 years too late' – and based the character off Fergus MacIvor on the chief in his novel *Waverley*. Scott wrote in his diary a few days after the wrecking:

> I have this day the melancholy news of Glengarry's death, and was greatly shocked. He played the part of a chieftain too nigh the life to be popular among an altered race.

According to the *Inverness Courier*, the funeral procession of five miles from Invergarry to Kilfinnan was followed by 1,500 men and 150 gentry, the coffin being carried breast-high by eighteen Highlanders. Glengarry's personal piper, Archie Munro, composed a lament, as did the blind household bard, Allan MacDougall.

In Edinburgh Sir Walter Scott was moved to compose

Glengarry's Death Song, an undoubted expression of his genuine affection for the dead chief, if not perhaps a work of the greatest literary quality.

~

Glengarry was aged only fifty-five when he died; the Glengarry portion of his overburdened estates were later sold by his son – Aeneas Ranald Euan – for £91,000 to Lord Ward, later 1st Earl of Dudley. 'And but for his son, who emigrated to Australia, that was the end of Glengarry'.

And the rock? Ever since that night of storm and shipwreck and death it has been known as *Sgeir Mcic ic Alasdair* – Glengarry's Rock.

Map references

- OS Landranger sheet 41. OS Explorer 291:

  Sgeir Mcic ic Alasdair NN 031 681.

Historical notes

- PS Stirling has often been confused with the slightly later Stirling Castle. This was common in vessels registered with similar or identical names prior to the Merchant Shipping Act 1894 – or indeed unregistered vessels. Plus there were several different craft named Stirling Castle in different parts of Britain within a short period.

- The somewhat motley group of 37 individuals who owned the Stirling illustrates the kind of highly localised enterprise formed with the sole intention of operating a steamship at that date. And it is interesting to note the involvement of both builder and master as shareholders in this specialist, single ship company of this experimental era.

- PS Comet – Henry Bell was a hotel and baths owner from Helensburgh, who in the winter of 1811 got the shipbuilders John Wood and Company, Port Glasgow, to build a paddle steamer. She was named Comet after the 'Great Comet' of that year, and the 28 ton vessel was 45 feet long with a beam of 10 feet. The two paddle wheels on each side were driven by engines rated at three horse power each, giving a speed in calm water of 4-5 knots; one source states the engines evolved from an experimental little steam engine which Bell installed to pump sea water into the Helensburgh Baths.

However, the success of this service quickly inspired competition and the Comet was outclassed by newer steamers and she was briefly transferred to a service on the Firth of Forth. She was lengthened and re-engined, then from September 1819 ran a service to Oban and Fort William via the Crinan Canal, a trip which took four days.

• The Comet was shipwrecked on 13 December 1820 at Craignish Point, with Henry Bell on board, but no lives were lost. One of the engines ended its working days in a Greenock brewery, and is now in The Science Museum in London.

• Robert Burns wrote a satirical poem about Glengarry in the *Address of Beelzebub*.

• Glengarry Clearances: John Prebble wrote that:

> In the years immediately following Culloden this Macdonnel country was one of the largest estates in the Highlands, ranging westward from Loch Lochy to the broken coast and white sands of Knoydart. A thousand young men were its warrior-roll but the contribution in coin to the chief's purse was little more than £300 a year.

• Marjorie Macdonnel, wife of the 14th Chief, was 'a shrewd and ambitious social climber' who required cash, not men. At her instigation the Clearances began in 1782 to make room for sheep-runs at vastly increased rents. Three years later 500 Macdonnels cleared from Glengarry sailed for Canada in the ship *Macdonald*. As rents were raised or leases not renewed tacksmen followed suit and took their followers with them to America and Canada. 'One hundred years later there

20,000 Macdonnels in Canada and next to none in Glengarry'.

- Post the shipwreck: Colonel Macdonnel's estate was much mortgaged and encumbered with debt. In 1840, after his only son and heir, Aeneas Ranaldson Macdonnel, had come of age he sold the Glengarry part of the estate to Lord Ward, later Earl of Dudley, for £91,000. In 1860 his lordship sold it to Edward Ellice of Glenquoich for £120,000 – a handsome profit! Some years later Aeneas sold the Knoydart estate to a Mr Baird; he emigrated to Australia, but is on record as dying at Inverie, Knoydart, in 1852. His two sons died without issue and a kinsman inherited as 19th Chief. The 23rd Chief, Aeneas Ranald Euan Macdonnel of Glengarry (13th titular Lord Macdonnel) lives in England.

- Admiralty Tide-tables were not published until 1833, so I obtained from the Hydrographic Office Tidal Prediction System TIDECALC the time and height of the tide [1220 and 0.38 metres] for the 17 January 1828.

Sources

- *Burke's Peerage, Baronetage & Knightage and Clan* Chiefs – 107th edition.
- *The Mariners's Mirror*, May 2000, Volume 86 No.2.
- *The Scots Magazine* – November 2001.
- Hydrographic Office Tidal Prediction System TIDECALC.
- *Somewhere in Scotland* – Alasdair Alpin Macgregor.
- *Carmina Gadelica* – Alexander Carmichael.
- *The Highland Clearances* – John Prebble.

South Rona

The widow Mackenzie & her guiding light

To the east of Skye, and north of Raasay, lies the isolated island of Rona, whose name in Norse means 'rough' – to which Martin Martin, in 1717, agreed:

> This little isle is the most unequal rocky piece of ground to be seen anywhere; there's but very few acres fit for digging, the whole is covered with long heath … and some mixture of grass; it is reckoned very fruitful in pasturage…

Indeed, in 1763 the Laird of Raasay is recorded as having kept a cowhand and 160 cattle on the island. But water is scarce, and in dry spells the islanders were forced to fetch water from Skye. For many years it belonged to the Macleods of Raasay, and the eldest son took the title of Rona; the island is often called South Rona to distinguish it from its namesake, the rock outcrop of North Rona, between Lewis and Orkney.

What South Rona does possess is that most desirable of things to mariners – a snug harbour. *Acairseid Mhor* is, without doubt, one of the snuggest harbours in the islands, and I have ridden out many a gale there, the wind whistling through the tops of the Scots Pines fringing the rocks. It is totally sheltered from all winds once safely inside, but the entrance is not easy to see, and a large rock lurks just below the surface for the unwary.

In the 16th century Rona became a refuge for pirates, making their base at *Acairseid Mhor*, which duly became known as *Port nan Robaireann* – 'Port of the Robbers'. They were tolerated by the Macleods of Raasay, for – as any Chief would – Raasay took a cut of the plunder in exchange for turning a blind eye. One pirate is said to have been *Calum Garbh MacLeod*, son of Macleod of Lewis, who based himself at Brochel Castle on Raasay in 1518 and used Rona as his raiding base.

Dean Munro, writing in 1549, said that the island was

full of wood and hedder, with ane havin [haven] *for heiland gallys in the middis of it, and the same havein is guyed* [good] *for fostering of theives, ruggairs & reivairs…*[to the] *spulzeing of poure pepill.*

By 1787 MacLeod of Raasay, desperate for cash, explored the opportunities for commercial fishing on the island. He wrote to the Duke of Argyll, then Governor of the British Fisheries Society stating that Rona was:

…one of the most advantageous places on this coast for a fishing station. It is surrounded with numbers of banks which are daily discovered by the country people who come to fish from the mainland, which makes me think there is an inexhaustible fund of them about the island. It is likewise supplied with the best harbours at every creek, both for large vessels and small boats.

Raasay was stretching the truth, for there was only the one good harbour! Anyway, nothing came of his ideas and in 1843 Rona and Raasay were sold to one George Rainy, who began clearing the population of Rona for sheep and higher rents. He wasn't very successful, for eight years later the population was still at 115 souls, reaching a peak of 180 inhabitants in 1891; many were families cleared from more fertile land on Raasay. The main settlements on the island were at *Doire na Guaile* in the south and half a mile to the north of *Acairseid Mhor*, at *Acairseid Thioram*, where there was a better spring for water. However, as its name suggests, that harbour dries, and it is also open to the north-west gales.

Which brings me to my Tale, which happened in the middle of the 19th century. Snugly at anchor in *Acairseid Mhor* during one fierce September gale, I dipped into that splendid 1937 volume, *West Coast Cruising,* by John McClintock, wherein was the following tale:

Many years ago – about the mid eighteen hundreds – an over-long summer drought made necessary a voyage to Skye for water, from which a Mr MacRae – accompanied by a friend and two serving-maids – was returning to Rona on a dark and windy night. Missing the entrance to *Acairseid Mhor* and safety, the boat was dashed onto the rocks and all onboard perished.

MacRae's widow thereafter kept a light burning at night to guide other seafarers into the harbour, until such time as a lighthouse was built at the northern end of Rona. *'In recognition of her kindly thoughtfulness Mrs MacRae was given a pension of £40 a year by the Admiralty'.*

Another version is given in *'Scotland Picturesque and Traditional',* published about 1930:

A fisherman's wife sits in her cottage, the only person on the island, for her husband and three sons are out fishing in the Minch. A winter gale has blown up, and as darkness falls and the roar of the waves on the beach grow ever louder, the woman's fears increase.

Wrapping a shawl round her head she goes down to the shore. Buffeted by the howling wind and soaked by torrential rain she peers out to sea time after time, hoping to catch a glimpse of the boat. She is comforted by the thought that they might have found shelter elsewhere, but at last, in a rift of the driving spray, she catches sight of a sail. With a great shriek of horror she realises her husband has mistaken the entrance, and that the north-westerly gale is driving the boat straight onto the rocks. There, the craft was reduced to matchwood in seconds, and all on board were drowned.

Returning in her grief to the cottage, the widow almost lost her mind. For she found she had neglected to close the door, and the wind had blown out the lamp which acted

19-1: View B from Admiralty chart 2570 of 1850; 'Widows Cot E.N.E. just in sight leads into Acarsaid More.'

as a guiding beacon into the safe waters of the harbour. Ever since then, mindful of others at sea, she lit at dusk a lamp in the window of her cottage until such time as a lighthouse was built at the north end of Rona. As reward for her diligence, the widow was made keeper of the light.

～

And yet another version is in that indispensable volume, *'Scottish Islands'* by Hamish Haswell-Smith:

An islander called MacRae was returning to Rona after fetching water from Skye when his boat sank and he was drowned. His widow, unsure of what had happened to him, for thirteen years kept a light burning at night in the window of her cottage at *Acairseid Mhor*. Eventually she was given a pension of £40 a year, and persuaded to live with relatives in the Braes district of Skye.

～

I was intrigued at these varying tales, but somewhat sceptical that the Admiralty would be so generous as to grant a pension of £40 a year – more than twice the pay of an Able Seaman. Letters flew – or more often crept – between Maolachy, The Admiralty, The Commissioners for Northern Lights and Register House. Finally, at the latter, were found letters from one Captain Otter – at that time charting the West Coast – addressed to *'Alan Stevenson Esq.'* Engineer to The Commissioners for Northern Lights. The true story was pieced together from his letters and the above accounts; it is somewhat more prosaic, if equally tragic.

Captain Otter wrote from HMS Comet at Lochalsh on the 28th of October, 1851, that he had *'taken an interest in a philanthropic widow'* ,who kept a light burning in her cottage window,

> *which clears all the rocks at the entrance of the harbour* [Acairseid Mhor]. *For ten years she has kept the light burning … and much oil is therefore expended… Many fishing vessels and boats owe their safety from the storm to the poor Widows lights,*

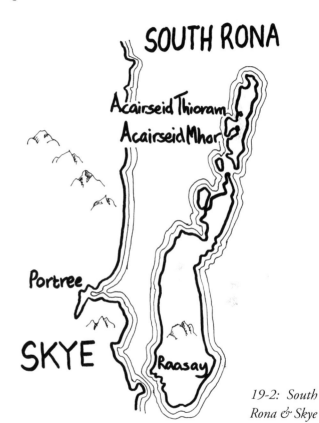

19-2: *South Rona & Skye*

when beating up the Sound of Raasay in long winter nights, and unable to contend against the terrific squalls that blow from the Skye shore, they anxiously watch for a glimpse of the narrow belt of light, which in clear weather is seen across nearly to the entrance of Portree Harbour.

The reason the widow kept a light burning in her cottage was that in 1840 there was just her family at *Acairseid Mhor*, all the rest being at *Acairseid Thioram*; the family were called Mackenzie, and they lived in a small stone house close to the present pier; the ruins can still be seen. That summer there was a severe drought, and Kenneth Mackenzie sailed his boat to Portree for water – he never returned. His widow Janet, refusing to believe he had drowned, every night kept a light burning in the cottage window to guide her husband safe into the harbour.

For twelve long years Janet Mackenzie struggled to raise her children, and each night faithfully lit the guiding lamp:

when her sons cannot procure a sufficient supply from the fish they catch, she is obliged to buy more [oil], besides on many occasions having to fall back on candle[s] … the only assistance she has ever received was £20 some years ago from the Trinity Board.

Captain Otter suggested that the Commissioners:

make her a present of a common agland lamp with a reflecter (sic), and supply her occasionally with a small cask of oil…' The Board, however, demurred to 'take any step which would tend to give such a prominence to the light shewn by the Widow … [which] … ought not certainly to be in the shape of a Light House Apparatus.

Anxious not to be outdone by their English counterparts however, the Board proposed that,

Having in view therefore, the example of the Trinity Board in this case, the safest course is to reward the praiseworthy exertions of this poor Widow by some pecuniary aid … I will suppose that she spends

about 20 or 30 shillings annually [on oil] in carrying out her benevolent purpose. Upon the whole I think the Board may safely repeat the grant of £20 which was made by the Trinity Board. Captain Otter will be very happy to take charge of conveying the gift to Mrs Mackenzie.

In spite of the money, in 1852 Janet Mackenzie gave up the struggle to wrest a living from Rona, and emigrated to Australia with her three sons. A check on the lists of those *'Emigrants Assisted by the Highlands & Islands Emigration Society'* from 1852-1857 failed to find any trace of Janet Mackenzie and her sons, or indeed anyone from South Rona. But it did turn up a further example of Captain Otter's philanthropy:

Family Shaw. Alexander 49, Marian 40, Alexander 6, John 2. Residence Portree. Estate Lord Macdonald. Ship Thames, Liverpool-Melbourne. Remarks: Very industrious man. Deposit Guaranteed by Captain Otter.

Whilst Mrs Mackenzie and her sons chose to emigrate, her daughter decided to stay, for she married a Rona islander called Macrae. They continued to occupy the widow's house by the pier, which for many years was marked on the old Admiralty chart 2570 as 'Widows Cot'.

In recognition of the needs of mariners a lighthouse was constructed at the north end of Rona, and first lit in 1857; it was automated in 1975. But the tale that the fisherman's widow was rewarded with the first keepership of the light remains just that – a tale.

~

In *'Leaves from Rowan's Logs'* for 1931 is a poignant entry:

…we all walked to Acarsaid Tioram and saw the deserted township with the primitive little church and school-house just as they had been left twelve years before. There were still school-books on the benches and writing on the blackboard.

In 1922 South Rona was purchased by the Scottish Board

of Agriculture for settlement by soldiers from the Great War. At that time there were twenty-two tenants and families, but a mere eight years later this had fallen to just two families. The last family, the Macraes, gave up the struggle and left Rona in 1943. However, it is possible these Macraes may not have been descended from the widow's daughter, for *'Leaves from Rowan's Logs'* states that the last Macraes only came to Rona about 1900.

~

So, elements of truth appear in all these tales from Rona. True, it was not a Macrae but Kenneth Mackenzie who drowned; nor did the serving maids perish, nor the Mackenzie sons. And in the splendidly melodramatic second tale the author appears to have confused *Acairseid Mhor* with *Acairseid Thioram*, for there is no beach at the former.

But, as in any old tale, it is the embellishments that grip one when narrating a good yarn!

Map references

- OS Landranger 24. OS Explorer 409:

  Acairseid Mhor NG 613 567

  Acairseid Thioram NG 613 580

Historical notes

Year:	1841	1851	1861	1881	1891
Population:	165	115	147	176	181

Year:	1922		1931	1971	1981
Population:	14 families		16	3	3

Year:	1991	2001	2011
Population:	0	2	3

- Admiralty chart 2570 – Sound of Raasay and Innersound (Northern Part) – was first surveyed in 1850. It shows *Acarsaid Chirm* (sic) both for the harbour and the village of some 11 buildings, set well back from the shore. But although a track is shown leading to *Acarsaid More* (sic), no track leads to the 2 buildings on the shore at *Acarsaid Chirm*. At *Acarsaid More* is marked 'Widows Cot' (sic).

- The 1929 revision has *Acarsaid Thioram* for the village; *Acairseid Thioram (Chirm)* for the bay; *Acairseid More* for the harbour and still marked 'Widows Cot'.

- In 1943 chart 2570 was again revised: it now had *Acarseid Thioram* (sic) in the bay and 'Solitary Cottage' instead of 'Widows Cot'.

- The first 6" Ordnance Survey of 1875 shows over 20 buildings at *Acairseid-thioram* (sic) on the hill but no track to *Acairsed Thioram*, marked in the bay. A track led to a building marked 'Lodge' which was some 200 yards north of 4 buildings on the shore at *Acairseid Mhor* (sic).

- The 1901 6" OS revision now showed the village as 'Dry Harbour' and a new track to *Acairsed Thioram* and buildings of 'Mission House' and 'School'.

- In May 1921 a group of ex-servicemen from Rona landed on Raasay and attempted to re-occupy the land from which their families had been cleared. The 'Rona Raiders' were arrested, tried and given jail sentences, but public support for them was strong and they were eventually freed and allowed to remain on Raasay. The next year the British Government bought both Rona and Raasay; however, most of Rona's inhabitants soon followed the Raiders to settle on Raasay. In 1943 the last crofting family left and the island had become uninhabited, with the exception of the lighthouse keepers who lived at its north end until the lighthouse was automated in 1975.

- On the east side of the island is a cave that was used for Sunday worship until the church was built in 1912. It continued to be used sporadically until 1970. The Gaelic name of the cave is *Uamh na gaisgeach* – 'Cave of the famous warrior'. In 1950 the cave still had stone 'seats'; the altar at the mouth of the cave; and a font fed by water drips from the roof.

- In 1992 Rona was bought from the government by a Danish owner, who is attempting to reverse decades of neglect. He has restored cottages at *Acairseid Thioram* for self-catering, and also Rona Lodge at *Acairseid Mhor,* where the island manager lives, providing B&B and bunkhouse accommodation.

Sources

- *A Description of the Western Islands of Scotland* – Martin Martin.
- *Scottish Islands* – Hamish Haswell-Smith.
- *West Coast Cruising* – John Maclintock
- *Scotland Picturesque and Traditional* – Eyre-Todd.
- *Leaves from Rowan's Logs* – Dr RB Carslaw.
- The National Archives of Scotland: NLC 2/1/26 of 26 November 1851.
- Admiralty chart 2551. 1850 Admiralty chart 2570 + 1929 and 1943 revisions.
- 1875 6" Ordnance Survey.
- https://en.wikipedia.org/wiki/South_Rona

Being two tail ends!

The tale of the Maggie Love

Before the smart new road to Mallaig was built the old one used to twist and turn, finding a route wherever it was easiest, at times hugging the sea, at times inland. Where the River Morar – the shortest salmon river in Scotland – meets the sea is a small creek, at Kinsadel. Here the road dropped in a hairpin bend to hug the shore – and on the west of the creek was until recently the final resting place of a once-fine sailing vessel. In 1982 *The Oban Times* reported that,

Age and uncaring people who tear away her planks for firewood are reducing to a mere skeleton a very familiar sight on the Morar Estuary – the derelict smack *Maggie Love*'.

The *Maggie Love* was a 'Fifie', a design of sailing fishing boat developed on the east coast of Scotland and used from the 1850s until well into the 20th century. Mainly used for herring fishing, they set long nets and drifted with the wind, waiting for the shoals of fish to swim into the nets – hence they were known as herring drifters. With their long straight keel and wide beam they were very stable and carried large sails; the two masts were set far forward and aft to give the maximum clear working space

20-1 Maggie Love bound for Soay

amidships – on the main was a huge dipping lugsail, while the mizzen had a standing lugsail.

The *Maggie Love* was – shall we say, as befits a lady – no longer in the first flush of youth when Sandy Johnston of Mallaig bought her. The railway came to Mallaig in 1900 and turned a bare dozen houses into a major fishing port; to service all these new boats Sandy founded a fuelling and ship-chandlery firm, now well-known. He bought the *Maggie Love* and converted her to become a coal carrier, for the newly constructed railway brought coal to the quayside. There the *Maggie Love* would embark loads of from thirty to forty tons, before sailing to Lochs Hourn and Nevis, Airor on the Knoydart shore, the Small Isles, Soay and similar isolated communities. Where there was a pier or jetty they would go alongside to discharge; where not they would anchor as far inshore as they could safely go on a rising tide and simply drop the coal overboard. Then at low water ponies with panniers or carts would come down to be loaded by hand – a laborious job, which might have to be carried out over several tides, but the coal was unaffected by its dowsing and burnt just as brightly!

Rogie Gillies was her skipper, assisted by Sandy from Mallaig Veag. Both men liked a wee dram before they set off and old Sandy Johnston always insisted that they sailed the smack with far greater proficiency when they were fortified with the warmth of a dram. Considering the hardships they endured, man-handling the huge sail and tacking into difficult inlets, it was no wonder they needed something to keep up their strength.

With her huge cumbersome mast and lug sail it says something that these men even sailed loads of coal across the Minch to Rodel, on the Isle of Harris. From there they negotiated the tortuous channel between the reefs and skerries of the Sound of Harris to the spectacular Amhuinnsuidhe Castle, right on the shores of West Loch Tarbert. At that time there was only a small and rough track to the castle and the districts beyond it, meaning nearly all provisions and guests came in by sea.

Although for years the *Maggie Love* with her billowing sail was a conspicuous sight plying her trade delivering coal from Mallaig along the coast, her days were numbered.

Just as steam drifters had replaced sailing drifters, so too did steam puffers replace the outdated sailing smacks, including the *Maggie Love*. The puffers were small cargo-vessels, about 88 feet long for the 'outside boats' which served the Minch areas; with their flat bottoms they could beach and then unload at low tide into horse-drawn carts brought alongside. For remote settlements without piers this was a huge bonus, and cargoes could include coal, lime and even a complete house's furniture when flitting. Return cargoes of farm produce and gravel were sometimes brought back, all loaded/unloaded by the ship's derrick. Puffers could carry over three times the tonnage of coal as did the *Maggie Love* – her days were over.

When the Great War started in 1914, the working era of the *Maggie Love* drew to a close and Sandy Johnston, at a loss as to what to do with his ship, sold her to Mr MacEachen of Kinsadel, for the princely sum of one hen and twelve chickens. She has lain at Kinsadel through the years, each year adding its toll to her dereliction as rigging mast and finally the very timbers of her hull vanished, exposing what is left of her ribs. But even yet, seeing the fine cut of her prow, one can visualise her ploughing through the seas in full sail, with Rogie's firm hand at the helm.

Map references

- OS Landranger 40. OS Explorer 398:

  Maggie Love NM 680 920

Historical notes

- Steam puffers were made famous by the Para Handy writings of Neil Munro – later a television series; and, of course, that classic film The Maggie, now on DVD. But like the Maggie Love, the puffer era too ended; in 1973 I helped unload a cargo of lime for the Island of Shuna from one of the last working puffers, the Eilean Easdale. At Amhuinnsuidhe Castle – after the demise of the Maggie Love – 120 tons of coal was delivered annually by the puffer Maggie Lough; but she too was superseded when the road was improved in the 1940's and lorries could deliver to the castle.

- A photograph of about 1955-1960 shows the stem and hull planking largely intact; in 1985 all that remained of the *Maggie Love* was her keel and a few bottom ribs. I admit to nicking one 3 feet length of rib, which is now the base of a sundial – so part of her is still working!

- Allan Johnston wrote in 2002 that 'There is nothing

remaining of this vessel today because of the new road … the stones in the *Maggie Love* were from the Isle of Lewis, used as ballast'.

Sources

- *Oban Times* column c. 1982.
- *The Clyde Puffer* – Dan McDonald.
- *West Highland Shores* – Maldwin Drummond.
- Personal letters from: Allan Johnston, grandson of Sandy Johnston: Tony Scherr re Amhuinnsuidhe Castle: Scottish Fisheries Museum, Anstruther.

Mrs Campbell 'of' Kilchurn Castle

This story was told me by 'an impeccable source' and has a total ring of truth about it!

~

20-2 Kilchurn Castle 1846

Pre-war, Kilchurn Castle – at the north end of Loch Awe – was in ruins and abandoned, apart from an old tinker woman who had built herself a shelter against an inner courtyard wall. True, it was only branches roofed with an old green tarpaulin – a 'harp' as they are known – thoughtfully abandoned by an Argyll Council road-gang. But the courtyard was well protected, and there was plenty of timber handy for a fire to make the shelter snug and warm. Loch Awe was mere yards away for water, so the old woman was probably as well housed as she had ever been.

There remained, however, the problem of food, and whilst she could beg the necessities from the neighbouring houses and the grand hotel in Loch Awe village, it remained a hand-to-mouth existence. What conjured up the idea I know not, but perhaps it was a chance remark overheard from Cook at some 'Big Hoose'. Wherever the idea came from, the old woman purchased one sheet of writing paper and an envelope – as one could in those days – and in her best copperplate hand wrote to Harrods for a small order for food. At the head of the letter she inscribed 'Kilchurn Castle, Loch Awe, Argyll, NB. Station: Loch Awe' and duly slipped it into a letter-box. Naturally, she attached no stamp, considering that Harrods could afford the cost more than her – and after all, was she not giving them an order?

On receipt of the letter, signed Mrs Campbell of Kilchurn Castle, Harrods promptly despatched the order by rail and, within a couple of days, the old tinker woman collected it from the station. Now, it is a couple of miles from Loch Awe village to the castle, and when you are old and rheumaticy carrying a box of supplies that distance is no fun. So Mrs Campbell arranged with the engine driver that he would stop the train where the castle track crossed the railway line and leave her parcels there. Problem solved.

Emboldened by the ease with which she had obtained her food parcel Mrs Campbell duly ordered another, this time rather larger – and another – and another. When the monthly account duly arrived the old woman, naturally, ignored it, and instead used it for a further order – after all, it saved her the one penny she could ill afford for writing paper and envelope.

Harrods being Harrods, and not wishing to lose such a prestigious customer, events went on for more than a year. After all, the individual sums were modest, for Mrs Campbell was shrewd enough to keep them so; and even if the total was by now well over one hundred pounds [at a time when a miner's wage was £120 a year] it was nothing compared to the sums owed Harrods by many of their customers.

However, the tone of the letters became steadily more demanding, and even hinted at despatching no further supplies. Suddenly, the orders ceased. Letters and accounts to the castle were returned marked 'Gone away'. Harrods finally decided to write off the sum as a bad debt. Yet the manager of the Food Hall, to whose ultimate responsibility the matter fell, was intrigued by the situation. He found that Loch Awe Hotel had some excellent salmon fishing on the Rivers Awe and Orchy, as well as fine views for his wife to paint, and so he booked them in to the hotel for his annual holiday.

Once safely arrived in Loch Awe he contacted the local policeman and discovered the truth about 'Mrs Campbell of Kilchurn Castle'. The old lady had died a few months previously – just when the orders stopped – but her body had not been found for some weeks. Clasped in one hand was an empty bottle of Harrods Own Whisky and there was a smile of peaceful contentment on her face.

When I recounted this story to Unicorn Pursuivant he responded with another – about the same period, and of a lady bearing the same name, but of vastly different social standing.

Old Mrs Campbell of Dunstaffnage was in reduced circumstances, even having to sell her estate of Inverawe, which had been in the family for 150 years. She moved to the relatively humble farmhouse of Fannans, where she lived in genteel poverty. She dined one night at Bonawe House, a couple of miles away, and after dinner the guests duly dispersed, either driving themselves in their smart motors, or summoning their chauffeurs. Mrs Campbell, however, put two fingers to her mouth and emitted a piercing whistle – out of the shadows emerged her last old retainer, pushing an ancient wooden wheelbarrow. Into this Mrs Campbell climbed with difficulty, for her arthritic old joints were complaining; finally settled, and ensconced on threadbare but well-padded velvet cushions, she was decorously wheeled down the road for the journey home.

A sting in the tail of Fionn the Fair & The Wicked Princess

With tales of a voyage, a picnic ending in patricide & a good maths puzzle

This is really just a variation on the joke that 'Scotsmen are better than Irishmen', but if you want a tale of a handsome hero, a beautiful (but wicked) Princess, her sad old father the King, a gale at sea, plus a good maths conundrum thrown in – then read on.

Long, long, ago there lived on Barra a band of heroes named Feinn, and their chief, not surprisingly, was called Fionn. Now whether he was the Fionn of all the other tales I don't know. I doubt it; maybe just a cousin, or maybe just another chief called Fionn.

Anyway, our Fionn was tall and exceedingly strong, as were all of his band. Each and every one was, of course, very handsome with fair hair and blue eyes, as becomes descendants of Norsemen. Before a man could join the Feinn he had to prove himself a mighty swordsman, strong enough to grip his great two-handed sword between thumb and forefinger and hold it out at arm's length without a tremor. He also had to jump a tree level with his own forehead; crawl under a tree level with his own knee without shaking a single leaf; pull a thorn out of his foot whilst running at full speed; and amongst all these activities, even when hunting with the spear, his hair must be tied neatly with a ribbon at the nape of the neck. Pretty smart chaps, eh?

On joining the band each warrior had to swear a great oath that he would never do harm to any woman, or refuse to marry one if she was poor; that he would be kind to the weak; that if he was killed in battle none of his friends should be expected to avenge his death; and that he would never refuse to fight single-handed against nine of the enemy.

The band was fourteen in number, and over their shirt and kilt they wore a plaid as a sleeveless cloak. The great two-handed sword was strapped round the waist, a shield was carried on the left forearm, and a dirk in the right stocking top; tough luck if you were left-handed. For hunting they exchanged the sword and shield for a spear, and I suppose they just hoped that they met no enemies.

All in all the Feinns were a pretty gung-ho lot, and the only difference between them and Fionn – apart from him being chief, and therefore the boss – was that Fionn had one special gift. Whenever he had a difficult decision to make Fionn would put his thumb on his wisdom tooth, and straightaway the answer would come to him.

Now, one day when they had run out of women to rescue or enemies to slay, Fionn was rubbing his thumb over his wisdom tooth when he said, "Let us put out our boat, prow to sea and stern to shore, hoist the speckled flapping sails, and visit Dubhan, King of Ireland."

And his men, having nothing better to do, and rather fancying a pint or three of Guinness, replied "Right-on Chiefie," nipped down to the galley, launched it, and two days later reached Ireland late in the afternoon.

There King Dubhan – alerted by Oban Coastguard – came down to the beach to welcome them. He noticed that Fionn had fourteen fair-haired warriors with him, so he immediately selected the best fourteen of his own dark-haired followers as an equal bodyguard. As the prow of the galley rode up on the shingle beach Fionn and his men leapt out and hauled the craft above the high-water mark.

"I am Fionn," he said to King Dubhan, "the son of a daughter of a sea-king."

"Hulloo," said the King, "Away up to the palace for a fish supper."

"Oh no, not bloody fish again," muttered all the Feinns. But they did so under their breath, not wishing to upset their hosts, who looked pretty ferocious – and big with it too.

But a surprise awaited them in the Great Hall, where a fire of huge logs roared up the vast chimney, and long tables were laden with all manner of good food. Now, as it was the height of summer, and being unused to central heating – for there were few trees on Barra – the Feinns soon worked up a muck sweat. So they piled their armour and plaids in one corner and set to the feast with a vengeance; oysters fresh from the sea, hare soup with lots of blood, roast venison straight from the great haunches turning on the spit, and a whole boars head carried high on the shoulders of two cooks. No chicken MacNuggets for our band of heroes, and they used their dirks to carve the meat straight from the joints, ate it with their fingers, and wiped their greasy hands on any passing wolfhound – which, as *everyone* knows, are just the correct height for wiping one's dirty hands on.

At the high table sat King Dubhan, with Fionn on his right, and on his left his only daughter, the Princess, black-haired, dark-eyed, with skin as creamy and smooth as ivory, and lips the colour of pink coral.

Once he had eaten his fill and let out an enormous belch in appreciation of the meal, Fionn turned to the King and said, "See here King Dubhan, I rather fancy your daughter, the Princess, and judging by the looks during dinner she sure has the hots for me. How about we get married?"

"It shall not be granted," said the King, "for never would I give my only child to the son of a sea-wolf (pirate)."

"Say not so," replied Fionn, "but await the morning."

The morning dawned sunny and calm, and the Princess asked her father; "Say Pops, why don't we launch the royal galley and show Fionn and his gang the seacliffs."

"Nay," said the King, "for the royal galley takes but the two of us and our fourteen rowers. Would you have me risk the lives of the noble Fionn and his men?"

"Scaredy-cat," replied the Princess, turning all her charm upon her father. "The sea is flat calm, and there's plenty of room for everyone."

Then King Dubhan, who could deny his daughter nothing, and not wishing to appear a coward, gave his consent, and the overladen royal galley set sail. Past the high headlands they went on a smooth sea, until they came to the great cliffs where the sea-birds nested in their tens of thousands, and where the winter gales sent huge waves booming into the caves.

There the King dished out as lunch enough Pot Noodles for everyone, all except the Princess, who delicately picked at a few lettuce leaves, for she was watching her figure – and so was Fionn. As for our hero, he had thoughtfully brought along a hamper of venison sarnies, a few hares legs, the odd roast swan, and a keg of beer, all just for him in case he felt peckish. Barely was lunch over when the sky darkened ominously, and the wind soon got up to a half-gale.

"We must lighten the ship O King, and some must be thrown overboard" cried the navigator, a man called Horse, for the simple reason he looked like one.

"Oh shit," said the King, but to himself, for Kings must not show they are worried, "we're in deep trouble." For he knew fine well that the galley was overloaded, and half of the occupants must be thrown overboard, or else all would perish. Yet he was loathe to give the order to any of his own trusty men; and equally loathe to be so discourteous to his guest as to say "Look, old bean, would you and your chums mind hopping overboard, so that the Princess and I and my merry men can all be saved?"

And so he sat, head in hands, whilst the spindrift blew off the wave-crests, and water began to break over the galley, and his men cried out "Some must go." Finally the King thought to himself "The Princess got us into this mess. She can bloody well get us out of it."

So he turned to his men, and to Fionn and his men, and shouted above the wind, so that all might hear.

"Let my daughter, the Princess, decide who shall be thrown overboard, and who shall be saved."

"Yes," replied all the men, "but be damn quick about it, for the water is already over the floorboards and our feet are getting wet." For in spite of all their macho posturing, at heart they were a load of woosies.

"That's not all that will be getting wet for some of you," thought the Princess, but aloud she said, "Let the chosen ones be by lot, but first I shall place you all in the galley."

Now, if you have been paying the least bit of attention to my story, you will remember that there were onboard Fionn and his fourteen fair-haired followers, the King and his fourteen dark-haired bodyguard, and, of course, the Princess. So she placed herself on the centre thwart, facing the stern, and allotted the men places as on the diagram (white circles Fionn and the Feinns, dark circles King

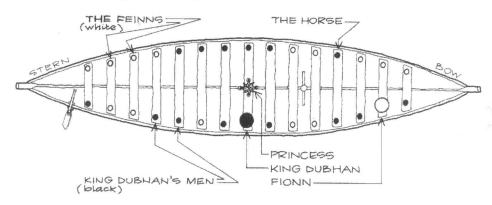

21-1 The galley layout

Dubhan and his men). The Princess began with four of Fionn's men on her right, starting at the stern, and allotting the men all round the galley until she finished with a single dark-haired warrior in the starboard quarter.

This Princess must have taken Higher Maths at Oban, for when she had finished, she said:

"Now, O my father, you shall count, beginning where I began, and every ninth man shall be thrown overboard."

So the King began to count, commencing with the first of the men in the stern on the port side, and every ninth man, when tapped on the shoulder, jumped smartly overboard holding his nose to stop the nasty salt water going up it. Old King Dubhan, thick as he was, soon noticed that every ninth man was in fact one of his own dark-haired men, and by the time he had counted fifteen times, he himself went overboard.

Patricide over, and having got what she lusted after, namely Fionn, he and the Princess in the royal galley sped before the gale for Barra. There they were duly wed amongst much feasting, and this was probably the bravest

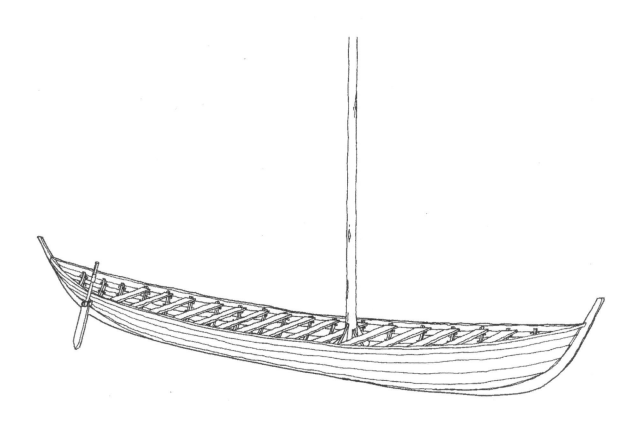

21-2 The Royal Galley

thing Fionn did, for he must have spent many a sleepless night with his murderess wife by his side, wondering if he was next. Or just maybe he didn't care – we shall never know.

For centuries the children of Barra played the game of the Wicked Princess on the sea-shore, drawing the galley in the sand, and using cockle shells for Fionn and his fair-haired men, and mussel shells for King Dubhan and his dark-haired followers. Maybe they still do? More probably it's on a computer game by now!

The placing of the men around the galley by the Princess is commemorated in a Gaelic poem, translated by Father John Macmillan as follows:

Four from the Fionns of glorious beautiful appearance,
Let them stand aside,
With five black men after them, from the dwelling of
Dubhan.
Two from Macumhal anew
And one from Dubhan – the Horse,
Three from the Fionn, of glorious beautiful appearance,
And one from Dubhan, put him out,

Fionn will not sit in the white stream
Without two black fellows on his left,
Without two others after them, of the habitation of Fionn,
Three blacks, one on each side of the Dubhan,
One fair of Fionn watching these,
Two black giants after that,
Two from Fionn and one from Dubhan.

Sources

- *Hebridean Journey* by Halliday Sutherland. Told to Halliday Sutherland about 1930 by Father John MacMillan, parish priest of Northbay, Barra born and bred.